PUBLIC INFLUENCE

A Guide to Op-Ed Writing and
Social Media Engagement

PUBLIC INFLUENCE

A Guide to Op-Ed Writing and Social Media Engagement

Mira Sucharov

UNIVERSITY OF TORONTO PRESS
Toronto Buffalo London

© University of Toronto Press 2019
utorontopress.com
Printed and bound by CPI Group (UK) Ltd, Croydon, CR0 4YY

∞ This book is printed on paper containing 100% post-consumer fibre.

Library and Archives Canada Cataloguing in Publication

Sucharov, Mira, author
Public influence : a guide to op-ed writing and social media engagement / Mira Sucharov.

Includes bibliographical references and index.
ISBN 978-1-4875-8746-8 (hardcover).   ISBN 978-1-4875-8745-1 (softcover)

1. Editorials – Authorship.   2. Social media.   I. Title.

PN4784.E28S83 2019   808.06'607   C2018-905770-X

We welcome comments and suggestions regarding any aspect of our publications—please feel free to contact us at *news@utorontopress.com* or visit our internet site at utorontopress.com.

North America	*UK, Ireland, and Continental Europe*
5201 Dufferin Street	NBN International
North York, Ontario, Canada, M3H 5T8	Estover Road, Plymouth, PL6 7PY, UK
	ORDERS PHONE: 44 (0) 1752 202301
2250 Military Road	ORDERS FAX: 44 (0) 1752 202333
Tonawanda, New York, USA, 14150	ORDERS EMAIL: enquiries@ nbninternational.com

ORDERS PHONE: 1-800-565-9523
ORDERS FAX: 1-800-221-9985
ORDERS EMAIL: utpbooks@utpress.utoronto.ca

University of Toronto Press acknowledges the financial assistance to its publishing program of the Canada Council for the Arts and the Ontario Arts Council, an agency of the Government of Ontario.

Canada Council **Conseil des Arts**
for the Arts **du Canada**

ONTARIO ARTS COUNCIL
CONSEIL DES ARTS DE L'ONTARIO
an Ontario government agency
un organisme du gouvernement de l'Ontario

Funded by the   Financé par le
Government   gouvernement
of Canada   du Canada | **Canadä**

Contents

Acknowledgements

I owe a debt of gratitude to many friends and colleagues. Thanks goes first to Mat Buntin, my outstanding editor at University of Toronto Press, whose superb vision and sage guidance helped this book grow from inception to print. Thanks goes too to Natalie Fingerhut at UTP who helped nurture the seed of the idea. Copyeditor Kerry Fast, production editor Christine Robertson, proofreader Gina Nicholls, indexer Siusan Moffat, and Anna Maria Del Col and her colleagues in sales and marketing made the entire process smooth and enjoyable.

Brent Sasley, Thomas Juneau, Marc Caplan, and Nathaniel Berman each read parts of the manuscript and provided thoughtful feedback. Three anonymous reviewers also helped make the manuscript stronger.

Joshua Busby, Chaya Halberstam, Patrick Thaddeus Jackson, Shaul Magid, Atalia Omer, and Tamara Cofman Wittes each offered helpful articles or conversations at key points in the project. Many friends and followers on social media answered my various crowd-sourcing calls for observations about your experiences and for that I am grateful.

Some of the issues covered here were workshopped at the Centre for International Policy Studies at the University of Ottawa, with Brent Sasley in the pages of *PS: Political Science and Politics* and on the London School of Economics and Political Science Impact blog, and with Lena Saleh in *Israel Studies Review*.

Thanks to my department chair, Jonathan Malloy, who supported the creation of my Political Opinion Writing course at

Carleton and to the students in all my courses who have to (or get to, depending on one's perspective) learn how to write op-eds and who continue to teach me a lot.

The many editors I've worked with in the opinion pages of various news outlets over the years have helped sharpen my op-ed voice. Thanks goes to Peter Beinart, Avital Chizhik-Goldschmidt, Ali Gharib, Rob Gilroy, Lisa Goldman, Yoni Goldstein, Charlotte Hallé, Jillian Jones, Basya Laye, Sara Miller, Andrew Phillips, Cynthia Ramsay, Michael Regenstreif, Sigal Samuel, Doug Saunders, Dahlia Scheindlin, Esther Solomon, Rhonda Spivak, Simon Spungin, Leonard Stern, Batya Ungar-Sargon and Rutie Zuta.

Peter Eisenstadt, Bernie Farber, Brent Sasley, and Joshua Schreier, co-authors of several op-eds I have written, have each helped me think through pressing topics in a new way.

Thanks to Dara Pavlich and Ryan Nadel, my younger and hipper cousins, who in December 2006 first introduced me to Facebook, and to my early mentor, Rex Brynen, who modelled fine scholar-social media use from the beginning of the platform.

Most of all, thank you to my family: to my parents and stepparents for their ongoing enthusiasm and curiosity about my creative projects; to my husband for his constant, loving support in every way; and to our two amazing kids who infuse my days with fun and meaning and give me added reason to want to write towards a better world.

M.S.
Ottawa, October 2018

chapter one

Introduction

In 1969, an editor at the *New York Times* invited a scholar to adapt the ideas from his recent book into an op-ed for the newspaper. The scholar agreed and submitted a draft. But when the editor presented some suggested edits on the op-ed, the scholar demurred. "I am afraid that I will have to abandon the project, reluctantly," said the scholar. "For some reason, I find it enormously more difficult to write 700 words than 7,000—a typical professorial defect, I suppose." The scholar was Noam Chomsky. He would go on, of course, to become one of the most prominent public intellectuals of the twentieth century and beyond.[1]

That was half a century ago, and while much has changed in the realm of public commentary owing to the digital revolution, one thing has not. There are many, many experts out there—academics, professionals, and graduate students training to become specialists in their field—who have much to contribute but who struggle with the idea of pivoting from strictly professional writing to the kind of writing and informal engagement that can reach a broader audience. And because we are now living five decades after Chomsky walked away from that particular op-ed opportunity, we also inhabit a time where the conversations stemming from public-commentary pieces, including op-eds, columns, blogs, short analytical essays, etc., regularly spill over into social media spaces. In turn, many of these social media debates shape much of what goes into informed and responsive public commentary. This book traverses the landscape of op-ed and related publishing, into the dynamics of social media conversations and back, to help you develop and sharpen your public engagement skills.

Why *Should* Experts Contribute?

Professors and related experts are plenty busy. So why should we spend time and effort contributing to op-ed pages and to related public-commentary outlets, and why should we engage our peers and the broader public on social media? Here's why. Experts have access to information and a depth of understanding useful for addressing an array of problems of interest to the public. When shared thoughtfully and judiciously, even personal experience can help illuminate thorny and polarizing issues. (I discuss the role of personal experience as a source of insight in chapters 3 and 4.) Using social media to weed out false and deceptive articles claiming to be news; arguing issues on their merits; bringing evidence to bear on arguments; clarifying hot-button terms and labels that are sometimes understood differently across audiences; and harnessing knowledge to make research-based arguments all mitigate against the decline of intelligent discourse and the erosion of an informed citizenry. All this, in turn, strengthens civil society, a key component of a healthy democracy. A free and open media, as is well-known, is one of the linchpins of democracy. Infusing the news media—and social media, for that matter—with expert voices that provide analysis, commentary, and public-policy prescriptions on a range of issues and from a range of perspectives enhances the role that the fourth estate can play.

While many of the calls for more expert assessments in the public sphere have focused on scientists, with issues like climate change looming large, this principle holds true across academic fields. A few years ago, *New York Times* columnist Nicholas Kristof tried to energize humanities scholars and social scientists to throw their hats into the ring of public debate. Kristof urged them not to "cloister yourselves like medieval monks—we need you!"[2] Because he aimed his pen at academics themselves, rather than at the gatekeepers of the op-ed pages, some scholars bristled. "We are right here!" screamed the headline of political scientist Erik Voeten's response piece. Voeten wrote, "They are easier to find than ever before."[3] The point of this book isn't to adjudicate the question of whether scholars in any particular field are sufficiently visible in the public sphere. The point is that now, more than ever, a healthy public sphere, including the formal public-commentary pages and the informal discussions taking place on social media, requires a powerful mix of reason, evidence, and compassion—all components of thoughtful expertise.

Yet none of this is easy. Shifting one's writing voice to connect with a broader audience poses one set of challenges. More challenging, perhaps, because of its unpredictability, is anticipating the social media reaction of your interventions and interpreting social media dynamics carefully enough to avoid getting buffeted by the harsh waves of changing ideas and assumptions so that you don't feel like you're getting slammed against the rocks. This book will help you navigate these sometimes choppy waters, with an eye to the emotional toll these activities can take on even seasoned experts.

My own experience with op-ed-writing and social media engagement has developed over the better part of the last decade. In addition to my regular research and teaching duties as a tenured professor of political science, I have published around 250 op-ed-style pieces at all levels: community papers, city papers, national papers, and global news outlets, sometimes as a regular columnist or blogger, and sometimes as a one-off freelancer. (I briefly discuss the differences between columns and op-eds in chapter 5.) In these op-eds, I have concentrated on the topic of my main fields of expertise: the politics of Israel-Palestine and the dynamic of Diaspora Jewish politics. But having a regular column at various times has allowed me to experiment with other topics that I feel deserve some attention as well. These have ranged from Indigenous issues to sexual assault and harassment to pedagogy and parenting. I have also developed a stand-alone course in my department on the subject of op-ed writing, and I now incorporate at least one op-ed assignment into every course I teach (and usually more than one, so students can improve their skills). My department is political science, so my course is called "political opinion writing," but in that course I define "political" broadly, and I can easily imagine a similar op-ed writing course adapted to many disciplines.

Aside from the crucial public-influence role that scholars and other experts can play in these domains, there is also the role that public-commentary writing and social media engagement can play in making us more knowledgeable and helping enhance our research and our research profile. Op-ed writing has brought me into contact with networks of people I might never have met otherwise. In turn, many of those people may not have had a chance to encounter my ideas had it not been for my public-commentary platform. Many personal examples come to mind, but one particularly memorable episode was an invitation to teach multiple sessions at a Jewish community seminar in Sydney and Melbourne, Australia, where I hope my audiences learned something from me and where I learned all sorts of things about Australia's Jewish community and its relationship to issues ranging from Israel-Palestine to Indigenous reconciliation. This opportunity arose directly from my public writings and social media engagement. From my public writing profile, I have developed a social media network, one that I inaugurated modestly in 2006 in the early days of Facebook when I struggled to find ten people I knew, and which grew once my regular public-commentary writing got underway and once the social media platforms themselves suddenly expanded.

For me, social media engagement has been mostly fulfilling. But it has also been stressful—at times extremely stressful. In the pages that follow, I will share what I have come to understand to be best practices in public-commentary and social media engagement. And I won't shy away from conveying the personal lessons I have learned, sometimes the hard way.

As for Noam Chomsky, we now know that he ended up blazing a path forward to the public-commentary pages after all. This book owes much to his legacy and to that of many other public intellectuals of all political and philosophical stripes who managed to overcome whatever initial hesitations they may have harbored about shifting their writing and engagement voice to reach a broader audience.

How to Use This Book

The book is divided into 12 chapters covering the landscape of public-commentary writing and its extension to social media. Some chapters focus more on one half of the ledger than the other; some chapters combine both. The first half of the book, roughly, focuses on developing your voice and getting it out there through formal op-ed and related channels. The second half covers how to manage the ensuing conversation via social media. I am aware that some readers may want to hone their public-commentary publishing skills and forego social media engagement; others, perhaps non-specialists who nevertheless want to engage in deeper and more productive conversations, may simply want to improve their social media engagement skills without contributing to op-ed pages. Still others, those who define their public engagement in an activist way, may appreciate the opportunity to see many of the dynamics they are already encountering be placed into a more analytical context. Most readers, I hope, will find the analysis of the interlocking landscape—between public-commentary writing and social media engagement—to be useful and informative. Here is a brief chapter-by-chapter summary so you can jump right in.

Chapter 2 introduces the idea of being a public commentator by helping leverage and expand your expertise. In this chapter, I suggest how to find your way into an ongoing conversation. I also lay out the differences in style, scope, and aims between academic writing and public-commentary writing and flag some risks in speaking out in these public forums.

Chapter 3 focuses on public-commentary publishing by demonstrating how to generate op-ed ideas and how to pitch them to a relevant outlet. The chapter also discusses rejection.

By analyzing four published op-eds, chapter 4 maps the terrain from idea to pitch to writing to publishing, focusing on the nuts and bolts of writing an effective op-ed and managing the ensuing conversation, even when the public reaction is unexpected. Understanding the dynamics of social media, something I cover in later chapters, will help prepare you for the various reactions you may receive to your ideas so you can amplify your message and help influence debate effectively.

Chapter 5 describes the features of various public-commentary platforms and provides examples, including social media, blogs, op-eds, podcasts, and additional outlets like current-affairs magazines.

By analyzing various op-ed writing styles using examples from several regular columnists, chapter 6 discusses how to select an effective public-writing voice. Which styles appeal to you and which do you think are most effective? Does storytelling invite? Does rage entice? Does sarcasm sell? This chapter will help you find your public voice.

Chapter 7 shifts the discussion from more formal public-commentary writing to social media engagement. I frame the chapter by discussing the emotional challenge and allure of social media engagement to examine the endemic problem of confirmation bias and suggest some tools for escaping echo chambers. Then I turn to the question of how to communicate your ideas to an evidence-resistant audience, before looking at the rising problem of social media interference through trolling and "bots" and examining the phenomenon of "fake news" (including suggesting why that phrase might not be the best term to use) and the particular role scholars can play in mitigating the spread of false content.

Chapter 8 surveys the ground of public-commentary writing and social media discourse to investigate the culture of political labels. While labels are a convenient way of organizing and categorizing perspectives, they can get lost in translation. Chapter 8 will examine six terms—white supremacy, privilege, Zionism, Islamophobia, ableism, and rape culture—to demonstrate how they are used and understood (and sometimes misunderstood) in popular discourse. The chapter suggests ways of transcending the polarization that language debates can evoke by demonstrating how to adopt a critical and clarifying stance, something that schol-ars are particularly well positioned to do.

Extending from a discussion of particular labels, chapter 9 examines some of the more diffuse dynamics motivating social media activism and how public engagement can be harnessed to make change. The chapter introduces and investigates concepts like "outrage culture," "virtue signaling," "slacktivism," "sham-ing," "tone policing," the charge of "white fragility," and the tac-tics of "calling out versus calling in" and concludes by laying out some concrete strategies for running your organization's social media presence, for those who currently are, or may one day find themselves, in a social media leadership position. The language and ideas underpinning online debate are changing quickly, and this chapter will both identify pitfalls and suggest ways to avoid them as you seek to influence the public conversation in produc-tive directions.

Chapter 10 is about dealing with the emotional aspects of social media. Putting ideas out there, whether through formal public-commentary writing or whether in the more informal forums of social media discussion, can lead to heated exchanges. When should you get angry? When should you step away? When should you resort to "blocking" someone altogether? And what happens if you get doxxed (the phenomenon of people publishing others' private information online for the purpose of intimidating and harassing)? The chapter analyzes some cases of employers reacting to con-troversial social media posts from faculty members and students and concludes by discussing the practice of taking a "social media detox," an increasingly popular phenomenon as many social media users seek to contend with the toll that consuming social media for so many of our waking hours can take on our personal lives.

Chapter 11 looks at how to best engage with social and pro-fessional networks in a constructive way on social media while navigating and maintaining actual friendships. It begins by trac-ing how social media platforms have evolved and thus how social media use has shifted. Drawing on personal examples, I identify strategies for how best to communicate ideas, both through formal channels and informal debate, with an eye to keeping personal relationships intact. Public engagement provides the opportunity to not only have elected officials and policymakers hear your message but also to sway the hearts and minds of people close to you. Figuring out a way to accommodate personal relationships will help broaden your reach in constructive ways.

Chapter 12 concludes the book. In this chapter, I recount a personal example of where public engagement led to a rupture with a particular audience and what I learned from that episode. I then discuss how the academy can better account for public commentary as an indicator of faculty productivity.

The appendix outlines how professors can adapt an op-ed course assignment to suit a more research-intensive course and reproduces the practice exercises I've inserted throughout the earlier chapters. The purpose of these exercises is primarily to help you help your students master the craft.

chapter two

Saying What You Want to the Right Audience

Because this is a book for scholars and other experts, an important first step to consider when working your way into op-ed writing is to think about how it differs from academic and other professional writing. Scholarly writing is often characterized by a certain formality and a type of insider discourse where the writer is writing for a limited audience of peers. Sentences can be long and complex. Paragraphs are often peppered with jargon and are usually accompanied by footnotes to situate the arguments within the broader scholarly literature. And scholarly writing is more often descriptive and explanatory, rather than prescriptive.

Good public-commentary writing and the social media engagement that flows from it employs a different style but is still governed by an important set of principles shared with scholarship. Any effective public commentator must still advance an argument, use logic, marshal evidence, anticipate one's critics, and deploy solid reasoning. While an op-ed does not have footnotes, digital news platforms allow for hyperlinks to be embedded into the piece; these are, in their way, a newfangled form of citations.

The main differences between academic writing and public-commentary writing are these:

1. *Brevity.* Aside from personal blog posts, whose length is determined by your own preference, op-ed writing is the most concise of the public-commentary styles, each piece usually running between 650 and 800 words. Other analytical pieces can run a

little longer, with editors generally laying out length options with the writer in advance. Editors of hard-copy publications tend to be stricter on word length. If you are publishing the op-ed in an online-only news outlet, you may have a little more leeway.

2. *Reach.* Public commentary is intended to reach a wide audience of non-specialists. While some online news outlets are experimenting with subscription-only services, reader access is usually more open than in academic publishing. A broader audience also means that you cannot expect op-ed readers to be experts in your field. So that you might need to include some background and explanation in the framing. But this must be done concisely. Most importantly, a wider reach means that your piece can have a broader impact.

3. *Immediacy.* Academic publishing is known to be notoriously slow from submission to publication. Public-commentary pieces, by contrast, sometimes appear a day or two after you submit them. This means that the ideas you are engaging with can and should be tied to the news cycle. Because most op-eds reflect on some aspect of current events, readers are likely going to be primed to be curious about what you have to say. It also means that the shelf life for a given op-ed may be short. But this isn't always the case. Some op-eds are considered "evergreen," meaning that they contain insights that last beyond the headlines of the week. (I discuss evergreen pieces, and how to make them enticing to editors who are concerned with immediate relevance and hence timeliness, in chapter 3.)

4. *Style.* Public commentators are typically striving for a certain intimacy with the reader. But given that the reader is not a fellow subject expert, the relationship must be earned. Make the prose inviting. Accordingly, make sure to avoid jargon altogether, or use it sparingly and explain it carefully. And unlike academic articles, which might garner a captive audience of scholars who need to review and cite the literature on the given research question before they embark on their own contribution, no one is required to read your op-ed or related analytical piece. So grab the reader's attention. Lay out your arguments clearly. The field is crowded, and readers will turn away if they are bored or confused.

5. *Inspiration to action.* In op-ed writing, versus other forms of public-commentary such as short, analytical essays, not only is it necessary to provide an argument that is compelling and interesting but you are typically trying to construct one that will spur the audience to action. Taking style and clarity seriously will help achieve this.

Consider these two excerpts. One is from an academic article I published in 2011 and the other is from an op-ed on the same topic I published five years later.

The role of values in political mobilization is a crucial yet understudied component of international politics. Constructivist scholars have stressed the role of ideas in shaping outcomes, pointing to norms residing at the international, societal, and interest group levels.... (March and Olsen 1998; Sending 2002; Muller 2004). But they have spent less time theorizing about how values—and value trade-offs—operate in the realm of foreign policy, particularly among interest groups. Acting in accordance with one's values helps maintain personal identity, and hence a sense of ontological security, where routines of action and relationships serve to maintain psychological well-being.... (Mitzen 2006; Lupovici 2008; Steele 2008). But as discursive currency in garnering public sympathy for policy pressure, values are also used instrumentally. By turning a lens on the case of "Israel advocacy," this article assesses how ethnic groups combine particularist and universal values to promote support for certain foreign policies. The evidence from the Israel advocacy case suggests that parochial values are more likely to be used in the service of in-group critique, whereas mainstream Israel advocates are more likely to draw on universal values to make their case. In doing so, the article encourages a more self-conscious focus on the affective motivations and strategic use of values, by expanding on the emotions-based turn in IR (Crawford 2000; Mercer 2006; Ross 2006; Bleiker and Hutchison 2008; Lowenheim and Heimann 2008; Fierke and Fattah 2009)—particularly the dynamics of intergroup sensitivity and shaming, and the literature on decision making and value trade-offs (Festinger 1957; Keeney and Raiffa 1993; Baron 2000; Bain, Kashima, and Haslam 2006). Doing so can also help connect with debates surrounding the identity-action constitutive chain introduced by constructivists (Wendt 1999); how personal and communal values shape, and are informed by, the dominant view of what is appropriate within global politics, how the national interest is conceived (Krasner 1978; McCabe 1999), how values-based loyalty can redefine the group (Tessman 1998), how religion shapes international affairs (Abrams 2001; Dionne, Elshtain, and Drogosz 2004; Thomas 2005; Fox and Sandler 2006; Banchoff 2008; Hurd 2008), how advocacy can strengthen personal identity (Teske 1997), and the relationship between advocacy and discourse, teaching and learning, and talking and listening (Muller 2004).[1]

In this passage, notice the jargon I used, the crowded sentences I wrote that didn't have space to breathe, and the rather invisible (or at least specialized) reader.

And now consider this passage from an op-ed I published five years later on the same topic:

Politics experts know that appealing to the values of the target audience can be an effective tool of persuasion. These may be shared religious values, as in the case of Bono's citing of Leviticus to encourage U.S. Senator Jesse Helms to agree to debt relief for developing countries as part of the Jubilee 2000 effort; or the kind of universal principle the blood diamond campaign deployed—getting consumers to see a symbol of romance as wrapped up in the gruesome violence of conflict.

When it comes to Jewish values and Israel advocacy, my own research points to something intriguing. Jewish groups who criticize Israeli policy often appeal to Jewish values, while Israel advocates often try to burnish Israel's image through the language of universal concepts like democracy, science, sovereignty and history, as well as, more recently, attempts to "brand" Israel through universal appeals like "LGBTQ-friendly" or "hi-tech nation."

Part of the reason for this counter-intuitive dynamic is psychological: those who identify with a group that challenges the accepted reading of a tradition and its values will first look for ways to even out the dissonance, to dissent from within that tradition, rather than leave the group altogether. Israel advocates, on the other hand, seek to appeal to a wide target audience's core values, deliberately moving away from

particularist associations. Often these values are chosen for their depo-
liticized nature, avoiding potential areas of controversy.[2]

Perhaps the biggest difference is that when I wrote the academic
article, I had my reviewers in mind. I wanted to situate my argument in as much academic literature as I could. I used jargon flu-
idly, wanting to signal that I was aware of the ongoing debates
embodied by certain key terms. In the op-ed, by contrast, I was
trying to make a connection with a broad audience. I wanted to get
the public to see things in a new light. And I wanted to persuade
and to move the members of that audience. (The remainder of that
particular op-ed shifts from an explanatory frame to a more prescriptive one, where I try to spur the reader to action.)

One final thing to consider is that frequent op-ed writing may
result in clearer and more inviting academic prose. This means that
as more academics jump into the public sphere, we may find the
differences between the two styles begin to narrow.

Are Op-Eds about Being Subjective?

The term "op-ed" stands for "opposite the editorial page," from
the days of broadsheet newspapers where the left-hand side of the
paper included short editorials penned collectively by the staff of
the newspaper, and the right-hand side contained signed pieces
whose arguments belonged only to the individual writer. Nowa-
days, we tend to use the term "opinion piece" and "op-ed" inter-
changeably, leading some people to assume that "op" is short for
opinion. No matter. It's still a form of opinion writing.

Beyond the question of the origin of the term, when some people
hear the terms "op-ed" and "opinion writing," they think that this
means that academic writing is objective while opinion writing is
subjective. This book is in part an attempt to challenge that notion.
I'd like to suggest that good public-commentary writing, along
with the effective social media engagement that can flow from it,
should be guided by the same objective rules as those governing
more formal expert-based writing, including scholarly books and

articles, relies on. It's just that op-eds differ in style, as discussed above, and they extend the analysis into a prescriptive mode. They tend to tell the reader what they, meaning society more broadly, or else the government, a particular organization, or a political party, should be doing. As for the tool of subjectivity— incorporating the writer's own experience into the narrative—I discuss this in chapter 3 as one way to draw the reader in and build your argument.

How to Find Your Way into a Conversation

To find your way into an ongoing public conversation, consider how your scholarly specialization can translate outward, and then identify a germane moment in current debates. Pegging an op-ed to a current event provides a much better chance that readers will be interested in reading the piece and, thus, that an editor will want to run it. The "why now" question is called the "news peg."

In many cases, how to make your area of academic expertise relevant to a broader audience may be obvious. The public is constantly hungry for accessible writing on topics ranging from parenting and relationships (psychology) to climate change (environmental science) to voter behavior and political scandal (political science) to medical ethics (law, bioethics, philosophy) to addiction (medicine, psychology) to public and foreign policy (politics, history, international relations) and to the economy (economics, public policy). Even fields that are more inward looking can have much to say about issues of public significance. Helen Young, a professor of English who received her PhD in medieval literature, saw such an opportunity when she published a short piece called "Why *Game of Thrones* Has a Race Problem."[3] Pop culture is always, well, popular, and race and racism are among the most pressing issues of the day. Medieval history is also having its time in the sun owing to current issues. News reports indicate that scholars of medieval history are fighting back against the weaponizing of medieval historical symbols by white supremacists, for example.[4]

How does one find a news peg? Take the example of election expertise. If there is an election campaign happening, then the news peg for a piece on voter behavior is obvious. But even between elections there may be an opportunity to share election-related expertise. The publication of a candidate's memoir, for example, can provide an opening for election experts to deepen and broaden the observations they had been nursing from the previous race. Contests for party leadership or moves to introduce campaign finance reform legislation are two other examples of events that occur between elections where you could insert your voice, all while pegging the piece to current events.

Once you have identified a topic about which you have something to say, try to see what others have been writing. Is there something that is missing from the current taken-for-granted understanding of a topic? Is conventional wisdom lacking? Is the current debate around a given issue coalescing around two sides, whereas you see a third? Any one of these can be an entry point.

Practice Exercise

Identify a controversial issue and consider what the two existing prominent sides of the debate are (I will call them argument A and argument B). Find at least one op-ed that advances argument A and another that advances argument B. Write a paragraph outlining the debate, indicating what the writer or writers on side A argue and what those on side B argue. Now tell the audience what's missing. Your argument C could be the basis of an op-ed.

Here's an example of where this method has worked for me. Some years ago I noticed I was frustrated by what I saw as a debate over the Israeli-Palestinian conflict that assumed two opposing sides. And while what has become known as the "two-state solution" (whereby Israel would withdraw from the West Bank, making way for the establishment of a Palestinian state there and in the Gaza Strip) was not at all new, I felt I could rejuvenate the debate. I could do this by showing how I personally identify with both national claims. The op-ed I wrote was called "I am a Zionist. And I am a Palestinian Nationalist." (Note that op-ed headlines are usually written by the editorial team, rather than by the writer.) While today I would write such a piece differently owing to the evolution of my own political perspectives, at that point the framing I used captured my personal views. It was also a provocative way to spur conversation.

Note that public-commentary writing can live on a long time. In recent social media debates, I have had that piece, now several years old, brought up by another person in a heated thread. In advancing opinions through op-eds and social media, be prepared to face the consequences of your opinions changing. But as long as the given piece is guided by standards of logic and evidence, I think it is a risk worth taking. People's views *do* often change. That's a natural part of a lifetime of thinking and learning; exhibiting opinion change over time can even be a way of modeling the values of intelligent and reasoned public engagement, something that helps break down polarization and reorients us toward informed analysis.

Four Types of Questions

The types of questions academics typically use to structure our writing—descriptive, explanatory, predictive, and prescriptive—are important parts of expert inquiry. Descriptive questions ask "what is it?" and "how does it work?" Explanatory questions ask "why is it this way?" and "how did this happen?" Predictive questions ask "what will things look like in the future?" and "what is the likelihood of a given event happening?" Prescriptive questions—the focus of most of this book—ask "how should things be?" and "what ought to be done (and by whom) to get there?"

The core difference between prescriptive questions and the other three types lies in the "is-ought" distinction. "Is" refers to how things *are*, how they came to be, or how they might turn out. "Ought" refers to how things *should* be. But while there is a difference between "is" and "ought," good analysts know that the "ought" actually flows from the "is." We construct informed pre-scriptions based on our understanding of the current situation, including how it came to be.

The is-ought distinction is not only useful for framing op-ed and related analytical pieces; it is also important when navigating debates on social media. Countless times I've noticed people talk past one other when debating a given issue because one person is talking about how things are and the other is talking about how things ought to be. Identifying an is-ought slippage as it's happening can constitute a helpful intervention for steering a debate onto level ground, whether it's a debate you're engaged in or whether it's one you're observing.

What Are Your Values? How *Should* Things Be?

Even a debate that seems outmoded, like the role of women in family structures, can provide fodder for a fresh take. In a *New York Times* op-ed called "Do Millennial Men Want Stay-at-Home Wives?" Stephanie Coontz, a history and family studies professor at Evergreen State College, traced the results from a new study revealing that, in her words, "fewer of the youngest millennials, those aged 18 to 25, support egalitarian family arrangements than did the same age group 20 years earlier." The rest of her op-ed links these findings to current trends in the workplace and includes a comparison of family-leave policies around the world. Coontz was able to take what seemed like a stale debate and inject it with new data and analysis.[5]

Coontz was not weighing in directly on the "ought" question about whether women should or should not stay at home. Still, she tipped her hand when she wrote: "Are we facing a stall or even a turnaround in the movement toward gender equality? That's a possibility, especially *if we continue to pin our hopes* on an evolution-ary process of generational liberalization" (emphasis mine). In her case, onto an underlying prescriptive argument (societies should strive toward gender equality) she placed a descriptive question (what are current attitudes?) and an explanatory question (why do millennials hold these attitudes?), finally landing on a supplementary prescriptive question: what kinds of policies should the US put into place to bring about more gender equality?

Target Audience

Identifying the target audience will help determine the optimal outlet for your piece. It can also work in reverse; the audience of an outlet with which you already have a relationship may determine a convenient way to frame the piece. When I had a regular spot at the *Globe and Mail*, I tailored my pieces to suit a primarily Canadian audience. When I had a regular spot in *Haaretz* (English edition), I thought about my audience as primarily non-Israeli and Jewish. (I say non-Israeli because Israelis tend to read the Hebrew-language press.) You might be seeking to write for a segment of the public that is already somewhat specialized. Readers of *Foreign Policy* or *Foreign Affairs* are more likely to be conversant in basic international relations trends and concepts, for example, than the average newspaper reader. Another consideration is political slant. Finding an outlet that has a clear ideological or philosophical orientation that matches yours is a mixed blessing; you will find many like-minded readers, but you will be less likely to have an opportunity to persuade the skeptics.

Second, whose interests are you trying to serve, and what are their guiding values? Do you see your primary role as fulfilling the national interests of your country? Or perhaps you feel you're there to serve the needs of a particular ethnic or religious group. This is a legitimate aim, but be aware that critics may accuse you of partisanship or tribalism. (Maybe this is okay with you.) Or perhaps you are guided by a particular value like justice, the rule of law, social justice, compassion, environmental stewardship, and so on.

While you may hold different values from some readers, an important tactic for being persuasive is to situate arguments in the broadest context of common values. What can everyone agree on? Trying to contextualize your points in terms of peace, human rights, civil rights, equality, prosperity, health, safety, or security can help persuade a skeptical readership, even where disagreements about policy issues are typically deep and wide. (I discuss persuasion further in chapter 7.)

The Risks of Amplifying Your Voice

Though bringing more expert voices to the public sphere enriches the level of public debate and thus is good for democratic discourse, putting yourself out there, even with appropriate credentials, carries some risk. The level of risk depends not only on what your general disposition is when it comes to public criticism, but also on various identity factors (real or perceived), including gender, racialization, minoritization, sexual and gender identity, and employment status.

The first risk comes from the uncomfortable feelings resulting from pushback. I discuss this much more fully in chapters 10 and 11. For now, I'll say this: getting criticized not only comes with the territory but can be a sign that the piece has spurred conversation where most needed. The importance of developing a thick skin is by now a truism in most professional fields, and this is no different. A related bit of advice one sometimes hears is "never read the comments." This might be useful on the anonymous message boards that some news outlets still run. Those comment pages can, indeed, feel like a swamp. But it's less useful, and harder to avoid, when you're trying to develop a social media presence. There, particularly on platforms where people use their real names, it is important to listen and engage thoughtfully with critics. If you have deliberately or inadvertently scratched a wound or been seen to contribute to some sort of structural oppression, it is important to account for this. (I discuss this further in chapters 10 and 11.)

I also encourage you to track from which political and communal direction the incoming criticism feels most stinging. Noting this privately can reveal which values you most care about and which professional, activist, or scholarly communities you most value. It doesn't mean that those folks are right, necessarily, but gaining more insight into what drives you politically and emotion-ally can be a valuable way to develop political judgments and cope with emotional upheaval, all while helping you stay true to what you actually believe in. (I discuss this further in chapter 11.)

In addition to the unpleasantness that sometimes comes from being criticized, there are the professional or even safety risks that may come from writing for public audiences. Having tenure helps buffer a writer from advancing controversial ideas. (I discuss the question of public writing in the context of tenure and promotion in chapter 12.) Having a job helps more than being on the market, and so on. If you are currently looking for employment or may be in a position to do so in the near future, consider potential future employers. Some employers may value an employee who chal-lenges accepted wisdom on a particular issue. And even construc-tive criticism directed at a certain type of organization or industry (say, a political party to which one otherwise displays sympathies or the university system more broadly) can signal that the writer will be an asset. But this can be risky too. The principle of academic freedom is supposed to protect a scholar from advancing contro-versial ideas. But not everyone agrees on where the boundaries between scholarly discourse and private comment lie, or what separates legitimate political outrage from hatefulness. (I discuss this further in chapter 10.)

Various identities a writer may hold also intensify the risk of speaking out. A writer's racialized or minoritized identity, their class, their gender and gender identity, and their sexuality and ethnicity are all potentially linked to various risks when it comes to remaining safe in the public sphere. And while those with more vulnerable identities may be at higher risk when speaking out, we must do whatever we can to support a diverse range of voices being represented in social media and on public-commentary pages. It means that we should be aware of various forms of ally-ship. (Chapter 10 discusses various ways to alert allies to instances that require support on social media.) It also means that we should use whatever privilege we have in various spheres to speak out in the face of bullying and harassment. Our democracies will be stronger for it.

chapter three

Developing Ideas and Pitching an Op-Ed

Once you've decided you want to jump into the public-commentary sphere, how can you land on a specific idea? In this chapter, I identify 16 ways to help you come up with ideas for op-eds and related pieces in your area of expertise. I list them here and include specific examples of op-eds in the footnotes. The rest of the chapter suggests how to select a suitable outlet, how to pitch your idea to an editor, and how to deal with rejection.

How to Generate Op-Ed Ideas

1. Watch the news cycle. A real-time event presents the best opportunity to pitch an op-ed.[1] Both good news and bad news can be occasions for analysis. Beware of giving the impression of ambulance-chasing, but in the wake of a tragedy, many readers will welcome sober analysis and some sense of what to do next.[2] The death of a state leader (whether the official is currently in office or not) provides an opportunity to pitch an op-ed taking stock of the person's impact and legacy.[3] The passage of a new law, signing of an executive order, or a debate over a bill before it becomes law can be an opportunity to weigh in.[4] A key speech from a leader can serve as a launching point for an analytical and prescriptive op-ed.[5] A public apology from an elected official, or calls for an apology about some historical injustice can provide room for contemporary analysis.[6] Consider a much-talked-about anniversary[7]

or one that has not been talked about enough.[8] Similarly, elections in most any state, province, or country provide an opportunity for analysis both in advance and immediately after.[9] Perhaps there are appointments or policy decisions that require interpretation as a new government takes shape.[10] Maybe there is a governmental commission that requires a response.[11] A significant global event like a refugee crisis provides an opportunity to discuss and analyze government policy and efforts by the grassroots to sponsor and welcome refugees.[12]

2. Remember: better late than never. Sometimes weighing in later than you wished you had can itself be part of the argument. For example, the case of Hassan Diab, a Canadian citizen who was detained for years in France after having been extradited for a crime on flimsy evidence, had garnered local and national attention long before I turned to it. So my coauthor and I wove the idea of not speaking out sooner right into the piece.[13] Six months later, authorities released Diab, and he returned home to Ottawa.

3. Consider partnering with an expected or unexpected coauthor. This can be done in a few ways. One is to coauthor with someone who you normally agree with, but who brings some sort of identity perspective you feel you lack to make the argument with credibility. Another is to find someone with whom you normally disagree. Depending on the issue, an argument from two writers associated with opposing political parties could be seen to hold even more weight. Consider an op-ed in the *Washington Post* on what the US should do regarding North Korea, coauthored by Jake Sullivan and Victor Cha. Sullivan served under Vice President Joe Biden, a Democrat. Victor Cha served under President George W. Bush, a Republican. That they were able to agree on policy advice lends credence to the idea that their prescriptions stem from a policy-informed view of the situation, rather than from a partisan one.[14] (Though beware of political fallout from stating your opinions. Six months later, Cha, widely considered President Trump's likely pick for US ambassador to South Korea, was passed over after he wrote another op-ed, this one opposing a "bloody nose" strike on North Korea.)[15] On another occasion, I partnered with a

coauthor with whom I had had robust and informal debates on a different topic. Formulating an op-ed with that person enabled us to approach a vexing issue in a new way.[16]

Another way to leverage a partnership is to pitch, with one or more colleagues, two or more debate-style pieces. "Room for Debate" in the *New York Times* does this with two or more writers.[17] Then there is Thomas Juneau and Roland Paris taking to the *Globe and Mail* to debate Canada's mission in Iraq.[18]

4. Make sure to find a current news peg, even if the piece is evergreen, meaning a piece that could be placed nearly anytime as the topic wouldn't expire. When my coauthor and I in the example mentioned above submitted our piece, the editor noted that it was an evergreen piece. On the one hand, evergreen pieces are good; readers may stumble upon them long after their initial appearance. (I continue to use this particular piece in my Israel-Palestine course syllabus.) But it also means that if you want to give your editor an incentive to move it up in the publishing queue, you have to find a current news peg to hang it on. So we rewrote the lede (the opening sentence) to incorporate mention of a recent appearance of Israeli and American NGO representatives at the UN Security Council. We framed our argument by identifying a policy question that those NGO speeches left out.

Note that an analytical piece lacking a news peg might still be of interest to editors of an academic blog, rather than to an op-ed editor. And if you can lengthen it into a piece with a non-time-specific analysis, you may be able to place it in the kind of current-affairs magazines and related outlets that I discuss in chapter 5.

5. Nurture a wide network, and be on the lookout for inside sources who can provide you with data others may not have. This happened to me when a member of a large and prominent Facebook group approached me with screenshots capturing a heated argument about Israel-Palestine. In the resulting piece, I presented the material in an engaging way, tried to inform readers about particular points in Israeli-Palestinian history, and made some political judgments of my own. (I erased any identifying info from the screenshots so as not to compromise the subjects' privacy. I discuss this piece in detail in chapter 4.)[19] Other sources I maintain

keep me abreast of NGO campaigns, for example, that I sometimes write about as a window into broader issues.[20]

6. If you strongly disagree with an op-ed, consider pitching an opposing piece. Many editors welcome pitches representing a different view on something they have recently published.[21] Publishing a range of opinions helps insulate an editor from being accused of being one-sided, and also ensures a broad readership.

7. If you have just published a new book or the results of a significant new study, consider boiling the findings into an op-ed, especially if you can hang it on a current news peg. Consider the example of Zeynep Tufekci, whose book, *Twitter and Tear Gas: The Power and Fragility of Networked Protest*, was forthcoming at the time, writing about the 2017 Women's Marches in light of her research.[22] Or James Loeffler, who condensed the arguments of his recently published book *Rooted Cosmopolitans: Jews and Human Rights in the Twentieth Century*, pegging the piece to Israel's 70th anniversary.[23] Both op-eds appeared in the *New York Times*.

8. Watch the buzz on social media. Watching debates unfold on social media platforms will give you a window into how people are talking about particular issues. Understanding how society thinks about issues can sometimes be just as important as the contours of the issue itself. Policy topics, whether health care reform, legalization of marijuana, refugee intake, gun control, or boycott, divestment, and sanctions (BDS) against Israel, largely depend on public opinion. A specific emerging social media trend, such as the #MeToo movement, can occasion a piece from your own experience shedding new light on the phenomenon.[24] Before #MeToo hit, I had written two pieces, one spurred by allegations against Bill Cosby, and later, one by allegations against a prominent Israeli journalist, stemming from my own experience of being a victim of sexual harassment and coercion.[25] Pegging my experiences to the headlines was a way of positioning my piece, which was really an evergreen piece, in the news cycle. Once the #MeToo hashtag emerged, I could repost those pieces in my social media feed if I wished. (If you do repost old material, it's important to tell readers that the piece is from a previous month or year. I discuss the phenomenon of old pieces being reposted without such cues in chapter 7.)

Noticing a more obscure hashtag emerge, especially one that is not getting a lot of media attention because it may be specific to one country or subculture, can be another opportunity for a pitch. I wrote another piece stemming from an Israeli hashtag aimed at raising awareness of sexual assault in the Israeli military.[26]

9. Related to the examples above, did something upsetting, disturbing, or surprising happen to you that pulls back the veil on broader social or political forces at work? Take the example of an op-ed writer who took his experience of being turned away by Israel's airport border control and wrote a piece about Palestinian identity, human rights NGOs, and the boycott movement.[27] Charles M. Blow, a *New York Times* columnist, gave a harrowing account of his son being stopped on his university campus at gunpoint, an incident that starkly illustrates contemporary racism.[28] We are a species of storytellers: sharing a personal story draws the reader in, is more likely to wedge in audience memory, and can make what seem like abstract issues into something concrete. As psychologists have shown, compelling stories not only draw and keep our attention; they also motivate us to take action.[29]

10. Annual events like holidays or other seasonal happenings pose an opportunity for an op-ed on some pressing issue. The back-to-school season can be an opportunity for professors to take stock of an educational, campus, or pedagogical issue. Christmas lends itself to discussing issues ranging from the role of religion in the public sphere to multiculturalism to consumer culture to poverty and hunger to issues around loneliness and mental health. American Thanksgiving provides an opportunity to write about topics including Indigenous issues, food ethics, and how best to navigate political conversations around the dinner table. Canadian Thanksgiving could be an opportunity to ask whether this is a truly ecumenical holiday or not.

11. If you're traveling, consider finding an off-the-beaten track tour that enables the telling of a less understood story about something of historical, social, or political relevance with contemporary implications. I have done this when I asked the founder of an NGO in Israel to show me the sites of destroyed Palestinian villages in the Tel Aviv area.[30] I wrote another piece after visiting a

coexistence school in Jerusalem and followed it up by interviewing some alumni.[31] Interviews can also be done by phone or Skype, once you've returned from your travels.

12. Make your travel local. Virtually all of us have access to some potentially illuminating places in our own cities or towns. These might be a historical site, a museum, a visible example of a knotty urban planning issue, or even a resident with an intriguing story that sheds light on some larger issue of public interest.

13. Watch for the release of films in your area of expertise. Even if newspapers run separate reviews, opinion editors may welcome an op-ed style piece hitting on a particular theme raised by a new film.[32]

14. Watch for the results of new surveys being published. Opinion pages require analysis and prescription from subject experts when these emerge. I wrote a piece when the Pew Research Center surveyed Israeli Jews.[33]

15. The fallout from an op-ed you have written might give you an occasion to write another piece about that first experience. This has happened to me more than once.[34]

16. Keep an eye on your own day-to-day experiences, and listen closely to your mental observations. What might start off as a private rant could turn into a well-argued piece if you build the argument carefully. One of my earliest op-eds was a piece I pitched to the *Ottawa Citizen* stemming from the three days I spent at the Ontario Universities' Fair, meeting with prospective students and their parents, and privately feeling bemused by how often parents spoke on behalf of, and instead of, their kids.[35]

Pitching to the Right Outlet

Once your op-ed idea is in place, it's important to consider the right outlet. If it's a local issue, a local outlet might be best. On the other hand, sometimes local papers are saturated with coverage by regular staff writers, and so another outlet, farther afield, might be interested in exposing their readers to a new topic.[36] Another option is to focus on platforms that cater to academic writers. One example is the Monkey Cage at the *Washington Post*. It features mostly political scientists, but their submission site says it is open to pitches on topics from other disciplines too. Note, however, that the style may need to be less like a regular op-ed and more about disseminating research in a neutral tone. Upon inquiry, the editors will convey their expectations.

If the pitch is time sensitive, as most are, emphasize that in the pitch. Be sure to let the editor know what the argument will be and why you are pitching the piece now: in other words, what the news peg is. If you don't already have a relationship with the editor, lay out your relevant credentials and/or what specific experiences you bring that will facilitate a fresh angle. Make sure not to simply rest on your laurels; credentials are no substitute for a compelling argument backed by logic and evidence.

Do not pitch to more than one outlet simultaneously. Editors don't like it. If you are awaiting a response from one editor, follow up in a couple of days. If you still haven't received an answer and feel you cannot wait, let the editor know that you are pulling the pitch before submitting it elsewhere. If you do submit to more than one outlet simultaneously without letting the first editor know and both accept it, pulling it from one editor may very well burn a bridge with them. It's too risky, and it is considered bad form. During the entire process from pitch to publication, make sure to stay close to your email; it's important to be able to respond quickly to the editor both at the acceptance stage and at the revision stage. (Sometimes editors will send you material they suggest you include, such as breaking news or links to other related stories on their site, while you are drafting.) If the editor replies affirmatively to your pitch and asks you when you can file, consider a turnaround time within a day or two if possible. The piece should remain fresh.

Once you submit the full piece, the editor will likely suggest edits or more extensive revisions. Often in an op-ed, revisions are a fairly simple matter: editors ask for clarification or elaboration, etc. Usually it's clear how addressing these points will strengthen the piece. If you strongly disagree with a request, let the editor know why, but remember that the editor will ultimately decide whether or not to run the piece. And while it may be obvious, check your piece carefully before submitting it. The editorial team will copy edit, but do proper due diligence first. Plus, an editor in receipt of clean copy is a happier editor and thus will be more likely to want to work with you in the future.

Sometimes an editor will ask to see the full piece before they make a decision, or you may decide that until you have a solid working relationship with an editor, the chances of success are greater with the full piece written. I tend to work via pitches; other colleagues I know prefer to submit full pieces for consideration.

As for payment, some outlets always pay, some never do, and some pay only if they solicit the piece. As for amounts, I have seen payment run between $50 and $250 in the United States, and between $75 and $300 in Canada. Don't be afraid to ask. If you have been paid at a certain rate before, either at that same outlet or elsewhere and hope to have a new editor match it, mention that. You can do this at the pitch stage or after the piece has been accepted, depending on how important the particular sum is to you.

Once the piece has come out, I encourage you to share it on social media and make sure to stay close to your accounts for a couple of days so you can engage productively with comments. Later chapters discuss social media debate strategies.

What about factual errors? If a reader points out an error in your op-ed, immediately let the editor know. If it's online, the editor can easily make a correction. (The editor will decide whether to quietly make the correction or whether to note at the bottom of the piece that a correction has been made.) Sometimes errors result from sloppiness on the part of the writer. Other times you may feel certain that something is true and thus didn't even think to check it. Other times, data may vary widely across published studies. It is essential to fact-check even if you don't think the facts need checking. Your political or ideological critics and challengers may make hay from the error. If this happens, thank them, apologize to whomever might require an apology, and move on. Do not escalate it into a pointless social media debate and don't appear defensive.

If you develop a good relationship with an editor and have published several pieces with them, consider suggesting a regular column in their outlet. If they have space and they like your writing, they may accept.

Finally, if you wish to reprint the piece elsewhere, discuss this with your editor. Every publication has different freelance agreements; there may be a required cooling-off period between the time that the piece first appeared and the time you are allowed to reprint it. In addition, the freelance agreement may stipulate that any reprinting must credit the original source. If you've made a few changes between the first piece and its reprinted version, you can say "a version of this piece first appeared in ..." at the bottom of the reprint. In short, discuss this with your editor.

Practice Exercise

Develop a pitch email to a hypothetical editor. The pitch should address the following questions: a) What is the issue to be discussed? b) Why now? What is the news peg? Is there something in the news or some upcoming event or anniversary that makes discussion of this particular event timely? c) What is your argument? d) How will you support and illustrate your argument? d) Why should readers care? What is at stake? e) Why are you the right person to write the piece?

Dealing with Rejection

Occasionally an editor will accept a pitch but then reject the finished product. The piece you write may not be what they were expecting from the pitch. At other times, an editor might reject the piece because they changed their mind, rather than because of any problem with your execution. In these cases, the editor may offer you a kill fee. I have been rejected a handful of times after submitting a full piece based on an agreed-upon pitch. It's never pleasant when this happens, but remember that rejection is part of the writer's trade. In most cases, I have been able to place the piece in another outlet.

Sometimes, it's just a matter of fit. I worked on a piece with an editor only to have it rejected after a few rounds of edits because the fit wasn't right for the subsection of the news outlet. It was frustrating, and I felt my time had been wasted, but later, I understood.

If your piece gets rejected, consider turning it around to another outlet as soon as possible. This might mean revising the opening or providing some additional data that is relevant to the geographic context of the new audience. A piece on student mental health, for example, headed to a Canadian outlet, should include Canadian data. If that outlet rejects it and you want to send it to an American outlet, *and* assuming the main argument is of general interest, swap out some (or all) of the Canadian data for American data before making what is hopefully a generalizable argument.

Unlike with journal articles, op-ed writers also have the advantage of developing a relationship with an editor who might be more amenable to accepting a subsequent pitch, knowing the quality of the writing and argumentation they can expect. (Scholars can theoretically publish in the same academic journal more than once, but they don't tend to do so as often.) This means that regular op-ed writing, particularly with the same set of editors, can, hypothetically, reduce your chances of being rejected. An editor can more easily come to believe in you and your product.

Part of how I became attracted to op-ed writing was wanting to find a way to insert my voice into an ongoing conversation, wanting to reach a wider audience, and enjoying the feeling that I didn't have to cover everything in a single op-ed. Another reason was that the pace of academic writing and the style and intensity of rejection was starting to wear away at my emotional buffers and suck my creativity dry.

While I would never make the argument that op-ed writing is for those who can't publish academic books and articles, I would suggest that jumping into the op-ed and more popular fray can be a good way to replenish one's energy if the pace of academic publishing is taking a toll. By way of example, a premier journal in my field has an acceptance rate of around 12 per cent.[37] Given the glacial pace of peer review, subsequent revisions, and editorial journal decisions, that kind of publishing can be emotionally taxing. Academic careers are long, and the rise of public-commentary writing and the increase of outlets through which to do it give scholars additional options. You may find that you can move easily between the two platforms at any given point. Or you may decide that some years of your career are best devoted to more popular forms of engagement and other years are better devoted to more traditional forms of scholarly publishing.

chapter four

Writing an Effective Op-Ed and Managing the Ensuing Conversation

This chapter will lay out the mechanics of constructing an op-ed and will suggest productive ways to manage the ensuing conversation. After laying out some general principles, some of which I've touched on in earlier chapters, I will examine four published pieces: a *Globe and Mail* op-ed by international relations scholar Thomas Juneau, two of my own pieces, one in the *Forward* and another in *Haaretz*, and a *New York Times* op-ed written by actor Mayim Bialik that had unexpected results.

General Principles

Here are some general principles to keep in mind when writing an op-ed.

1. As I've discussed, while the form is different from traditional academic essays, in overall aim an op-ed is not much different. I like to think in terms of questions and answers. I'm posing a question—ideally a puzzling one—for my readers, and laying out an answer (my argument). On rare occasions, I might pose a question I don't directly answer; in those cases, I use the question to spur a related conversation. For example, after discussing a grassroots initiative by Open Hillel, a Jewish student group, to resist the political constraints introduced by a few large donors, I wrote the following:

Assuming there is truth to the dynamic that the Open Hillel leadership has identified, namely that a small cadre of large donors is increasingly managing the Jewish institutional agenda, a dynamic I have seen firsthand in other Jewish institutions, we still need to ask whether the engines of these institutions would be able to survive without these types of donors, outsized say and all.

[Rachel] Sandalow-Ash [a co-founder of Open Hillel] believes they can: "It will take some creative reformulation in terms of … cultivation of new donors, and a grass-roots approach to fundraising." Sandalow-Ash thinks "there's a choice to be made here. I don't think we are inevitably tied to the whims of donors. I think if Jewish communities made their priorities clear, many would support that."[1]

I didn't fully answer the question in my piece. Instead, I used a possible answer to highlight the work of a particular grassroots group. In a sense, the piece functions to constitute an answer: if enough people read it and get inspired, more people would presumably donate to these countercultural groups, thus giving rise to the outcome Sandalow-Ash says is possible. In this way, my op-ed represents a mix between analysis and activism, which is another way of thinking about the role of opinion writing in society. Nevertheless, do this sparingly; to build trust between writer and reader, it is helpful to answer the actual question that you pose to the greatest extent possible.

2. The lede should identify a news peg, making clear to the reader why you're writing what you're writing *now*. As discussed in chapter 3, you may have written a piece that was not inspired by any particular news event. But there is a higher chance of getting it published if you find a current event to peg it to. We'll discuss this further in the case of Thomas Juneau's op-ed, showing how he took it from evergreen to current.

3. Place your argument near the beginning. The reader should know where the piece is going long before they reach the end. We always hope readers will read the whole piece, but in reality many readers read the first paragraph and skim the rest.

4. Make sure to anticipate the critics: what would those who disagree say? Be explicit about their hypothetical counterarguments. Cite the arguments directly if they have already been articulated, or anticipate them for the reader. Be sure to cast the critics' arguments as iron person, rather than straw person, versions. The stronger the counterargument, the more powerful your rejoinders, and thus your overall argument, will appear.

5. Don't be afraid to write in the first person. Writing personally can serve to create a relationship with the reader. Of course, some op-ed writers favor a more dispassionate tone, removing themselves entirely from the narrative. Find a style that works for you.

6. Don't be afraid to tell the reader what you don't know. If we simply do not yet have all the evidence, acknowledge that. Just make sure that your lack of knowledge doesn't stem from laziness. Do whatever research you need to to write the most well-supported piece you can.

7. Vary the sentence length, but keep sentences shorter where possible. Avoid the passive tense. Be conversational. Be punchy.

8. Make sure to show the reader what's at stake. Why should the reader care? A given debate might seem narrow or arcane to the audience, so reveal what the broader public implications are.

How to Read an Op-Ed

Keeping those general principles in mind, I'll now turn to analyzing four op-eds in detail. The first task in writing good op-eds, of course, is to read many other op-eds. When reading the following pieces, ask yourself these questions:

1. What is the author's overall question? The writer may have phrased it as a question with an actual question mark, or the question may be implicit.
2. What is the author's answer to that question? Think of the answer as being equivalent to the author's argument.

3. How does the author find their way into the conversation? For example, does the author note that some people argue X, some people argue Y, and here's what they are missing? (The "here's what they are missing" is the author's argument/contribution). Or does the author simply say, "many people believe X and here's why they are mistaken?"
4. How does the author support their argument? Do they adequately use logical reasoning and empirical evidence?
5. Does the author anticipate and rebut their critics' arguments?
6. Does the piece deploy any notable stylistic devices? As a reader, do you connect with the author's voice? Does the author manage to draw you in?

Op-Ed Sample #1: How Much Should We Spend?

Thomas Juneau's piece in the *Globe and Mail* on Canadian military spending is reprinted below with permission, followed by my discussion of it. The *Globe* prefers pieces on the shorter side, and Juneau's op-ed is a concise 615 words.

OPINION: Canadian Forces Reality Check: Time to Do Less with Less

THOMAS JUNEAU

The Liberal government announced on April 6 that it is launching public consultations to inform the drafting of its new defence policy. In launching the review, Defence Minister Harjit Sajjan emphasized that defence policy must be shaped by the defence needs of the country.

This is as it should be. In practice, however, defence policy is more often than not hijacked by domestic politics, the capture of the process by bureaucratic and other interests, and the world view of whoever holds power at the time. Given that the timeline of weapons procurement is measured in decades, new governments are also boxed in by the actions—and inaction—of their predecessors.

What would be the foundation of the new defence policy if Mr. Sajjan's wise guidance is followed? Contrary to the assessments of the opening chapters of the past two defence-policy documents under the Stephen Harper and Paul Martin governments, Canada is extraordinarily safe. Few countries in history have benefitted from a position as secure as ours.

This is not to suggest that the Canadian Armed Forces (CAF) do not serve a purpose. The country has some defence needs, notably in monitoring our borders and contributing to the defence of North America alongside the United States. The CAF are also an important tool to help Canada pursue influence abroad. Sound defence policy, moreover, cannot entirely dismiss the possibility that threats could arise in the future. But the reality that Canada is a fundamentally secure country implies that there is no strategic rationale for increasing today's already small defence budget.

That today's international security environment is not peaceful is irrelevant, or at least it should be. What matters is that there is no conventional direct military threat to Canada, neither now or for the foreseeable future, while other, lesser threats are limited.

It is a matter of when, not if, terrorists try to strike Canada again. But the best defences against terrorism are law enforcement and intelligence, not frigates and fighter jets. A resurgent Russia threatens Eastern Europe—but not Canada. We should keep an eye on the evolving balance of power in East Asia and should certainly increase our diplomatic and commercial presence there—but our defence interests are limited. Instability in the Middle East will continue for decades. But none of the region's many conflicts pose a direct military threat to Canada.

In this context, Canada has the rare luxury of being able to use its military to pursue opportunities, not in response to direct threats. With its security guaranteed, Canada can and should aim to be a reliable ally to the US and to NATO, and to support vulnerable partners in hotspots throughout the world. But this does not justify the investment of large amounts of additional money for defence.

The pursuit of Canada's international interests would be best served through enhanced investments in diplomacy and development. For a fraction of the investments in major military kit, Canada can get a better bang for a smaller buck.

On the defence side, this implies that the CAF should, in the coming years and decades, do less with less. This may be unfortunate or unpalatable to some, but it is the logical consequence of the fundamental reality of Canada's secure position. To better equip the CAF to support Canada's international objectives, enhanced investments in defence diplomacy—notably in capacity-building and training programs—would provide the government with relatively inexpensive but highly valuable tools.

The foundation on which sound defence policy should be built, in sum, is a level-headed assessment of the defence needs of the country. Let us hope that the current policy review recognizes that on this basis, Canada is in a highly enviable position.

Published 14 April 2016 in the
Globe and Mail; updated 24 March 2017.

Juneau opens by identifying a news peg: "The Liberal government announced on April 6 that it is launching public consultations to inform the drafting of its new defence policy." The key word here is consultations. What soon becomes clear is that this op-ed is Juneau's way of contributing to this consultative process.

Next, Juneau does something that is a gift to debates everywhere: he reminds us that there is a difference between the "is" and the "ought." (This is something I discussed in chapter 2.) He notes that "in practice ... defence policy" results from various forces: domestic politics, "bureaucratic and other interests," leaders' worldviews, and even previous policies.

This is a descriptive and explanatory statement; it is the "is." But this op-ed isn't meant to primarily describe or explain. Instead, it's meant to prescribe. He nods to these important explanations of policy before turning to the meat of the piece, his prescriptions. "What would be the foundation of the new defence policy if Mr. Sajjan's wise guidance [which Juneau paraphrases as 'being shaped by the defence needs of the country'] is followed?" So now we know that the rest of the piece will be devoted to Juneau's view of how the next defense-spending cycle should proceed. In laying it out this way, Juneau also relies on the clear question-and-answer method of structuring an op-ed, something I encourage you to try, especially when getting started. Including an actual question mark will force you to clearly demarcate the purpose of the piece.

How soon do we get the answer to Juneau's clearly posed question? He states it gently in the paragraph that contains the question, when he writes, "Canada is extraordinarily safe. Few countries in history have benefitted from a position as secure as ours." By the end of the following paragraph, we see it stated much more firmly: "the reality that Canada is a fundamentally secure country implies that there is no strategic rationale for increasing today's already small defence budget."

As Juneau builds a case to support his argument that the defense budget should not be increased, he is careful to anticipate his critics. He does this multiple times:

- "Contrary to the assessments of the opening chapters of the past two defence-policy documents under the Stephen Harper and Paul Martin governments, Canada is extraordinarily safe."
- "Sound defence policy, moreover, cannot entirely dismiss the possibility that threats could arise in the future. But the reality that Canada is a fundamentally secure country implies that there is no strategic rationale for increasing today's already small defence budget."
- "That today's international security environment is not peaceful is irrelevant, or at least it should be."
- "The best defences against terrorism are law enforcement and intelligence, not frigates and fighter jets."

- "A resurgent Russia threatens Eastern Europe—but not Canada."
- "We should keep an eye on the evolving balance of power in East Asia and should certainly increase our diplomatic and commercial presence there—but our defence interests are limited."
- "Instability in the Middle East will continue for decades. But none of the region's many conflicts pose a direct military threat to Canada."
- "The CAF should, in the coming years and decades, do less with less. This may be unfortunate or unpalatable to some, but it is the logical consequence of the fundamental reality of Canada's secure position."

In all of these moves, Juneau manages to defend his position (summed up in the pithy phrase "doing less with less") by acknowledging those who already do or might want to disagree.

Stylistically, the piece is punchy. Juneau makes good use of the small but mighty three-letter word "but." The following paragraph uses it four times: twice to open a sentence, and twice to open a clause after an em dash. Juneau is choreographing a brief dance for the reader: here's what some people think, and here's why they are wrong. His use of the word "unpalatable" to describe why some might disagree with his argument is also strategic: it's as if he's suggesting that they are moved by visceral feelings of distaste, whereas his argument, he is implying, rests on logic and evidence.

> It is a matter of when, not if, terrorists try to strike Canada again. But the best defences against terrorism are law enforcement and intelligence, not frigates and fighter jets. A resurgent Russia threatens Eastern Europe—but not Canada. We should keep an eye on the evolving balance of power in East Asia and should certainly increase our diplomatic and commercial presence there—but our defence interests are limited. Instability in the Middle East will continue for decades. But none of the region's many conflicts pose a direct military threat to Canada.

Juneau concludes by reminding readers what underwrites his analysis: a "level-headed assessment of the defence needs of the country." Yet he is not above emotion; his final sentence injects a bit of feeling – urging the authors of the upcoming defense policy review and, by extension, the op-ed's readers, to realize that "Canada is in a highly enviable position."

~

The overall impetus for writing the piece, Juneau said when I asked him, was his "longstanding frustration," dating from his time working for the Department of National Defence, "with the dominant view in the media by defence commentators, that Canada should spend more on defence." For too long, Juneau thought, that view had gone unchallenged. "Spend more on defence, but why?" Talking in vague terms about how the world is a "dangerous place," and how "Canada must do its part" he thought, wasn't sufficient.

He found the first assumption, about looming danger, "false and misleading," and he found the second one vague. "So my starting point," he said,

> became that even though the world may be dangerous (in itself, this is debatable), Canada itself is actually remarkably safe. And to the extent that we do face threats, most of them cannot be dealt with, primarily at least, through military means. So I tried to take the main arguments often heard in favour of increased defence spending—resurgent Russia, terrorism, rising China, etc.—one by one and explain why I didn't think they actually justified more money for defence.[2]

But to increase his chances of getting a piece like this published, Juneau needed to find a news peg for what was essentially an evergreen idea (I discussed evergreen pieces in chapter 3). That news peg appeared when the government announced it would be drafting a new defense policy.

Op-Ed Sample #2: Alphabet Fights

One evening I received a private message from a friendly acquaintance. Conversation in a social media group she was in had recently become heated over the subject of Israel-Palestine. I was familiar with the group from the media (it is the same group I discuss briefly in chapter 9), where relations had become tense during the summer of 2017 over the issue of race. Tensions had erupted again with the publishing of a children's book called *P is for Palestine* by one of the group's members. The friend told me that she had collected 50 pages of screenshots. I was intrigued.

So I contacted an editor I'd worked with before. I mentioned that I had screenshots from an anonymous source. I also included a link to a basic news piece about the events. (Because we have an ongoing professional relationship, my pitch was less fully developed than if I were pitching cold.) I also mentioned that I personally knew the anonymous source so that my editor could rest assured that this would not be a broken-telephone situation. Including a news link in the pitch, as I did, is helpful for two reasons: editors can quickly get a sense of the scope of the actual event in case they are not aware of it without having to search from scratch, and it's a quick way of reassuring the editor that you won't be reproducing the news but, rather, analyzing it and making some prescriptive arguments.

My editor accepted right away. Here is the piece, originally published in the *Forward*. (Note that there were hyperlinks in the online version that did not make it into this reprinted version.)

Upper East Side Moms Facebook Group in Turmoil— Over Israel and the Palestinians

MIRA SUCHAROV

The Forward, 20 November 2017

The topic of the Israeli-Palestinian conflict is stirring controversy in unusual quarters.

A Facebook group of moms on Manhattan's Upper East Side that is known for tense exchanges (along with stroller recommendations, nanny discussions and million-dollar apartment advertisements) is teetering on the edge of dissolution with the publication of a children's book. And according to anonymous group member sources, the moderators of UES Mommas (with over 27,000 members) are discussing closing the group due to the political tension that erupted as a result.

Last week, Golbarg Bashi, an Iranian-Swedish professor of Iranian studies at Rutgers University, took to the UES Mommas group to announce the launch of her book *P Is for Palestine.*

Conflict began simmering from the very title.

"How is there an alphabet book in a nonexistent Palestinian language?" one member asked. (The book is in English.)

"You should buy a plane ticket to Palestine then," another snarked. "Let me know when you find one."

Someone suggested that Bashi should have written about the Kurds instead.

And there was sheer racism: "Nothing more racist than Muslims!!!!!!!" Many members called for the post to be taken down.

Then the lightning rod that is the name of Linda Sarsour, the Brooklyn-based Palestinian-American activist, appeared. (Bashi had tagged Sarsour in one of her posts.)

"Linda Sarsour??? LOL d is for delusional I is for Israel s is for sue me. ..." And, in a fit of absurdity: "Linda Sarsour??!!!! Was Hitler not available to write a blurb?"

O for obsession, anyone?

There were some attempts at compassion: "Congratulations on your book and please know that many who love Israel also would celebrate your achievement, care about your safety and rights as an American and support you in this endeavor!"

Eventually, tired talking points emerged, like the possibly apocryphal quote attributed to Golda Meir: "Peace will come when the Arabs will love their children more than they hate us."

According to the crowd-funded video for the book (a copy of the published version wasn't available before this article was published), the author writes that "A is for Arabic, B is for Bethlehem, D is for 'Dabkeh, a delightful dance.' There's also Gaza and Yallah and 'Miftah, a key of return'" [punctuation in original].

The word that landed with a thud in the mom's group, though, was intifada. "I is for Intifada, Intifada is Arabic for rising up for what is right, if you are a kid or grownup!" the book says.

In response, some mommy group members shared memories of terror attacks in Israel.

Does invoking the intifada mean celebrating violence?

As with many things related to Israel-Palestine, the answer is complicated. The first intifada (1987–1993) consisted largely of rocks, Molotov cocktails, general strikes, tire burnings and graffiti. It wasn't without bloodshed, though. Nearly 300 Israelis were killed, including 175 civilians. But Palestinians bore the brunt of the violence: Nearly 2,000 Palestinians were killed (with 359 of those being killed by other Palestinians).

As I have detailed in my book *The International Self: Psychoanalysis and the Search for Israeli-Palestinian Peace*, the first intifada showed Israelis that how the army suppressed the uprising challenged society's values of fighting "wars of no alternative" and deploying only purity of arms. The intifada arguably humanized Palestinians in the eyes of Israelis and paved the way for the 1993 Oslo agreement.

During the final year of that uprising, I was attending the Hebrew University. To get downtown, we sometimes took the bus route that cut through East Jerusalem. One American friend from those days recalls rocks being thrown at her bus. "Were you scared?" I asked. "Kind of," she said. "But mostly I felt like it was wrong to be driving through there when we could take a longer route and not flaunt our freedom."

Fast-forward seven years, and the second intifada was much more violent. Frustrated by lack of progress in the 2000 Camp David talks between Yasser Arafat and Ehud Barak, followed by Ariel Sharon's visit to the Temple Mount, Palestinians ramped up their use of force. One thousand Israelis and 3,000 Palestinians died during that four and a half year uprising.

So does *P Is for Palestine* celebrate violence? Possibly. But not necessarily. Resistance to the occupation involves a lot more than the use of force. And it surely involves much more than wanting to hurt Israelis out of a sense of hatred. There is, after all, personal and collective freedom at stake.

And if it does celebrate violence, even implicitly, and if we are going to censure a book for celebrating the intifada as child's play, then we might want to rethink letting our own kids walk around in Israel Defense Forces T-shirts, a common fashion staple among young Diaspora Jews. I'm probably not the only teen of my generation who had gotten her hands on army-issued IDF surplus and wore it to Jewish summer camp, awash in a sense of tribal solidarity.

For every Diaspora Jew or Israeli frightened by the threat of Palestinian violence and the "intifada" word, there are many more Palestinians terrorized by those who wear the IDF uniform and order administrative detention and home demolitions and carry out night raids. And if violence is unacceptable, then there are other, more peaceful means to pursue resistance.

And last I checked, activists like Linda Sarsour are at the forefront of those efforts. So something tells me that this fight isn't actually about violence after all, but about wanting those who are seeking their freedom to just go away.[3]

My first task, as I was poring over those screenshots, was to get a sense of the trajectory of the debate so I could summarize it for the readers in a concise and engaging way. To do that, I needed to select some choice quotations. I tried to retain a wry voice throughout that section.

In the next section, I posed one of the trickiest questions directly. Given that much hay had been made in the mom's group from the children's book page saying "I is for Intifada," I needed to ask, "Does the inclusion of the Intifada mean celebrating violence?"

Here's where I drew on my own scholarly understanding of the situation in Israel-Palestine to answer the question I had posed. First, I outlined what each of the two Palestinian Intifada uprisings (1987–1993 and 2000–2005) had entailed in terms of casualty figures and scope of violence. Referring to my own book, I also included some analysis of the importance of the first Intifada in humanizing Palestinians in the eyes of Israelis. Then I included a reference to my personal experience living in Jerusalem as a student at the Hebrew University during the final year of the first Intifada and included a quotation from a friend and fellow classmate from that year who spoke on condition of anonymity.

Knowing that the audience of this particular publication, the *Forward*, is primarily Jewish North American, I tried to make a point about the optics of I for Intifada by turning the lens on a popular Diaspora Jewish symbol, Israel Defense Forces souvenir T-shirts. I concluded by pointing to what I saw as the hypocrisy of casting Linda Sarsour, a Palestinian-American activist, as an enemy of the Jews, as some of the Facebook group members had done. I alluded to Sarsour's support of nonviolence. If the issue was really violence, I suggested, then perhaps people should look more kindly on activists who have specifically supported non-violent efforts. This was my way of taking to task those readers who opposed the Palestine solidarity movement for reasons that I found specious.

Op-Ed Sample #3: The Words Keep Coming

Here is another op-ed example. It started with a pitch I sent in May 2017 to my editor at *Haaretz*. Because we've worked together many times, I did not introduce myself (as you should do if you're pitching to a new editor).

Hi [xxx],

Are you interested in a piece about the disciplining of conceptual boundaries in the Israel debate in Canada's Jewish community?

Something unusual happened this week. The editor of the *Canadian Jewish News* felt compelled to write an editor's defense of his decision to publish my last column.

http://www.cjnews.com/perspectives/opinions/yonis-desk-response-controversial-column?platform=hootsuite

The criticisms he got—which were apparently intense and numerous, had been about my use of the term "occupation." *Haaretz* readers may forget how narrow the boundaries of discourse are in some Diaspora communities.

The piece would:

1. talk about the disciplining of boundaries

2. discuss the red lines that Canada's national Jewish newspaper has over the Israel debate (excluding Jewish Voice for Peace–like voices officially—in Canada the group is called Independent Jewish Voices).

3. Discuss whether the term "occupation" should be controversial, considered a matter of opinion, or else a description of fact (not surprisingly, I will argue the latter). [If this were an editor who wasn't already very familiar with my work, as we've worked together many, many times, I wouldn't have included the "not surprisingly" phrase.]

4. What Jewish communities in the Diaspora (on various sides of the issue) feel is at stake in the use of the term occupation, and what I feel is at stake.

Let me know what you think … thanks for considering.

When I submitted the actual piece, I included this disclaimer to my editor: "Here it is. I probably pitched about four or five sub-points to you; in the event, I felt the piece had room for two or three." Though over-promising can carry some risk, most editors will realize that some refining goes on during the writing stage, and they probably prefer a tighter piece than one that tries to cram in too many ideas.

Here is the piece, as published in *Haaretz*:

OPINION: In Diaspora Jewish Communities, Just Don't Call It the "Occupation"

MIRA SUCHAROV

Haaretz, 10 May 2017, 11:47 a.m.

What's in a word? If you're a Diaspora Jew, and the word has something to do with Israel, apparently a lot.

After all the column-writing I've done, something unprecedented happened last week. Owing to significant reader criticism, my editor at the *Canadian Jewish News* felt compelled to publish a note defending the running of my latest piece. The source of the complaints? That I used the word "occupation."

Two issues cry out for attention here.

The first concerns what the nature of Jewish community dialogue is, and should be, around matters relating to Israel and Palestine. The second—how is it that for so many in the Jewish community and more generally, the term "occupation" is regarded as a matter of opinion, rather than fact.

I often hear the familiar refrain that, to Diaspora Jews, Israel is like our child and so we shouldn't criticize the country publicly. But it's a weak metaphor. The State of Israel is no helpless infant: it has millions of citizens that it must serve and protect, and millions of non-citizens under its control. When it comes to civil rights and human rights, all states must be held accountable as adults.

But even if we did accept the Israel-as-child metaphor and thus agree that Diaspora criticism of Israel should be done en famille, I have to ask: where are these vigorous intra-community debates actually happening? With a few notable exceptions, they certainly aren't taking place in our day schools, summer camps, JCCs, Federations, synagogues or campus Hillels.

The fear of the word is not confined to North America. Chemi Shalev recently described how the term "occupation" is becoming taboo among many Israelis. But that doesn't give Diaspora Jews a free pass to gloss over it as well; nor can they, evidently, leave the debate over the occupation to Israelis. In fact, the discourse in Israel is moving in Orwellian directions: the head of Army Radio has now forbidden the station's journalists from using the term "West Bank." So who is having the conversations that need having?

Curiously, in my piece, I restricted my discussion of Israel to the post-1967 occupation, and did not touch what I would assume to be the far more provocative, if not radioactive, subject of 1948 or the question of restitution for the Nakba. I did, however, compare the 50th anniversary of the Israeli occupation with Canada's 150th birthday (since both fall this year), arguing that we need to end the occupation just as we need to honor the truth and reconciliation demands toward the Indigenous Peoples of Canada.

Perhaps reminding my fellow Canadian Jews that I am well aware that our own country is not free of social justice imperatives had the opposite effect. And even though I made no mention in my piece of who may or may not have indigenous status in Israel-Palestine, perhaps collective defense mechanisms kicked in, activated by the emotional discomfort of thinking about how we, as, Jewish immigrants, benefitted from Canada's settler-colonial project.

And what about the occupation?

Let's start with Gaza, the most obvious candidate for "non-occupied" status after Israel's 2005 withdrawal. Though Israel withdrew all its ground troops and settlers then, the state maintains a naval, air and, along with Egypt, ground blockade around the Strip. And despite having a political body—Hamas—ruling day-to-day affairs in the territory, Gaza is still dependent on Israel for its electricity needs; the state supplies Gaza with electricity (charging the PA $11 million per month as Israel refuses to deal with Hamas on this issue). So while it's not the kind of ground occupation we see in the West Bank, it is still a serious situation of external control.

Over in the West Bank, Palestinians do not have freedom of movement. Israel maintains a network of 59 fixed internal checkpoints well within the West Bank (meaning they cannot be simply seen as quasi-border controls protecting pre-Green Line Israel from the territories), as well as additional surprise checkpoints, hundreds of roadblocks, and some separate roads—nearly 60 kilometers of West Bank roadway is fully or partially barred to Palestinians. The separation barrier, which in some areas separates Palestinians from their land, and leaves dozens of communities either partially or totally encircled or else West of the barrier altogether, further restricts movement.

The Oslo agreement, which divided the West Bank into three sections, does not negate the fact of occupation. The PA controls Area A, which constitutes around 18 percent of the West Bank, and is where most West Bank Palestinians live. Area B's security matters are controlled by Israel, with the PA having civil control. Israel controls all facets of Area C, which represents 60 percent of the West Bank; here, 300,000 Palestinians and over 300,000 settlers live. But despite this tripartite division, one should not forget that the Israeli military can—and does—enter or exit any part of the West Bank at will.

Most importantly, and though the degree to which they are governed by Israeli military law is most apparent for Palestinian residents of Areas B and C, Palestinian residents of the West Bank are under Israeli military law while Israeli settlers are under Israeli civil law.

This is occupation.

Now, we can debate what should be the fate of Israeli settlers if Israel did withdraw, how the question of Palestinian refugee return should be adjudicated, how access to holy places in Jerusalem can be ensured, and how both peoples, and every individual, can be protected culturally and physically in the event of a one-state or two-state agreement.

But to deny that the West Bank is under military occupation right now, and has been for 50 years, is to deny the most basic of facts. It is also to raise another troubling point: If occupation isn't the right word, I can think of another term that captures things equally well, if not better. But I don't think those same readers would prefer to hear it.[4]

I chose to include this piece in this book to demonstrate that the many discussions we have on op-ed pages, in casual conversation, and on social media can sometimes illuminate important social dynamics in and of themselves. In this piece, I managed to interpret community language dynamics as a window into politics, while informing readers about the nuts and bolts of a contested issue—the occupation. I included facts and details that aren't necessarily widely known about how the occupation plays out in practice. This two-pronged goal of informing and analyzing can underwrite many policy prescriptions and served to underscore my own prescriptive argument—that calling a thing what it is can help uncover instances of injustice.

Op-Ed Sample #4: Saying Sorry

Here is an op-ed that created more negative buzz than the author probably intended: Mayim Bialik's 13 October 2017, op-ed in the *New York Times,* called "Being a Feminist in Harvey Weinstein's World."

As the #MeToo campaign was winding up, actor Mayim Bialik took to the *New York Times* to share her experiences in Hollywood. Bialik gained child-star fame in the early 1990s through the NBC sitcom *Blossom.* She now co-stars in the CBS sitcom *The Big Bang Theory.*

In the piece, which I will quote from, but not reprint in its entirety (I encourage you to do a search and read the entire piece), Bialik opens by mentioning that she is "shocked and disgusted" but not surprised by the allegations against Harvey Weinstein. She acknowledges that "industry profits on the exploitation of women—and not just on screen."

She then turns personal, saying that she "grew up constantly being teased about my appearance." She talks about her own behavior: she "made conservative choices as a young actress." She adds, "I followed my mother's strong example to not put up with anyone calling me 'baby' or demanding hugs on set. I was always aware that I was out of step with the expected norm for girls and women in Hollywood."

She continues:

> I still make choices every day as a 41-year-old actress that I think of
> as self-protecting and wise. I have decided that my sexual self is best

reserved for private situations with those I am most intimate with. I dress modestly. I don't act flirtatiously with men as a policy.

And then, in what I suspect was in response to a suggestion by her editor to clarify that she is not trying to blame the victims, she writes "Nothing—absolutely nothing—excuses men for assaulting or abusing women."

But then, seeming to undermine that claim, she writes, "But we can't be naïve about the culture we live in." She concludes:

> If you are beautiful and sexy, terrific. But having others celebrate your physical beauty is not the way to lead a meaningful life. And if—like me—you're not a perfect 10, know that there are people out there who will find you stunning, irresistible and worthy of attention, respect and love. The best part is you don't have to go to a hotel room or a casting couch to find them.

The reaction was swift and angry.[5] Within a week of her op-ed appearing, Bialik had issued a public apology.

Any op-ed, particularly one written by someone famous, can lead to an outcry. Opinion pieces are there to challenge and provoke. But there was something specific about this piece, I think, that led to more backlash than constructive give-and-take. The problem, as I see it, is threefold.

The first and most important problem is that Bialik's argument answers a different question than the one she implicitly poses at the beginning. Her argument, in other words, her "answer," is to buck the norms of beauty standards by not wearing makeup or getting manicures (as a child actor, anyway), and by making what she calls "conservative choices." But the implicit question at the beginning—the one hanging on the news peg—is how to prevent more Harvey Weinstein-type figures from preying on women in Hollywood. Dressing conservatively does not prevent rape. And if she believes that it does, she needs to provide evidence to support this controversial claim. (I, for one, have looked at the evidence and not surprisingly, it doesn't.)

The second problem is that she conflates her choices (to present conservatively and to avoid hotel rooms or the proverbial "casting room couch") with appearing nontraditional, at least as she describes it. She talks about being teased about her appearance growing up, about not being "a perfect 10," and about being "prominent nosed." So is it her behavior that we should interpret as being determinative? Or is it her (in her description) unconventional looks? And if it is the latter, how does this help us better understand what we, as a society, should be doing differently?

Finally, Bialik signals that she is not trying to justify violence against women in Hollywood. But the argument she is advancing, namely that she has avoided being the victim of sexual violence because of her conservative choices, paints a picture of causality. Causal explanations are not exactly the same as justifications, but they can appear so close in the mind's eye—particularly pertaining to questions of sexual assault—that she needs to realize that and issue more than a perfunctory preemptive statement that seems out of place as her actual argument unfolds.

After It Hits the Stands: Managing the Ensuing Conversation

This book is about the conversation that can, and hopefully will, ensue from your public-commentary pieces. It is also about how to maximize your social media use to generate op-ed and other public-commentary ideas and to enhance your research and research profile more generally. After publishing an op-ed or related piece, consider sharing it on social media. Though as sociologist Kieran Healy notes, the press-release format of social media where you hop on just to share a piece you've written and then hop off again is the least effective way to engage with the medium. This means that "occasional appearances to drop a link to one's new article into the public sphere," Healy writes, "will likely be ignored."[6]

You can also expand your reach by letting your organization's communications department know about your latest piece. They are frequently looking for ways to promote the creative output of their employees. Some op-ed and related essay writers develop an email list of friends and colleagues to whom they regularly send their pieces. I don't find this method appealing, but it may suit your style. And because email is considered more invasive than a social media stream, be sure to let recipients know how to unsubscribe from your missives.

You can also engage with commenters on most news outlets' websites, but there anonymity is even more the norm and therefore commenters tend to be both harsher and less thoughtful. I would discourage you from spending much time on those comment forums, unless it's a professional blog that attracts insiders from within your field and with whom you have, or can develop, actual professional relationships.

After publishing and sharing your op-ed, analytical essay, blog post, or podcast, hopefully a conversation will emerge. You may not feel you have the time to engage with commenters on your social media feed, but I encourage it for these reasons:

1. It's a good way to build up a following.
2. Commenting on a piece on social media platforms brings the piece up, along with the comment, into view again for friends and followers, enabling those who missed it the first time to see it again.
3. It can lead you to broaden and deepen your ideas, resulting in potentially new op-ed or research topics, or a refining of your current thinking on an issue.
4. It's a way to honor the readers and the time they've taken to read and comment. (Of course, one isn't always sure that those who comment have actually read the piece.)

Not all commenters will approach you in the spirit of healthy debate. I discuss how to deal with social media blowback, where some conversations are more constructive than others, in more detail in chapter 10.

Writing in a public outlet may be sufficient; it may be that you have had your say and have little desire to continue the conversation on social media. That is fine. This book, though, seeks to lay out the social media possibilities of public engagement, both as a way of deepening and broadening your reach and as a way of generating new ideas. While surfing social media can feel like a waste of time (I discuss social media detoxes in chapter 10), keeping plugged into social media is a good way to get a sense of what people are talking about, which news stories they are sharing, and how they are reacting to various issues. You might even change your mind on some subject you've written about, thus enabling you to write a new piece describing that shift.

It is always a risk that one will get lulled into a false sense of reality occasioned by one's self-constructed echo chamber. Recall that Facebook, at least, uses elaborate algorithms that prioritize posts by people you most interact with. This leads to more echo chambering and more strengthening of the silo walls. In chapter 7, I lay out specific strategies for escaping the echo chamber. For now, keep in mind that honoring the conversations generated by public commentary, especially if commenters are coming at the issue from a range of perspectives, is probably the most powerful strategy of all.

Reactions to op-eds vary wildly. Keep tabs on what people are saying and try to be gracious in responding. If you see comments about the piece on Facebook or Twitter, defend your flank without sounding defensive. It's a fine line to walk. If the piece lands in unintended ways, there's nothing wrong with issuing a follow-up piece that seeks to clarify or even apologize for how it was taken.

Mayim Bialik did this when she published an apology on Twitter:

> Let me say clearly and explicitly that I am very sorry. What you wear and how you behave does not provide any protection from assault, nor does the way you dress or act in any way make you responsible for being assaulted; you are never responsible for being assaulted.

She concluded with "I am truly sorry for causing so much pain, and I hope you can all forgive me."[7]

As a reader, I find her apology heartfelt and genuine, and I think it's a sign of a healthy society that she was able to hear how her words sounded to many. I do wonder about the role of her editors at the initial stages. Did they do due diligence in determining whether the argument she made was really the one she intended to make? As discussed above, the piece conflated multiple issues:

what it's like to be teased about one's appearance, the reasons one might wish to forego certain aesthetic affectations, and the reasons for, and proper response to, the spate of sexual harassment and assaults in Hollywood and other places where power and success are concentrated. These are four separate issues that formed a risky admixture in an op-ed in one of the nation's top newspapers.

As for Juneau's column, he tells me that reactions to his piece "were mixed." There was the "usual truckload of insults on Twitter, the comments section of the *Globe [and Mail]* website, and … direct emails." People accused him of being, as he paraphrased it, "willfully blind to the dangers of the world." Some delivered a version of "thank God real men are out there to defend the country while weenie academics like you write rubbish." Others accused him of being a Liberal Party hack testing ideas on the government's behalf.

But Juneau also got a lot of positive feedback. Many people thanked him "for finally saying out loud what many people think but few say publicly." And, he added, "Not surprisingly for me, but maybe surprisingly for others, I got much positive feedback from within the Canadian Forces, where some—but obviously not all—agreed." Finally, he got the "ultimate compliment" when he learned from friends and former colleagues that the piece was "extensively discussed" in the halls of government.[8]

Sometimes managing the conversation arising from one's public writings can feel overwhelming. Such was the case for Ta-Nehisi Coates, who shut down his Twitter account after being on the receiving end of criticism from Cornel West. Coates is the author of *Between the World and Me* and *We Were Eight Years in Power*. West, more than two decades Coates's senior, wrote *Race Matters*. In an op-ed West published in the *Guardian*, he characterized Coates as being part of the "neoliberal wing" of the "black freedom struggle," the latter with which West also identifies. He contended that by ignoring "the centrality of Wall Street power, US military policies, and the complex dynamics of class, gender, and sexuality in black America," as well as "the black elite's refusal to confront poverty, patriarchy or transphobia," Coates's view was "too narrow and dangerously misleading."[9] Further, West wrote, Coates "fetishizes white supremacy."

In this case, the final straw in the feud between these two public intellectuals was an op-ed by West in the *Guardian* attacking Coates. As the debate migrated to Twitter, including the white supremacist Richard Spencer retweeting West approvingly, Coates decided to leave Twitter and his 1.25 million followers altogether. "peace y'all. i'm out. I didn't get in it for this," Coates tweeted.[10]

As for me, not long after I published that *Haaretz* piece analyzing the occupation and sharing my woes about my *Canadian Jewish News* readership, I decided to quit my *CJN* column. I discuss this further in chapter 12, but for now I'll say it was a bittersweet decision. Since leaving my post entailed cutting off my voice to an important audience in my community, it is a decision I remain ambivalent about.

Finding the Right Platform: Op-Eds, Blogs, Social Media, Podcasts, and Other Outlets

Knowing how to generate ideas, how to pitch, and how to construct an op-ed are key skills for getting your message out. The digital revolution has meant that more lower-cost space on more platforms is available for advancing your ideas and potentially having an influence on important policy debates. But op-eds are not the only public-commentary form. This chapter provides an overview of the current landscape of public-commentary outlets, both written and podcasts, to help you find the most effective way in. As this book tries to show, op-ed and related publishing is interconnected with social media. Op-eds and other analytical pieces get shared and discussed on social media, and social media provides fodder for op-ed writers and other public commentators to take the temperature of society on a given issue and, thus, to contribute to an ongoing conversation. The chapter concludes with a brief overview of social media platforms.

Op-Eds

This chapter situates op-eds within the broader landscape of public commentary, and so some of this section will serve as a review of what has been discussed in previous chapters. Op-eds are usually uniform in length, typically 750 words, though some hard-copy newspapers ask for as little as 600 to 650 words. Others, especially if they are running the piece online, may allow up to 1,200 words. If the piece is to be published online, consider including hyperlinks. These enable the reader to check your sources and read through for further background and context. For revenue reasons, though, news outlets like to keep their readers on their own platform for as long as possible. This means that editors might insert hyperlinks (or encourage authors to insert hyperlinks) that bring the reader to other pieces within the same paper rather than take them to another outlet altogether. My astute students note that this can seem like the op-ed writer is stuck in her own echo chamber, so keep in mind that this practice may be editor driven.

Columnists, as opposed to freelance op-ed writers (which is what most scholars who dip into this medium are), are given dedicated space at regular intervals by the news outlet to publish what is for all intents and purposes an op-ed on a subject of the writer's choice. The functional difference is that a columnist doesn't generally have to pitch the idea before writing about it. A staff columnist is a salaried writer for the given outlet. Other columnists may be full-time employees elsewhere and maintain a regular spot in the given outlet once or twice per month. (While maintaining a full-time, tenured position, I have had regular columns at different frequencies and for different lengths of time in at least four outlets.) Other op-eds are one-off pieces that the author pitches to an editor. Some pieces are directly solicited by the editor.

Are there differences in form and style between columns and op-eds? I haven't generally thought of my op-eds as being fundamentally different in aim and scope from my regular columns; nearly all have been of a similar length and style, and all have demanded that I make an argument and deploy logic and evidence to support my points. But *New York Times* columnist Bret Stephens argues that there is a key difference between columns and op-eds: "An op-ed should never be written in the style of a newspaper column. A columnist is a generalist, often with an idiosyncratic style, who *performs* for his readers. An op-ed contributor is a specialist who seeks only to inform them."[1] Though I didn't change my style when I was writing in one capacity or another, you may find that Stephens's comments resonate. (His comments might also be more applicable to salaried columnists who are more closely associated with the newspaper's brand.) I'll leave it to you to decide.

The best way to establish a relationship with a new editor is to pitch them an idea for a piece or to write a whole piece and submit it in its entirety for consideration. If you have had success publishing with them, they may be receptive to the idea of a regular column.

Blogs

If op-eds are traditionally the domain of media outlets, there is also the less formal forum of blogging. A neologism that emerged from "weblog," blogs first came onto the scene in the late 1990s, with many bloggers focusing on US politics. Some well-known American bloggers have since migrated to senior editorial positions, like Ben Smith (now editor in chief at *BuzzFeed*), and Matthew Yglesias (co-founder of *Vox*). The format of blogs is fluid, with length and hosting platforms varying, and sometimes there is not much difference in form and style between blogs and op-eds.

Blogs exist in at least four forms: blogs run by a single blogger; blogs that bring a group of writers together; blogs hosted by traditional news outlets; and blogs appearing on the website of an organization. Unlike traditional op-eds, which tend to run from 650 to 800 words, blogs are less constrained by length. If you run a personal blog, by definition there are no editorial restrictions or gatekeeping, whether on length, topic, or anything else. On the other hand, running a personal blog means getting no editorial support for copy editing or any other editorial improvements. While blogs are sometimes seen as a less professional form of op-ed writing (something I'll discuss in the book's conclusion in the context of tenure and promotion), some scholars value blogging as a way of getting their ideas out on current issues in a consistent and timely way. And social media posts themselves can be a form of micro-blogging.

Here are some examples of news outlets that host blogs. *Huff-Post* (formerly *The Huffington Post*, which is one of the outlets where I got my start, long relied on the work of unpaid bloggers. This business model brought heat on the news organization with a class action suit against it launched by bloggers in 2011, who demanded that they be paid for their work. The judge dismissed the suit in 2012.[2] However, as of January 2018, *Huff Post* is no longer keeping unpaid contributors, and instead will run a more conventional opinion section where the editors have invited readers to contribute unsolicited pitches; authors whose pieces are accepted will be paid. It is not yet clear whether this includes unsolicited pitches and submissions.[3]

The *New York Times*'s Blog Directory lists blogs on topics including news and politics, technology, culture and media, and health, family, and education.[4] The Monkey Cage brings together political scientists to analyze politics; it started out as a stand-alone blog before it was taken over by the *Washington Post*.[5] Another *Washington Post*–hosted blog is the *Volokh Conspiracy*, comprising law professors.[6] The *Daily Beast* ran a blog devoted to Israel-Palestine called *Open Zion*, where I frequently blogged before it closed in 2013. The *Times of Israel* runs a large blog page, though in an unusual and, to my mind, disconcerting move, the paper places a disclaimer at the bottom of each piece distancing itself not only from the opinions of the writers (which is not unusual), but from the facts as well. Any of these current blogs might accept pitches from those outside the core group of contributors; it's worth contacting their editors if you think your work is within their areas of focus.

Then there are blogs hosted by institutions that aren't media outlets. An example is the teaching blog page I have contributed to at Carleton University. Being on the web, blogs like these are publicly accessible but rely on the institution's social media reach or on the writers themselves to direct additional traffic toward it through their own social media pages.[7] Another example of a blog hosted by an organization that is not a news outlet is the series of blogs hosted by the Brookings Institution.[8]

Other blogs are independently run and hosted by an individual. Daniel Drezner, a professor of international politics at The Fletcher School of Law and Diplomacy at Tufts University who currently blogs at the *Washington Post*, has been a pioneer in the world of scholar-blogging. Many of us owe him a debt of thanks for chipping away at the thick walls between scholarly research and public engagement. In the blog's earlier stages, Drezner's commitment to public engagement had been thought of as risky. When he was denied tenure at the University of Chicago in 2005, many people speculated that his blogging had something to do with it—they wondered whether his university viewed the very act of blogging as unbecoming of a scholar, rather than there being anything objectionable about what he had written in the blog. As Drezner wrote on his blog the day after he received the news, "who the hell knows?" in answer to his question "WAS IT THE FRIGGIN' BLOG??!!"[9]

Other scholar-blog examples are Cornell University's Tom Pepinsky's political science blog and the eponymously named blog by Chris Blattman of the Harris School of Public Policy at the University of Chicago, whose blog is subtitled *International Development, Economics, Politics, and Policy*.[10] The blog *National Security Law: Canadian Practice in Comparative Perspective* is run by Craig Forcese of University of Ottawa's Faculty of Law.[11] *Mediamorphis* is run by Carleton University journalism and communications professor Dwayne Winseck.[12] *Saideman's Semi-Spew* is an international relations and ethnic-conflict blog run by Stephen Saideman, an international affairs professor at Carleton University.[13] Nervana Mahmoud blogs about Egyptian politics at *From the Middle East to the British Isles*,[14] Cheryl Rofer blogs about nuclear policy at *Nuclear Diner*,[15] and Josh Marshall runs *Talking Points Memo*, a blog covering a wide range of political issues.[16]

Some blogs bring groups of scholars and analysts together. *WorthWhile Canadian Initiative: A Mainly Canadian Economics Blog* is a project of five economics professors in Canada.[17] *Lawfare: Hard National Security Choices* is edited by Benjamin Wittes of the Brookings Institution.[18] *PrawfsBlawg* is run by a group of legal scholars.[19] Other international relations and related politics blogs include *Duck of Minerva, Just Security, Political Violence @ a Glance, Lawyers, Guns & Money, Crooked Timber, Think Progress, The Diplomat, Open-Canada*, and *E-International Relations*.[20]

In an academic article, Brent Sasley and I have explored the scholarly identities that inform blogging.[21] Brock University sociologist and Canada Research Chair Andrea Doucet marked her academic appointment by starting to blog, an activity she compares to being a tortoise racing against the proverbial hare. "I am not a blogger," she writes. "I am a scholar who blogs. Sometimes. And slowly. I like to think that I can move with the grace and speed of the hare. But I'm still guided by the mantra of the tortoise: 'Slow and steady wins the race.'"[22]

One thing to note is the gender imbalance in the list of bloggers above. A few years ago, Taylor Marvin and Barbara Walter set out to investigate why almost all senior bloggers in international relations were men.[23] They concluded that most IR faculty, especially tenured professors, at top-rated research institutions were men, and international affairs blogging reflected this gender breakdown; that women were invited to join group blogs at a lower rate than men, and they also accepted at a lower rate; that the vicious nature of online criticism directed at women bloggers took on a disturbingly gendered cast; and that women were less interested in blogging for a variety of reasons, including a possible reduced propensity to share strong opinions and a lower propensity to self promote.

Some organizations have attempted to increase the visibility of women as well as people of color in public commentary. Running parallel to scholar Saara Särmä's attempt to draw attention to the marginalization of women from public-commentary spaces in her satiric takedown of what she calls "manels" (all-male panels), *Foreign Policy Interrupted* gathers together public commentators who are women, as does #WomenAlsoKnowStuff, and POCAlsoKnowStuff is aimed to increase the visibility of people of color in the public-commentary realm.[24]

Podcasts

This book focuses more on the written mode of public commentary. But an increasingly prominent way of finding one's voice, literally, is through podcasts. Sometimes the written word can translate into a podcast, and a podcast can be a good opportunity to promote your writing. Podcasts are an exploding genre, and there are too many to list here, so I'll focus on those that bridge scholarly concerns with popular ones. Benjamin Walker's *Theory of Everything* is an eclectic mix of ideas; *Ideas* is from CBC; *In Our Time* and *Thinking Allowed* are both from BBC. *Aca-Media* is an academic discussion of media. *Tel Aviv Review* sees hosts Gilad Halpern and Dahlia Scheindlin interview scholars about their recent books. *Cited* is about "higher education and research" and "the birth, life and death of academic ideas." *Scholarly Kitchen* is about scholarly publishing.[25]

Practicing History is about the scholarly craft of the discipline; *Memory Palace* is about "the past"; *Sean's Russia Blog Podcast* is run by Sean Guillory, a PhD in Russian History. There's *Radio War Nerd* by Gary Brecher about war; *Uncivil* about the US Civil War; and *Intrepid* for parallelism about national security, hosted by Stephanie Carvin at Carleton University and Craig Forcese at University of Ottawa.[26]

Scene on Radio has devoted a season to race and whiteness, and another to gender and masculinity. *Gastropod* focuses on food science and history; *The Nostalgia Trap* focuses on the life and work of individual scholars, *Ottoman History* is about, well, just that, and *Rational Security* covers national security and foreign policy issues and is hosted by Tamara Cofman Wittes, Benjamin Wittes, and Susan Hennessey, all of the Brookings Institution. Other related podcasts are *War on the Rocks* and *The National Security Law Podcast*. *Arms Control Wonk* is hosted by Jeffrey Lewis and Aaron Stein. *Treyf* (where I've appeared as a guest) bills itself as "a debatably Jewish podcast," *Judaism Unbound* is about progressive Judaism, and *Frankely Judaic* is about Jewish Studies research out of the Frankel Centre at University of Michigan.[27] *Dissent Magazine* hosts *Hot & Bothered* about the politics of climate change and *Belabored* about labor politics. *Religious Studies Project* takes a social scientific approach to religion. *Lingthusiasm* is about linguistics, and *Lexicon Valley* is about language. Malcolm Gladwell's *Revisionist History*; *Freakonomics Radio*, hosted by Steven Drubner and Stephen Levitt; and *Dan Carlin's Hardcore History* also occupy the space between scholarly and popular.[28]

A proper guide to creating podcasts would necessitate a whole other book, and while I have been a podcast guest once, I have not produced my own. For now, I'll point out the article "How to Start Your Own Podcast" by Patrick Allan and the book *Podcasting for Dummies* by Tee Morris and Chuck Tomasi, which both provide a sense of the basics.[29]

Other Analytical Forums

In addition to op-eds, there are many other forums that enable scholars and other experts to bring their written analytical skills to bear. Examples include *The Atlantic, Foreign Policy, Foreign Affairs, The New Yorker, The New Republic, The Walrus, Time, Newsweek, Mother Jones, NOW, The Awl, The Weekly Standard, The Nation, Prospect, Maclean's, Vanity Fair, New Statesman, Rolling Stone, Bloomberg,* and *Harper's.* The Monkey Cage, discussed above, falls under this category too. *The Economist* can be an outlet for scholarly informed analysis, but it usually invokes a no-byline policy. Even *Teen Vogue,* in the wake of the election of Donald Trump, has emerged as a forum for smart political analysis.

A good example of a piece that deploys the kind of argumentation discussed in this book, but which is longer than an op-ed, is "'Republican' Is Not a Synonym for 'Racist.'" by Peter Beinart in the *Atlantic.* Here is a snippet: "Liberals and conservatives may never agree on whether or how deeply bigotry infects American conservatism. They don't need to. What America needs is a conservatism whose devotees feel less stigmatized, and who earn that lack of stigma by trying harder to disentangle their support of small government and traditional morality from America's history of bigotry. To make that possible, liberals and conservatives each need something from the other."[30]

A final genre to note here is "explainer journalism," pieces that seek to unpack and illuminate a current issue. Some are written by staff at the news outlet and others bring in scholarly voices. *Vox* is an example of a good explainer platform.[31]

Social Media

Various social media platforms have come and gone. MySpace (purchased by Time Inc. in 2016) was *the* place to be from 2005 to 2008, and to say that its popularity and relevance has waned might earn this sentence the understatement-of-the-year award. Twitter is widely seen to be an important professional medium where the action happens. But because it allows for more anonymity, some people find Twitter's level of discourse to be overly hostile. Anonymity enables users to depart from the social conventions they would use in face-to-face interactions. Basic politeness, for one, tends to fall away. Plus, tweets are usually public, whereas other platforms have more elaborate privacy settings.

The brevity requirements of Twitter (the platform has recently doubled its character limit to 280 characters per tweet) intensify the dynamic of harsh exchanges. Of course, there is always the possibility of writing a stream of tweets that are meant to be read together, known as a "tweetstorm," or "threading." If you don't make clear that they are intended to be read in a string, either by numbering them or by replying to yourself to indicate that you are continuing into the next tweet, followers can easily misunderstand. Added to this is the fact that each tweet becomes its own mini-website with a dedicated URL, and if you don't fully convey the intended meaning in a single tweet, the risk of being misunderstood is great. This is what I, along with Brent Sasley, argued happened in part to a scholar named Steven Salaita, whose job offer at University of Illinois Urbana-Champaign was rescinded in 2014 after he wrote tweets that were highly critical of Israel's attacks on Gaza.[32] (I discuss these dynamics further in chapter 10.) Since then, Twitter has improved its functionality around misunderstandings: it has introduced a "comment" space to add commentary above a retweet, thus enabling users to indicate whether they are endorsing it, challenging it, or engaging with it in new ways, and Twitter has made it easier to link threads together using its threading function.[33]

By contrast, Facebook discourages anonymity. Users are required to use their full name, although using a pseudonym or only a first and middle name is possible. The latter trend is more common among younger users and may be an especially prudent move for teens and young adults. Facebook also allows for lengthier posts and comments. While snark and pithiness have their place on all social media platforms, Facebook encourages a more wide-ranging, free, and open discussion.

The culture of Facebook encourages personal photo sharing, and even the name of the platform (which emerged from the "face books" that undergraduate students on some college campuses received at the beginning of the year to learn classmates' names) reminds users, however unconsciously, that we are all human beings. Perhaps for these reasons, Facebook is considered to be the less "fashionable" medium, in the words of Kieran Healy, though for these reasons it also remains my personal favorite for engaging with others on matters of social and political importance. Compared to Twitter, Facebook has a much wider reach: Healy notes that 21 per cent of Americans with good internet access (87 per cent of Americans identify themselves as having good internet access) use Twitter, but the number jumps to 72 per cent in the case of Facebook.[34] However, all these more intimate aspects of Facebook must be seen in light of recent disturbing developments whereby the social media giant has come under fire for hosting false news and as having been targeted by Russian hacking, something I discuss in chapter 7.[35]

Instagram and Snapchat, very popular among younger users, are primarily intended for photo and video sharing. Perhaps this image-heavy and text-light approach is what appeals to younger users, who may not be as interested in the political debate aspect of Facebook and Twitter. It remains to be seen whether this is a function of age or generation; today's teens may grow into the platforms that their parents currently occupy. Or maybe they will see the emotional toll it has taken on us and decide that that kind of conversational space is not for them. (I discuss the emotions of social media in chapters 10 and 11.) Or maybe our generation will eventually improve our own social media practices and leave a healthier digital landscape for our children and students to inhabit.

chapter six

Striking an Effective Online Voice

Once you determine an optimal publishing platform, you will need to develop your public voice. Are there some public writing styles that you think work better than others for connecting with readers and delivering your message? In this chapter, I consider various voices out there among op-ed writers. I mostly draw on the work of regular columnists, since that is a helpful way to identify a pattern of stylistic techniques. I review the style of seven columnists in the United States, Canada, and the United Kingdom, followed by an analysis of an unusual single op-ed that was delivered in full satire mode and published in a non-satirical outlet. I analyze the styles, but I won't evaluate their effectiveness; I consider it a matter of personal taste. Thus, you will need to settle on a voice that works for you. Following that discussion, I suggest strategies for developing your own social media style.

Thomas Friedman: Folksy Wordplay

Consider *New York Times* columnist Thomas Friedman's distinctive style, one that relies on metaphors and wordplay to describe the state of the world, as he toggles back and forth between the abstract and the concrete. Here's a recent example:

> ... as this column has been arguing, "climate change" is the right analytical framework for thinking about how we shape policy today. Why? Because we're going through three climate changes at once:

We're going through a change in the actual climate—disruptive, destructive weather events are steadily on the rise.

We're going through a change in the "climate" of globalization—going from an interconnected world to an interdependent one.… In this interdependent world, connectivity leads to prosperity and isolation leads to poverty. We got rich by being "America Connected" not "America First."

Finally, we're going through a change in the "climate" of technology and work. We're moving into a world where computers and algorithms can *analyze* (reveal previously hidden patterns); *optimize* (tell a plane which altitude to fly each mile to get the best fuel efficiency); *prophesize* (tell you when your elevator will break or what your customer is likely to buy); *customize* (tailor any product or service for you alone); and *digitize* and *automatize* more and more products and services.[1]

Friedman's style is catchy, but it has also caught the attention of satirists and more cutting critics. Political theorist Jade Schiff has described Friedman's columns as "folksy travelogue pseudo political vapidity."[2] Friedman's style has led readers to write essays devoted to the theme of how to create your own Thomas Friedman column.[3] His presentation is so distinctive that some readers see him as manufacturing recycled content wrapped in fancy packaging. In *Gawker*, Hamilton Nolan wrote a piece titled "Thomas Friedman Writes His Only Column Again."[4] It's not clear whether it's the actual repetition of content or the way he delivers it that leads to these critiques. But it's worth considering that the type of stylistic repetition that Friedman deploys may be leading critics to make negative inferences about the originality of the messages he's trying to convey.

Margaret Wente: Snark

Against Friedman's earnestness is the sarcasm of Margaret Wente. A columnist for the *Globe and Mail*, Wente relies on snark to expose what she sees as absurdity and hypocrisy. Consider the following passage from her column "Why Treat University Students Like Fragile Flowers?"

After identifying a series of accommodations that universities now offer students who face mental health challenges and an array of disabilities, Wente concludes with this: "… we are socializing young adults for fragility, not resilience. We're telling them that we don't expect them to endure unpleasant feelings such as anxiety, exam stress and feeling overwhelmed, or unpleasant speech that makes them feel bad, or unpleasant experiences such as failure. We'll send them to the cuddly room to kiss the puppy and make it better."[5]

In laying out a case for reducing the number and extent of accommodations, Wente mocks students and university culture, as she sees it. Wente's style isn't for everyone; some find it insensitive and even offensive. One advantage it possesses, though, is that it penetrates: she makes her points memorably.

Heather Mallick: Slightly Funnier Snark

Heather Mallick of the *Toronto Star* also uses snark to get her points across, though she laces it with a good dose of humor and, in the process, connects with readers in a new way. In a piece critiquing a policy being rolled out at a high school northwest of Toronto where ninth-grade students will be invited to negotiate their grades, Mallick writes,

> Recall the now-dismissed education theory that children shouldn't be praised for their results, but for the hard work they put into being lousy at things. "Good work!" we say to the toddler who can't quite blow bubbles.

Mallick continues: "This column blows bubbles, and I didn't even work hard. My best columns are the ones I'm on fire for. Flames are engulfing me now."[6]

Charles Blow: The Slow Burn

Charles Blow, also of the *New York Times*, writes in what Judaic studies and English professor Ranen Omer-Sherman calls a "distinctive incendiary style of slow-burning outrage, a rhetoric that owes to a certain political-prophetic mode."[7]

Here is a passage from Blow's piece "Dispatch from the Resistance":

> I often hear from Trump enthusiasts and accommodators that at some point resistance must submit, that the time for outrage is term-limited, that at a point, complete opposition registers as unfair and unpatriotic.
>
> This always settles on me in a most unsettling way. How is it, precisely, that right becomes less right and wrong less wrong simply by the passage of time and the weariness of repetition?
>
> How is it that morality wavers and weakens, accommodates and acquiesces?
>
> It seems to me the oddest of asks: Surrender what you know to be a principled position because "moving on" and "moderation" are the instruments that polite society uses to browbeat the radical insisting on righteous restoration.
>
> I see no value or honor in this retreat.
>
> I don't even think my crusade is a personal one, although it must be said that every day that I wake and recall that a bigoted, sexist, intolerant, transphobic scoundrel is president, my stomach turns and my skin crawls.[8]

Blow's prose is a moral call to action that operates at the personal and collective level.

David Brooks: The Columnist Who Academics Love to Hate (and Who I Love to Teach)

One particular columnist I like to assign in class because of his accessible style and knack for storytelling is also someone academics love to poke fun of: David Brooks, also of the *New York Times*. Political theorist Jade Schiff, the one who has strong opinions about Thomas Friedman, calls David Brooks's style "patient condescension."

Brooks took heat in 2017 when he wrote a column about upward mobility and cultural codes. When Brooks published the following paragraph, the internet exploded:

Recently I took a friend with only a high school degree to lunch. Insensitively, I led her into a gourmet sandwich shop. Suddenly I saw her face freeze up as she was confronted with sandwiches named "Padrino" and "Pomodoro" and ingredients like soppressata, capicollo and a striata baguette. I quickly asked her if she wanted to go somewhere else and she anxiously nodded yes and we ate Mexican.[9]

Using what Brooks may have thought was an everyday, relatable anecdote ended up triggering outrage among readers. It was a fortuitous moment for me, as I was in the middle of designing the syllabus for my op-ed course, and so we had lots to talk about that semester. Brooks's style may have gotten under the skin of some readers, but his piece and the various response op-eds succeeded in drawing attention to the issues he raised as well as to some issues his critics felt he had overlooked in his answer to the important question of how class structure is maintained.[10] Since Brooks isn't in the snark business, it's not clear to me whether he realized the effect the phrase "ate Mexican" would have on his readership. If you're going to offend, it's best not to be blindsided. This suggests that if your intended style is earnest and direct, then be extra careful with your choice of wording and the anecdotes you use.

Rex Murphy's Rants

Rex Murphy of the *National Post* likes to rant. Consider this paragraph where he discusses Hillary Clinton's post-election memoir. Here, tongue firmly in cheek, Murphy summarizes her account of the reasons she lost the race:

(a) The Russians, (b) James Comey, (c) Neanderthal sexism, (d) Global warming, (e) The invention of email, (f) The *terra incognita* known to explorers as Wisconsin, (g) John Podesta's texting habits, (h) Donna Brazile's slack delivery of debate questions, often mere hours before her debates with the superannuated socialist stooge, (i) The pathetic feminizing of Ghostbusters, (j) Robert E. Lee, (k) Bill and Loretta's tango on the tarmac—"How's the grandchildren?" "I beg your pardon," (l) The socialist grouch Bernie Sanders promising shinier ponies than she was promising, (m) The Russians again, (n) Film distributor, *auteur*, Anthony Weiner, (o) Chronic iron deficiency, (p) Failed séances with Eleanor Roosevelt, (q) Cell phones, (r) The Siege of Khartoum, (s) Sunspots, (t) The high visibility of the shuttle service between secret Wall Street speeches and public speeches denouncing Wall Street, (u) Obama holding her back on lacerating Bernie as a 'fifth-columnist' Democrat, (v) That g-d d—ed basket of deplorables, (w) Obama, for not going prime time to attack the Russians, (x) Charlie Rose's sleepy monotone, (y) The Knights Templar, and (z) A miserable campaign where nobody performed up to par except Hillary.[11]

It's hard not to avert your eyes from that paragraph.

George Monbiot: Outrage Cassandra

Or consider the *Guardian*'s George Monbiot, whose writing style political theorist and international relations scholar Anthony Burke describes as "Outrage Cassandra fuelled by a relentless injection of high octane facts."[12]

Here is Monbiot writing about Hurricane Harvey:

In 2016 the US elected a president who believes that human-driven global warming is a hoax. It was the hottest year on record, in which the US was hammered by a series of climate-related disasters. Yet the total combined coverage for the entire year on the evening and Sunday news programmes on ABC, CBS, NBC and Fox News amounted to 50 minutes. Our greatest predicament, the issue that will define our lives, has been blotted from the public's mind.

This is not an accident. But nor (with the exception of Fox News) is it likely to be a matter of policy. It reflects a deeply ingrained and scarcely conscious self-censorship. Reporters and editors ignore the subject because they have an instinct for avoiding trouble. To talk about climate breakdown (which in my view is a better term than the curiously bland labels we attach to this crisis) is to question not only Trump, not only current environmental policy, not only current economic policy—but the entire political and economic system.

And then the facts:

> We know that the severity and impact of hurricanes on coastal cities is exacerbated by at least two factors: higher sea levels, caused primarily by the thermal expansion of seawater; and greater storm intensity, caused by higher sea temperatures and the ability of warm air to hold more water than cold air.
>
> Before it reached the Gulf of Mexico, Harvey had been demoted from a tropical storm to a tropical wave. But as it reached the Gulf, where temperatures this month have been far above average, it was upgraded first to a tropical depression, then to a category one hurricane. It might have been expected to weaken as it approached the coast, as hurricanes churn the sea, bringing cooler waters to the surface. But the water it brought up from 100 meters and more was also unusually warm. By the time it reached land, Harvey had intensified to a category four hurricane.[13]

Moral outrage is best delivered with evidence-based argumentation, and Monbiot excels at this.

The Use of Satire

A related tool is what is now the nearly lost art of satire. Consider this, by Lisa Pryor writing in the *New York Times*, rendered in the best tradition of Jonathan Swift. The headline writers, in on the joke, helped Pryor's piece along by naming it "Heterosexual Couples Deserve Our Support":[14]

> Difficult as it might be to admit, there is some evidence that in an ideal world, and with all things being equal, one particular family arrangement does appear to have a slight advantage when it comes to raising children.

The reader is expecting Pryor to say a mother and a father and then ... bam!

> Of course I am speaking about lesbian parenting, which multiple studies have shown confers certain advantages on children.

After presenting data to support her point, she writes:

> We do not live in a perfect world in which every child has access to this ideal. Regardless of what laws we have in place, the reality of contemporary society is that it includes a wide variety of family types, including families headed by heterosexual couples.

And then:

> Worse still, heterosexual pregnancies typically come about as a direct result of a particular sex act heterosexual adults engage in for the purpose of their own pleasure. Despite years of warnings, public-education campaigns and public-health expenditure, heterosexual couples continue to indulge in this practice knowing full well the consequences and without apparent regard for the cost to society.
>
> They should be allowed to continue to marry and continue to raise children on one strict proviso—that they do not prevent those who are not heterosexual from doing the same.

Her column uses satire rather than snark and manages to delight the reader through the humorous element of surprise, while still managing to deliver a serious message.

Finding Your Op-Ed Voice

Perhaps there's a particular style you already favor. Or your style may evolve over time. My writing voice, for example, has become less earnest and tentative over the years. I try to keep the writing tighter and punchier. In part, this move has been a function of my evolving politics. But it's also because I want to ensure I keep the attention of my reader in a crowded digital landscape.

In coaching readers on op-ed submissions, Trish Hall of the *New York Times* puts it this way: "Write in your own voice. If you're funny, be funny. Don't write the way you think important people write, or the way you think important pieces should sound."[15] There's a certain pleasing paradox in what she's saying. Important pieces are often the ones that don't sound important: they are the ones where the author has sufficient confidence to talk directly to the reader in a way that makes clear that the author has something useful to say and a persuasive way to say it.

Practice Exercise A: Conversational Voice

FRIEND: What's your opinion about x?
YOU: I think y about x.
FRIEND: Really, huh? Why do you think that?
YOU: Because of z, a, and b.
FRIEND: But what about c? Doesn't that change things?
YOU: Yeah, I can see why you'd think c would make a difference, but it actually doesn't. Here's why.

Use the above six-line script to write a persuasive paragraph that brings a conversational voice directly to the reader. Replace the variables with ideas, remove your friend's dialogue, and smooth out the transitions.

Practice Exercise B: Urgent Voice

Take the paragraph you wrote above, and rewrite it in a blunter and more urgent voice. Which of the two paragraphs feels like a better fit for you?

Finding Your Social Media Voice

On social media, you might decide to use snark or humor, though those methods are somewhat risky. The rapid-fire nature of many social media conversations can lead people to misunderstand tone. Sarcasm is particularly risky. Emojis or even gifs (available to the social media user but not necessarily to the public-commentary writer) can help soften your tone, though beware the question of image: not everyone thinks emojis are suited to conveying a professional demeanor.[16]

Putting out a social media post and commenting on, or responding to, others' posts have different social norms attached. When posting (versus commenting on someone else's post), you are introducing a conversation. It's natural to want to receive a lot of "likes"—who doesn't like a well-timed like?—but be prepared for others to push back or disagree. Being able to then host a robust conversation or debate is a useful skill to develop.

When commenting on others' posts, be prepared to have the original poster (what's known on social media as the OP) be prickly if you push back or disagree. (This is where calling in versus calling out can be helpful. I discuss this further in chapter 9.) You are well within your rights to disagree with a post publicly, but this carries some social risk. If you don't want to be the first one to stick your neck out, wait to see if a debate between others develops. Beware the pile-on though. If one occurs, consider playing a bridging role: this can be particularly constructive if things are heating up. (I discuss the dynamics of shaming in chapter 9 and of navigating personal relationships on social media in chapter 11.)

Deploying Vulnerability

While it's important to project a certain amount of confidence and authority in one's public commentary and social media persona, one way of drawing the reader in is to deploy vulnerability. This needs to be done carefully and can be trickier for women, given existing stereotypes fuelled by sexism and misogyny.

Writers in various spheres have discussed how vulnerability can be useful in leadership positions, for example, and, drawing from feminist methodologies, in academic writing. Still, in writing about college admissions essays, *New York Times* columnist Frank Bruni criticizes what he sees as "a tendency toward runaway candor and uncensored revelation, especially about tribulations endured and hardships overcome, among kids who've grown up in the era of the overshare."[17]

In an op-ed context, I have used my own emotions to advance a bigger political point. Here's a piece I wrote in *Haaretz* challenging Israel's new law seeking to ban BDS (boycott, divestment, and sanctions) activists from entering the country. In the piece, I speculate how I would feel if I were to move towards embracing BDS and if I were banned upon arrival:

> I am picturing what I will feel like if I am indeed denied entry on my next visit, as I insist that my interrogation is conducted in Hebrew—my favorite language on earth to speak. I will probably feel a mixture of anger, frustration and shame. I will feel great disappointment that I cannot visit the people—family and friends—and places—urban and pastoral—that I love.
>
> I will probably wish I had sought citizenship during one of the three years I lived in the country while I was in my twenties. I will probably feel a sense of cognitive dissonance that the country to which I remain attached and yet so resentful for its early blindness over injustice and its continued slide to illiberalism has now used the same siege mentality I once studied and researched dispassionately—to bar me from its fortress walls. In short, I will feel bewildered, shaken and unmoored.[18]

Drawing on my own reactions was a way to illustrate the broader political issues at play between Israelis and Palestinians and between Israel and global activists, both Diaspora Jews and others.

On social media in particular, showing that you're struggling with something can be an invitation to others to share their own experiences. I have run a thread like this on the topic of anxiety. Not only did I get the personal support I was seeking in that moment, I also believe I helped others, both those posting and those lurking, to know that they are not alone.

Dropping the F-Bomb: Is It Ever Appropriate to Swear on Social Media?

Different people have different opinions on whether swearing is appropriate in professional and semi-professional settings. In fact, this question—about professors swearing in the classroom—has made it into an engaging op-ed, as Jordan Schneider, writing in the *Chronicle of Higher Education*, writes,

> I curse in class. Not every other word, but probably more than would be deemed appropriate by many. And I'm OK with that. While it might not be the most formal use of language, I don't plan on stopping, and I think there are good reasons to keep at it. So here, briefly, is why I curse in class.
>
> Part of it is the subject matter. I teach English, usually freshman composition and introductory literature courses. A big part of my classes consists of engaging students and getting them to feel safe and comfortable enough to express their own opinions. I can urge my students to tell me what they really think in class, but that command is contradicted by their 12 or so years of bad experiences and past failures on that front. They need to believe that I mean it, and speaking like they speak is one way to get past that wall—a wall that is real, strong, and will not be paid for by Mexico.[19]

While I've got my own opinions on this, I figured it would be helpful to see if my personal view squared with what others thought. That is the tricky thing about trying to give etiquette advice: etiquette by its nature is collective wisdom about what's appropriate, and what's appropriate, in turn, is a collective idea reflecting the dominant norms governing social life. So I put the question to my social network: "Hivemind," I posted. "What's your opinion on dropping the F-bomb on social media—in commentary and discussions of social and political life, real-world events, etc.? (And does it differ if it's your wall versus others'? Whether it's in a post versus a comment?)"

Not surprisingly, the answers varied from saying that it's unnecessary and unprofessional, to saying that it should be used sparingly, to saying that one should use whatever word is needed to make the point, to actually using the F-word in the answer.

If you're on the job market or are soon to be, I suggest keeping the language clean. Beyond that, I think it relates to personal style. Along with snark, rants, storytelling, alliteration, and emojis, you'll need to decide what works for you: a careful, seemingly thoughtful presentation or a blunter, elbows-out vibe. It should go without saying that careful thought and reason should guide everything you do, but it may feel more comfortable to have reasoned thoughtfulness guide your ideas, with your delivery conveying a more spontaneous, edgier feel. Try out a few different voices and see what kinds of conversations arise from each and which feels most satisfying and productive. Your public writing voice in formal public commentary and on social media will soon feel like a natural way of expressing what you most care about.

chapter seven

Avoiding the Echo Chamber and Communicating Your Ideas to an Evidence-Resistant Audience

It says a lot about the dynamics of social media that the phrase "confirmation bias" appears in a dictionary specifically devoted to that medium. Oxford's *A Dictionary of Social Media* defines confirmation bias as a "tendency to selectively attend to information that confirms one's expectations or beliefs and to discount that which does not." Tellingly, the definition concludes with "see also 'echo chamber.'"[1] Confirmation bias results in a common inclination to interact more frequently with people we already agree with.

On social media, the result is the kind of echo chamber that is even more insidious than the old kinds we had when people subscribed to a certain liberal newspaper over its conservative counterpart, or vice versa. This is because the sheer volume and cacophony of voices we experience on social media—the crisscrossing conversations on different topics without regard to what came before—gives the illusion that we are being exposed to more varied perspectives than we actually are.

This chapter will identify some tools for escaping the echo chamber in your own social media and public-commentary reading travels. I discuss how to communicate research and ideas, whether informally on social media or more formally in op-eds and other related writing, to an audience that is presumably also as vulnerable to confirmation bias and echo chambers as you are (more so, even, if they haven't read this book!). I conclude by showing how the kind of critical engagement required to escape echo chambers can also help combat the problem of "fake news" and why that term is itself problematic.

The Emotional Cocktail of Social Media

A recurring theme in this book is emotions: the emotions around rejection (chapter 3), the emotions around managing friendships and navigating social capital on social media (chapter 11), the emotions of political outrage (chapter seven) and outrage fatigue (chapter 9), and the emotions of social media addiction (chapter 10). The emotional intensity of the social media experience is what keeps us hooked and is what can, despite our best intentions, keep us locked in our silos.

Social media gives rise to a swirl of emotions. Consider the 2016 Pew report investigating social media user habits. More than one-third of social media users, the study reveals, are worn out by the amount of political content they encounter, and a majority (59%) "say that their social media interactions with those with opposing political views are stressful and frustrating—although 35% find them interesting and informative."

Most distressingly, engaging with other opinions results in an increased feeling of alienation and polarization, with "64% say[ing] their online encounters with people on the opposite side of the political spectrum leave them feeling as if they have even less in common than they thought," though "29% say they end these discussions feeling that they have more in common than they might have anticipated."[2]

The good news from this study is that in their social media travels, users are encountering those with different political perspectives. The bad news is that the emotional toll reported by social media users suggests that there is a heightened risk that people will seek out information that confirms their views, gravitate to users who post such information, and avoid others so as to save themselves the heartache.

I know the feeling firsthand of not wanting my beliefs to be challenged on social media. Here's a recent example. One of my favorite shows is *Stranger Things*, the nostalgia-drenched horror-sci-fi-fantasy-comedy-drama on Netflix. One of the terrific aspects of the production is the attention the show's writers and designers have given to mid-1980s period detail. So when a character in season 2, which is set in 1984, referred to Kentucky Fried Chicken by its acronym, "KFC," I felt a pang of righteous indignation. When my friends and I used to trek along Grant Avenue in Winnipeg's River Heights neighborhood to buy a boxed meal of chicken, fries, coleslaw, and a dinner roll, we *always* called Kentucky Fried Chicken by its full name. The acronym KFC, I was sure, came into vogue much later.

So I did what I often do in these instances. I took to Facebook. "No one, in 1984, called Kentucky Fried Chicken 'KFC,'" I posted, referencing the show. Within minutes, my wall was filled with counter evidence. "I recall my secretary saying it in the mid-80s," one older Facebook friend wrote. Another said that he had said it then too. One Facebook friend offered an "oral history," as he called it, to show that, as a "thermal poultry control technician" for Colonel Sanders, he recalled the abbreviated version being used in the American Midwest in the mid-80s. Then another Facebook friend, who was only a year old in 1984, found a 1978 *Business Week* article that referenced the acronym KFC. More and more evidence poured in.

I offered some counter arguments. Maybe there were some mitigating explanations? Was there was a difference at that time between Canadians and Americans? Did the particular region within Canada or the United States have something to do with it? More than wanting my beloved Netflix show to get the period details right, I noticed that *I wanted to be right*. I had locked myself into a position and now I felt I needed to defend it. This is a low-stakes example of recognizing how people have a tendency to seek out confirming evidence while being resistant to evidence that contradicts one's beliefs.

A related dynamic is the challenging mixture of emotions that comes with trying to persuade a skeptical audience of something upsetting. To illustrate this, let's take a more serious example: debates around the antiracist movement Black Lives Matter (BLM).

Let's say that one evening you find yourself in a social media debate about BLM with someone who is doubting the urgency of the cause. To weigh in on this issue, you want to find and share data supportive of BLM to persuade your interlocutor, along with whoever else is reading the thread. Don't forget that in addition to those who are conversing on a given thread, there are nearly always other, silent readers who are reading, watching, and hopefully learning.

What kind of data would be required to convince someone of the justness of BLM's basic cause? The movement describes its mission this way: "to build local power and to intervene in violence inflicted on Black communities by the state and vigilantes." It's a mission that relies on the premise that there clearly is a problem: "We are working for a world where Black lives are no longer systematically targeted for demise."[3] If someone doesn't believe that Black lives are "systematically targeted for demise" by US law enforcement, then it is unlikely that that person will be supportive of BLM. This means that the empirical proposition that American law enforcement officials are more violent toward Black individuals is the place to start.

You might begin by posting an article like "What the Data Really Says about Police and Racial Brutality" from *Vanity Fair*.[4] While *Vanity Fair* is a popular source, not a scholarly journal, that article provides a summary and links to 18 independent studies on the matter. This also serves to address the problem that academic journals tend to be gated, and not all of your social media interlocutors will have access to a university or college library.

But there's an emotional paradox at play. Just as you may be driven to find and share information to support your proposition, the facts of the matter may induce a sense of distress, including anger and outrage. It is, after all, distressing, angering, and outrage-inducing to read about racialized police brutality. I'm also aware that some readers of this book may know that from first-hand experience and don't need this book to tell them. Add to this the expectation that people who agree will "like" the post or a comment you make on someone else's post, and the swirl of emotions is intense and confusing indeed.

One feature of social media is that the "like" button is an awkward tool to use when wanting to react supportively to someone's unhappy news. As I was writing this, many Facebook friends were sharing articles about the death of Erica Garner. Her father, Eric Garner, had died at the hands of New York City police. Since her father's death, the younger Garner had become an antiracist activist in her own right.[5] It didn't feel right to click "like" on such an article, though I wanted to find some way to signal solidarity with the cause of antiracism and opposition to police brutality.

If you have this dual concern—that you will receive less feedback if followers are reticent about "liking" the post because it is an unpleasant topic and because you don't want to be thought to endorse something with which you disagree, you may be tempted to share only articles you agree with. This further contributes to echo chambers.

Facebook's extension of additional reaction emojis, including icons for "love," "wow," "sad," and "angry," has helped to some extent. Twitter's retweet function now includes an opening space to write commentary. (Previously, many users included a boiler-plate "retweet does not equal endorsement" phrase on their profile.) Still, plenty of ambiguity remains. This ambiguity underscores another reason why we should give people the benefit of the doubt on social media. If we are puzzled over something someone says through words or emojis, try inquiring. (I discuss "calling out and calling in" in chapter 9.)

Echo Chambers: That Warm, Fuzzy Feeling

Because political arguments can be distressing, it's natural for us to seek out people who think like we do. Through what's come to be known as social identity theory, social psychologists have demonstrated how powerful these pulls toward in-groups and out-groups are. Studies have shown that individuals favor their in-group even when it is derived from nothing more meaningful than who overestimated and who underestimated the number of dots scattered on a page. Consider then how much more powerful are pulls toward groups sharing a common identity, including ideology. In this way, social media is no different.[6]

Add to that Facebook's elaborate algorithms, and it's more likely you'll see the posts of those with whom you share common ground. While some people consistently comment on a post they disagree with, it's more common to engage with a post you agree with, at least by clicking "like," and Facebook sees this. The direct-message function (and we tend to message people we feel fondness for), as well as Facebook's ability to target ads according to user tastes and preferences, results in an echo chamber without us even realizing it.[7] By the time you read this book, the formulas may have changed yet again, since Facebook has recently attempted to respond to user complaints by reorganizing its news feed.[8]

Fearing the echo chamber enabled by social media and the internet more generally, Cass Sunstein argues for an "architecture of serendipity." He writes,

> To the extent that social media allow us to create our very own feeds, and essentially live in them, they create serious problems....
>
> Self-insulation and personalization are solutions to some genuine problems, but they also spread falsehoods, and promote polarization and fragmentation. An architecture of serendipity counteracts homophily, and promotes both self-government and individual liberty.[9]

From Sunstein's call for serendipitous encounters, one can either give up on social media altogether, or one can strive to nudge one's social media use in more diverse directions. While Karlsen, Steen-Johnsen, Wollebaek, and Enjolras prefer the term "trench warfare" over "echo chamber" to describe social media dynamics, the effects are similar. They write that the internet "not only provides the opportunity to discuss issues with like-minded people, it also increases the possibility of doing so with people who hold considerably different points of view." The result is that "people will interact and engage in debate with others who hold opposing political views, but this will only serve to strengthen their initial beliefs."[10]

Analyzing the Pew study I discussed earlier, Jack Karsten and Darrell M. West contend that the "echo chamber is not necessarily born of a refusal to consider opposing viewpoints, but has developed out of the negative political climate and of the desire to avoid confrontation."[11]

Finally, the degree to which one inhabits an echo chamber depends on one's ideological tendencies. Research suggests that liberal social media users are stuck in an echo chamber to a greater degree than are conservative users. As Bakshy, Messing, and Adamic write, "of the hard news stories shared by liberals' friends, 24% are cross-cutting, compared with 35% for conservatives."[12] And "the likelihood that an individual clicks on a cross-cutting content relative to a consistent content [is] 17% for conservatives and 6% for liberals, a pattern that is consistent with prior research."[13] Interestingly, these researchers cast doubt on the inherent value of being exposed to a wide variety of views: "Although normative scholars often argue that exposure to a diverse 'marketplace of ideas' is key to a healthy democracy, several studies have found that exposure to cross-cutting viewpoints is associated with lower levels of political participation."[14] I can't adjudicate that debate here; I will simply note that it is something worth researching further.

Ten Ways to Escape the Echo Chamber

Here are ten ways to resist the seductive pull of the echo chamber:

1. Among your social media contacts on, try to include those with whom you sometimes disagree. If you do articulate disagreement, keep it respectful. To go outside of your comfort zone to "friend" or accept a friend request from those with whom you might have sharp disagreements, consider using the separate settings that are available for various categories of friends (e.g., acquaintances) when posting private information. This can give you more peace of mind in accepting a broad array of friend requests in the first place, mitigating concerns about giving your critics or challengers too much access to private information, although even some people who agree with you can harbor ill will. Use privacy settings judiciously in general.

2. If you notice a thread with a lively debate, read it carefully
   and consider the various perspectives being advanced, even
   if you don't want to weigh in. Facebook, for example, has a
   setting on every thread you can activate that will notify you of
   a subsequent comment even if you have not participated in the
   thread directly.
3. If the idea of debating people directly makes you squeamish,
   consider posing nonthreatening questions, questions that can
   spur others to share their perspectives. "Can someone please
   relay to me the strongest criticisms of supply-side economics?"
   Or "I really want to understand the position of those who
   oppose same-sex marriage." Chances are there are social media
   participants who are longing to teach.
4. Read public commentary by numerous writers in a variety
   of outlets, particularly those you know hold or promote
   philosophical perspectives different from your own.
5. Follow a variety of news outlets and organizations. On
   organizational pages (and on some personal profiles, depending
   on the user), Facebook offers a "follow" button in addition to
   a "like" button. This feature can help reduce the echo chamber
   as participants can expose themselves to different perspectives
   without having to signal allegiance to those views.
6. When debating people you disagree with, find opportunities to
   show agreement as well as disagreement.
7. Don't underestimate the value of humor, especially of the self-
   deprecating variety. But avoid mocking, belittling, or insulting
   your interlocutor. Remember that sarcasm rarely works on social
   media.
8. Consider hosting a thread on a particular hot-button issue.
   Point to a real tension you're struggling with and let people
   from various perspectives weigh in. If engaging in these
   intense debates is unpleasant, outsource it! Let those who enjoy
   debating duke it out while you and the others watching have a
   chance to follow along, critically assess the interventions, and
   learn from the interaction. When hosting, though, you are
   ethically responsible to do proper social media housekeeping,
   which means following the conversation and calling out

any personal attacks or anything else that crosses the bounds of decency. Keep in mind that if it's on your thread, you can delete particularly egregious comments, though in some circles, deleting a comment is considered bad form, particularly if there's a sense that work (what's often called emotional or intellectual labor on social media) went into the comment or the responses to it. This is particularly the case given that deleting a comment also automatically removes any responses to that comment. Sometimes Facebook groups have explicit rules about deleting set by the moderators in consultation with the group's members.

9. Have some social media friends you can have robust but friendly debates with who are also friends in real life (or "IRL," as social media parlance goes). This can help you maintain actual interpersonal rapport and serve as a reminder that the stakes are lower than they seem through the glare of the computer screen.

10. If your positions are critiqued, take note as to whether criticisms from the left or the right sting more. This can help you map your own political positions on a particular issue. Doing so also reveals where you might wish to expand your knowledge.

Practice Exercise

Find an online debate on social media, and read through the comment thread. Consider the points of agreement and the points of disagreement. Are people disagreeing on evidence, interpretation of evidence, or on basic values? Write a comment to add to that thread hypothetically that describes and illuminates the nature of the debate.

Communicating Your Research to an Evidence-Resistant Audience

Given that your audience might be stuck in their own echo chamber and susceptible to confirmation bias, it's likely that they will seek out sources they already agree with. So, through social media engagement and your own public commentary, how can you successfully reach readers who don't already agree with you? How can you persuade more people?

The least uphill strategy is to be decidedly narrow in your scope of reach, writing for the already converted but the not-yet-active. While it's a less ambitious goal, you can still make a difference by furnishing those who share your worldview with stronger data and arguments to use in their activism. This is one way to make a difference.

But if you can, try to influence those who don't agree with you. Nothing replaces solid argumentation, the marshaling of evidence, and the expert deployment of logic. Whether you're writing an op-ed, a longer analytical essay, or a tweet or Facebook post, you need to ensure that your writing accomplishes all of these things. But there are some additional strategies that can be used to increase the chances of persuasion.

The first is at the placement stage: consider placing a piece in an outlet where the majority of the readership subscribes to different views from what you are proposing. Despite the reputation of particular outlets as representing a particular philosophical line, most editors value some diversity in their opinion pages. This can work to an extent, but it is also important to establish credibility and readership in outlets where a sympathetic audience exists. Gaining reach is a two-pronged task: establish a base of allies who will want to help promote your ideas because they are sympathetic to them, just as you will sometimes need to direct your megaphone toward the skeptics.

Once you've secured an outlet, consider how to best frame your arguments. One tactic is what behavioral scientist Robert Cialdini calls "pre-suasion," priming the audience with a related message before delivering the meat of the argument. As Cialdini explains, consumers who were shown pictures of soft pillowy clouds were more likely to be drawn to want to purchase luxuriously soft sofas compared to those who were shown pictures of hard metal coins. The coin-exposed group, on the other hand, was more likely to be drawn to cheaper furniture models.[15] For op-ed writers, this means introducing the piece by setting a scene or recounting an anecdote. For social media users, this can be done by opening a post by acknowledging what potential critics might be wondering.

These cognitive mechanisms inform the ideas of business-school coaches like June West writing on the blog of Darden School of Business at the University of Virginia. West suggests a five-step model, which she attributes to Alan H. Monroe, who developed it in the 1960s: Attention, Need, Satisfaction, Visualization, and Action. The service provider (or, in our case, the writer or social media user) must grab the attention of the audience, show them how the proposal will fulfill and satisfy some need of theirs, help them visualize the benefits, and make clear what action they need to take to get there.[16]

In chapter 3, I talked about telling a story, particularly a personal one, as one way to shape an op-ed. Powerful storytelling can disarm an audience that may otherwise be poised to reject your argument. As Michael F. Dahlstrom argues, "although the plural of anecdote may not be data, the anecdote has a greater chance of reaching and engaging with a nonexpert audience."[17] Narratives are also "associated with increased recall, ease of comprehension, and shorter reading times."[18] For these reasons, Dahlstrom points out, science education is increasingly coming to incorporate narratives as a delivery device, a device already widely used in the media.

To get through to "people who deny the facts, in science and other life areas," Gleb Tsipursky suggests a five-step model he calls EGRIP: Emotions, Goals, Rapport, Information, Positive Reinforcement. Start by tapping into their emotions (What do they care about? What are they anxious about?) by deploying empathy through active listening. Next, establish what Tsipursky calls "shared goals" (e.g., we both want peace, we both want prosperity; show you care about the other person's well-being). All this, he says, helps build rapport. Only then should you consider sharing the actual information. Doing so before building this rapport through empathetic listening can backfire, Tsipursky notes, resulting in the other person holding on to their beliefs even more tightly. Ideally, the facts and information you choose should be tailored to the original interests they expressed. If you think your hypothetical reader (or social media interlocutor) is concerned about something that the proposal wouldn't normally address, make sure to address it. Tsipursky gives the example of a climate change denier who is worried about manufacturing jobs being lost to other locales because of environmental regulation in the United States.

Tsipursky concludes:

> After all, as I told [the climate-change denier around the dinner table], the scientists are simply finding data, and it's government officials and business leaders who decide what to do with it. The key here is to show your conversation partner, without arousing a defensive or aggressive response, how their current truth denialism will lead to them undermining in the long term the shared goals we established earlier.

Tsipursky's advice aimed at conversational settings needs to be adapted for our purposes, given that op-eds require that the argument be presented near the beginning. But the spirit of the advice—identifying shared goals and values and understanding what is motivating the difference in values—can help anchor your arguments.

Finally, for social media debates in particular, Sean Jones cites another catchy formula from Lady Helena Kennedy, QC: "Prep. Position, example, reason, repeat position." Jones explains that it's crucial to get the facts down cold. Look for common ground. Be prepared to defend your position. "Lead with your best point," and keep it simple. Stay focused, and "[d]eal with one point at a time." Conclude by repeating your position. "Be courteous and thank them for 'talking.'"[19] (In chapters 10 and 11, I discuss how to navigate personal relationships on social media, where the goals of persuasion may be complicated by family and friendship dynamics.)

Fake News

While I'm pretty sanguine in this book about the role of social media in society, and I personally gain much enjoyment from it, there is no doubt that it has a dark side. In addition to the echo chamber tendencies discussed above, the friendship challenges I discuss in chapter 11, and the harassment and doxxing dynamics that can occur (see chapter 10), there's also a real threat that an article or post circulating on social media is an outright falsehood. The remainder of this chapter will discuss "fake news," how to avoid it, and what a better term might be to describe it.

One of the most striking examples of fake news spiraling out of control over the last couple of years is what's become known as "pizzagate." Here's Amanda Robb's shocking account in the *Rolling Stone*:

> [On 4 December 2016,] armed with an AR-15 semiautomatic rifle, a .38 handgun and a folding knife, [a man] strolled into [a Washington, DC pizza] restaurant and headed toward the back, where children were playing ping-pong. As waitstaff went table to table, whispering to customers to get out, Welch maneuvered into the restaurant's kitchen. He shot open a lock and found cooking supplies. He whipped open another door and found an employee bringing in fresh pizza dough. Welch did not find any captive children—Comet Ping Pong does not even have a basement—but he did prove, if there were any lingering doubts after the election, that fake news has real consequences.

The man in question, Edgar Maddison Welch, was convinced that he was on a mission to rescue children from satanic and sexual abuse rituals perpetrated by Hillary Clinton. It sounds like a case of psychosis. But the culprit wasn't neurologically or chemically imbalanced: he was responding to fake news spread via a Facebook post, a tweet, *InfoWars*, a conspiracy-theory outlet, and then in an interview on *Breitbart* before spreading to other right-wing outlets.[20]

This is one of the most well-known incidents of fake news spiraling out of control. But the rot goes deeper. At the time of this writing, allegations of Russian interference in the 2016 US election are being investigated. What we do know from a *New York Times* report is that a "shadowy company linked to the Kremlin" purchased over $100,000 worth of Facebook ads (representing 3,000 ads on hot-button issues).[21] All of this coincided with alleged Russian hacking into the Democratic National Committee computers.[22] And now, fake Russian accounts have been found to have penetrated social media to spread posts about the gun control debate in an effort to sow discord in the wake of the Florida school shooting in February 2018.[23] Whatever culpability particular social media platforms may have had, as users we must be cautious.

The issue of bots (robotic social media accounts), botnets (clusters of bots), and trolls is increasing. Bots roam mostly on Twitter but can pop up on Facebook as well. In reflecting on bot-type interference in the 2016 US election, Ben Nimmo at the Atlantic Council describes it this way: "It throws a smoke screen over the whole idea of one man, one vote. Somebody who controls 10,000 bots or 100,000 bots, they are controlling 100,000 voices and they distort the debate."[24]

Another very specific form of trolling is racist impersonators of Twitter users who present as a member of a particular racial or ethnic group by using and abusing someone's actual name and photo to portray that group in a negative light. Yair Rosenberg, a journalist for *Tablet* magazine who found himself in the antisemitic crosshairs of neo-Nazi Twitter trolls during the 2016 election, has written about partnering with a web developer to create an "Imposter Buster" bot. Unfortunately, he writes, Twitter blocked the invention.[25]

In December 2017, Twitter rolled out a new set of rules intended to block hateful accounts affiliated with racist and white supremacy ideas and organizations of the alt-right. As Don Moser in *Rolling Stone* described it, the rules sought to ban

"logos, symbols, or images whose purpose is to promote hostility and malice against others based on their race, religion, disability, sexual orientation, or ethnicity/national origin," as the company put it—and proscribed not only "specific threats of violence," but even mere association with "groups that use or promote violence against civilians to further their causes."[26]

In the wake of the new rules, however, there was confusion on the part of social media watchers as to why some groups were banned but others were spared the rod.[27]

About the term "fake news," some analysts have urged us to abandon the term altogether. Claire Wardle and Hossein Derakhshan argue that the term is "woefully inadequate to describe the complex phenomena of information pollution." They also point to the fact that politicians use it as a way to delegitimize outlets or articles that present them or their policies in an unfavorable light. Wardle and Derakhshan explain that "it's becoming a mechanism by which the powerful can clamp down upon, restrict, undermine and circumvent the free press." Donald Trump's frequent use of the phrase is a case in point.

By way of an alternative, Wardle and Derakhshan suggest the following terms:

- Mis-information is when false information is shared, but no harm is meant.
- Dis-information is when false information is knowingly shared to cause harm.
- Mal-information is when genuine information is shared to cause harm, often by moving information designed to stay private into the public sphere.[28]

In a similar vein, David Uberti argues that "political celebrities and partisan publications have used [the term fake news] to discredit the press wholesale." He prefers terms like "misinformation, deception, lies."[29]

Even as I was in the midst of writing this chapter, I fell for a piece of false news. It was 13 December 2017, and a Facebook friend had shared an article that looked like it was from the *Washington Post*, announcing a long-awaited name change of the Washington Redskins NFL franchise to the Washington Redhawks. Critics have long asserted that the name "Redskins" is racist toward Native Americans. I didn't re-post the article, but I did message a professional colleague based in Washington, DC a "go Redhawks!" sign-off, as we had been in the midst of a research query exchange when I saw the article. I then posted the same exclamation, replete with a pink-hearts background on Facebook for my entire network to see. I was surprised when, an hour later, I hadn't received many reactions. I scrolled through my feed and noticed that the friend who had originally posted the article had retracted the piece, announcing that she had discovered it was fake news. I, too, posted a retraction and messaged the colleague with clarification. (He told me that he had been puzzled, indeed.)

Later that day, calling it an act of "culture jamming" (a term used to denote subversive and often anti-consumerist campaigns), the hoaxers issued a press release:

> "We created this action to show the NFL and the Washington Football franchise how easy, popular and powerful changing the name could be," says Rebecca Nagle (Cherokee Nation), one of the organizers of the stunt. "What we're asking for changes only four letters. Just four letters! Certainly the harm that the mascot does to Native Americans outweighs the very, very minor changes the franchise would need to make."[30]

I went back to the original article to see how I'd been fooled. Looking closely, I finally noticed the subtle giveaway: the URL used was washpostsports.com whereas *Washington Post* uses washingtonpost.com. What made this even harder to detect was that the *Washington Post* often refers to itself as WaPo. (Googling "wapo" will bring up the *Washington Post* website.) So it had not seemed all that odd to me that the *Post* might use a shortened URL for its sports coverage. While I read the *Washington Post* frequently, I almost never read the sports coverage (another factor to keep in mind: make sure to be extra cautious to verify sources or sections you aren't familiar with).

I was initially angry and embarrassed when I discovered the ruse. But once I realized that the hoax was done for social-justice consciousness-raising rather than to sow harm, I felt a little better. (Readers might think it unethical; I won't weigh in on that here.) Whatever your view of the methods used by the hoaxers in this case, it proves that one must always be on alert. If there is something that seems doubtful, try plugging the issue into snopes.com, a site that weeds out rumors.

So how does false news operate? Another survey from the Pew Research Center reveals that nearly one in four (23 per cent) Americans have shared a made-up news story (either knowingly or inadvertently).[31] As Benedict Carey explains, "social media algorithms function at one level like evolutionary selection: Most lies and false rumors go nowhere, but the rare ones with appealing urban-myth 'mutations' find psychological traction, then go viral."[32] This phenomenon is reinforced by the fact that "likes," comments, and "shares" all release a "tiny bit of dopamine" to the user.[33] There is the resulting risk of a self-reinforcing loop; this can happen with any sort of news, but if it's a false story, the effect can be particularly pernicious.

The *Globe and Mail* provides some pointers for spotting the difference between real news, false news, and satire. They also have a quiz you can take to test yourself. Charmingly, they note that it's not cheating to use Google while taking their test, since "that's part of the exercise."[34]

In the spirit of combatting the false news trend, a group of thought leaders has created a "pro-truth" pledge, using a "crowd-sourcing accountability" mechanism. The pledge urges users to verify the facts before sharing, cite the "whole truth" (seek balance), cite and "share your sources," defend others "when they come under attack for sharing true information" (even if you "disagree with their point of view"), urge others, with compassion, to stop sharing "unreliable sources," and "celebrate those who retract unreliable statements."[35]

There's a final source of news that can feel misleading but isn't technically false news: that is news outlets "re-upping" an earlier piece on social media without indicating in any obvious way that it's an old article. I almost got caught in such a web, something that nearly led to this book's readers being misinformed. One night in late December 2017, I was scrolling through my Facebook feed and came across a piece the *Atlantic* had posted, an essay by Ta-Nehisi Coates criticizing the planned HBO *Confederacy* show (see chapter 9).[36] It was date-stamped by Facebook as "6 hours ago." That was all I needed to infer that it was a new article. It seemed that the show was back on the front burner. "Oh my!" I thought. "I better go back and revise the section I wrote that details the success of the #NoConfederate campaign." But then I remembered that it was best not to rely on the Facebook date-stamp and that I should instead check under the byline to see when the article had been published. August 4, it said, making it nearly five months old. No revisions were needed to my chapter on the hashtag campaign after all. But I was reminded of how careful we must be in scrutinizing social media, even with seemingly reliable sources. Ultimately, these platforms are only as valuable as their users make them.

chapter eight

What You Need to Know about Political Labels

Labels are an important way of organizing political perspectives. They can also be a convenient way of signaling value commitments, articulating policy preferences, and building coalitions. But in op-ed and related public-commentary pages, and especially on social media, labels sometimes get lost in translation. Some labels are used mostly by critics of the phenomenon (e.g., racism, sexism, ableism, antisemitism, settler colonialism, Islamophobia, homophobia, political correctness); others are used by both adherents and critics of the idea (e.g., Zionism, socialism, capitalism, feminism, multiculturalism), though sometimes in different ways. Still other concepts, like privilege, intersectionality, whiteness, heteronormativity, toxic masculinity, rape culture, indigeneity, and even words like justice and peace, are understood differently by different users, with some critics bristling at some of the terms altogether. In short, a label with which you identify may be understood differently by others, and a label that other people use to describe you may not resonate with your values or self-image. Labels can thus serve a political and cultural function in two ways: they signal to like-minded folks that the ideas you're about to present are meant in the spirit of furthering a joint cause. Or they can be deployed as a weapon to suggest that the ideas of another person shouldn't be taken seriously.

Not only do labels serve political and cultural functions, they serve grammatical and rhetorical purposes too; labels are a convenient shorthand for capturing a set of qualities. Brevity is the stuff of op-ed writing and social media engagement. But this comes with a cost: labeling someone or something to frame the conversation and signal a set of values can end up foreclosing discussion and impeding critical thinking.

This chapter will draw on six terms—white supremacy, rape culture, privilege, Zionism, Islamophobia, and ableism—to illustrate how, in the op-ed and public-commentary pages and on social media, various hot-button terms have themselves become the story. In the case of all of these terms, it helps to define them explicitly, according to your intended meaning. In many cases, different understandings of a term lead to misunderstandings. While terms are helpful for capturing dynamics that we want to spotlight, particularly when the dynamics are more structural and thus, paradoxically, often less visible, focusing on specific policy debates helps clear up some of the conceptual confusion that bedevils so many of these discussions.

White Supremacy

I will start with a term being heard more and more these days, especially following the neo-Nazi march in Charlottesville, Virginia, in August 2017. In the weeks and months following those harrowing events, commentators and activists tried to make sense of the apparent resurgence of far-right sentiment that had culminated in a car ramming that killed a counter protester named Heather Heyer. Activists are shining a light on aspects and practices across society that point to an implicit and explicit propping up of structural power favoring whites and disadvantaging people of color. The fact that critics of President Trump see him as cozying up to elements of the racist far-right (sometimes known as the alt-right) is only intensifying the dynamic.

Though it is hardly a new phrase, the term "white supremacy" is heard more and more in op-ed pages and on social media. "Is Trump a White Supremacist?" was the headline of one piece by *New York Times* columnist Charles Blow. His takeaway: "Either Trump is himself a white supremacist or he is a fan and defender of white supremacists, and I quite honestly am unable to separate the two designations."[1] Writing in the *Washington Post*, here's N.D.B. Connolly:

> This weekend's white power march in Charlottesville, and the march's attendant terrorist attack, reminded the country of the persistence of white supremacy, our country's 'scissors.' Right at the country's founding, racists cut black and indigenous people out of liberalism's contract. Black bodies and Native American land did not deserve the protection of contract. They deserved bondage and expropriation.[2]

Even *Teen Vogue* hosted an article by Lauren Duca called "How 'Nice White People' Benefit from Charlottesville and White Supremacy."[3]

The trouble is, white supremacists tend not to embrace the label of white supremacy. Alt-right leader Richard Spencer, for example, is on record preferring the term "identitarian" or member of the "alt-right."[4] Identity politics is seen by many to be the purview of minoritized populations, so Spencer knows what he's doing in casting "white identity" as just another form of ethnic allegiance.[5] A somewhat more neutral formulation when discussing white supremacists has become "white nationalists."

Assuming we all agree that racism should be actively opposed, how do we deal with the debate over whether white supremacy is a useful term to describe society writ large, or even to describe the views of a single, prominent individual like Spencer? Proponents of the use of the term (and by this I don't mean supporters of the actual ideology) argue that using the term is crucial in shining a light on a deeply broken aspect of society. Naming it, the logic goes, is the first step in fixing it. Opponents of the broad use of the term, even those who claim to oppose racism, argue that to paint society with such a broad brush is unhelpful and can lead to defensiveness and entrenchment by those best poised to help.

While debating the use of terms can feel like a dangerous distraction from actually addressing the scourge of racism, there is some good that comes from it. It can lead to more conscious awareness over the issue of "whiteness," something that is often taken for granted. In a better understanding of the cultural and political production of whiteness may lie the key to understanding the structuring ideology of racism.[6]

Rape Culture

A similar debate has played out among proponents and opponents of the term "rape culture." Is it a helpful or problematic term? While the term dates from the 1970s, the debate took on particular resonance at my own university in 2016, as Carleton was in the midst of drafting a new policy on sexual violence. Two op-eds published in the *Ottawa Citizen* at the height of the debate illustrate the differences.

Take Robert Sibley's piece. Rape culture, he writes, referencing the Ontario government's definition (he doesn't reveal whether or not he agrees with this definition), refers to "dominant ideas, social practices, media images and societal institutions [that] implicitly or explicitly condone sexual assault by normalizing or trivializing male sexual violence and by blaming survivors for their own abuse." Then Sibley argues against the use of the term in Carleton's sexual violence policy.

> But is it reasonable—and responsible—to claim the "culture" at Carleton University is dominated by ideas, practices, imagery and institutional arrangements that condone sexual assault, trivialize sexual violence or blame the victim? ... I have no special purchase on how women on campus perceive their circumstances. Some may well feel themselves under constant threat. But individual feelings, or even individual experience, don't necessarily reflect collective reality.

Sibley goes on to cite statistics of sexual assault at Carleton, statistics he argues reveal a very low incidence of sexual violence on the campus. Based on the empirical case he has outlined, Sibley concludes, "it is an exercise in ideological extremism to suggest Carleton University condones rape culture, tacitly or otherwise."[7]

Now consider Madeline Ashby, also writing in the *Citizen*, a few days before Sibley. She asserts that the term "rape culture" should be used in Carleton's policy document. Rape culture, Ashby writes, is the "culture that enables and encourages" sexual violence. She then lays out an empirical case of her own, citing examples of rape culture.

The problem is, none of the cases she cites had anything to do with Carleton specifically. They include the scourge of missing and murdered Indigenous women in Canada; the convicted serial killer Robert Pickton; a case at Stanford University; a case in East Long-meadow, Massachusetts; a case in Boulder, Colorado; the case of CBC broadcaster Jian Ghomeshi; and the case of actor and comedian Bill Cosby. Ashby concludes:

> Students, advocates, and activists aren't asking Carleton for a lot. What they're asking for is an admission that this is the culture we all live in, and that it's our responsibility to change it. Part of that responsibility is first acknowledging that there is a problem with campus rape, both in Ontario and elsewhere, and that problem grows in a culture—just like strains of a virus need a hospitable growth culture to flourish in. And if administrators need victims to speak up, they need to speak out, first.[8]

The concept of "culture" means something that is specific to a particular time or place. As it does not vary across time or place, breathing, for example, is not a cultural code. On the other hand, handshakes, bowing, giving high-fives, or dueling to settle disputes are examples of cultural signifiers that have waxed or waned across time and vary across geographic locales. The problem is thus, in my view, that the rape culture debate quickly bypassed this important conceptual point, leading to much shouting across the divide. In other words, was rape culture something specific to Carleton, or is Carleton simply reflecting the broader society? If the debate had been more focused on understanding how labels were being used, if the debate had focused on rape culture as permeating society writ large, including *all* college and university campuses, there may have been less pain and frustration. People could have more easily come to a resolution on the wording of the document, and, most urgently, on how to approach the issue of sexual violence. In other words, we may have found that Sibley and Ashby, and thus those on either side of the debate, were both right.

As for Carleton's policy on sexual violence, in the end the document did mention rape culture, but only once, in a list of definitions near the beginning. In other words, the term was defined in the document but never used. It was an odd compromise revealing more about the debate I've laid out than it does, unfortunately, about the issue.[9]

Privilege

Undergirding the ideas of white supremacy and rape culture is the more basic idea of "privilege," another ordinary word that elicits a lot of heat. "Check your privilege" is a phrase we hear more and more frequently. Not everyone who ostensibly has privilege wants to acknowledge that they have it, according to proponents of the use of the phrase. Critics of the use of the phrase argue that those who are being accused of having privilege don't necessarily have it, and if they do possess privilege, it's not for the structural reasons that those who embrace the term point to.

Like white supremacy and rape culture, the concept of privilege is not new. But it has been brought to the fore in renewed ways as debates over race and gender have risen to the forefront of societal consciousness. This has partly been a function of the activities and consciousness-raising of Black Lives Matter, the Women's March, and the #MeToo movement. The trouble is, not everyone can agree on what privilege is and on who has it.

The least controversial definition of privilege is arguably economic. In capitalist societies, having more money than others provides basic material opportunities. This is straightforward. But whether intergenerational wealth transfer undermines the ideal of the merit-based society is another issue worthy of deeper consideration.[10]

More controversial is the idea of privilege occurring as a function of gender or race. The term "male privilege" became popular in the feminist lexicon in the 1970s, later followed by the term "white privilege." Here's a current example of male privilege being discussed. On the site *Everyday Feminism*, Maisha Z. Johnson outlines "160+ Examples of Male Privilege in All Areas of Life." Johnson writes,

> Our current cultural expectations, legislative system, and social programming work to sustain a hierarchy that constantly places men on the top. Consequently, men consistently achieve, succeed, and benefit at the expense of every other gender. That's called male privilege.
>
> But here's the thing about male privilege: it hurts everyone, including you. This is because accessing male privilege often requires you to conform to a toxic norm of masculinity.[11]

And then there are those who seek to identify overlaps between types of privilege, the flip side of the concept of intersectionality. Coined by Kimberlé Crenshaw in 1991, the term "intersectionality" refers to the way that overlapping identities affect the experience of individuals. Writing about black women in particular, Crenshaw set her sights on feminism and antiracism work: "The failure of feminism to interrogate race," she wrote, "means that the resistance strategies of feminism will often replicate and reinforce the subordination of people of color, and the failure of antiracism to interrogate patriarchy means that antiracism will frequently reproduce the subordination of women."[12] A few years earlier, Peggy McIntosh had pointed to the collection of attributes of privilege, introducing the "knapsack" metaphor to indicate the kind of invisible tools of access that whiteness and maleness confer.[13] More recently, activists have sought to add gender identity and sexuality to create the "cishet" moniker (cisgender and heterosexual) to the proverbial knapsack that we each carry, with some knapsacks being fuller than others. The "cishet" moniker can be tacked onto white, male, able-bodied, and so on, to indicate increasing levels of privilege.

All these identities can be mixed and matched. In his op-ed "White Economic Privilege Is Alive and Well" in the *New York Times*, Paul F. Campo writes:

> Is the white working class losing economic ground because of policies intended to improve the lives of black people? Anxiety and resentment

among some white voters about those policies certainly seemed to benefit Donald Trump's campaign last year, with its populist, ethno-nationalist message.

The problem with this belief is that it is false. The income gap between black and white working-class Americans, like the gap between black and white Americans at every income level, remains every bit as extreme as it was five decades ago. (This is also true of the income gap between Hispanic and white Americans.)[14]

Yet some have sought to resist the concept. Here's commentator Brendan O'Neill:

> How's this for dark irony: throughout 2015, "white male privilege" was the buzzphrase on every rad tweeter and liberal hack's lips, as they fumed against the easy, pampered lives allegedly enjoyed by human beings who had the fortune to be born with a penis and pale skin. Railing against "white men" and their cushy existences has become the stock-in-trade of many feminists.
>
> Yet toward the end of 2015 it was revealed that there's a social group in Britain more derided and less successful than pretty much every other social group. Guess who? Yep, young white men. Especially young working-class white men. A large sector of the group that the new identity-politics mob loves to ridicule for sailing through life unmolested and unchallenged is actually having a rough time.
>
> Consider this: 18-year-old women are 35 percent more likely to attend university than 18-year-old men; and where 37 percent of black school-leavers go to university, only 28 percent of white school-leavers do.[15]

Princeton student Tal Fortgang also sought to resist the assumptions embedded in the idea of racial and gender privilege:

> I do not accuse those who "check" me and my perspective of overt racism, although the phrase, which assumes that simply because I belong to a certain ethnic group I should be judged collectively with it, toes that line. But I do condemn them for diminishing everything I have personally accomplished, all the hard work I have done in my life, and for ascribing all the fruit I reap not to the seeds I sow but to

some invisible patron saint of white maleness who places it out for me before I even arrive. Furthermore, I condemn them for casting the equal protection clause, indeed the very idea of a meritocracy, as a myth, and for declaring that we are all governed by invisible forces (some would call them 'stigmas' or 'societal norms'), that our nation runs on racist and sexist conspiracies. Forget 'you didn't build that'; check your privilege and realize that nothing you have accomplished is real.[16]

Tongue in cheek, Fortgang then went on to outline the "privilege" he came from, outlining a harrowing story of his family's legacy of Holocaust trauma and survival. (Related but left unspoken in his piece is the question of whether light-skinned Jews consider themselves, and should be considered, white, a hotly debated topic, especially since the events in Charlottesville in the summer of 2017.)[17]

It is hard to debate a concept like privilege because in its true sense, it implies some sort of causal and constitutive force that is hard to measure because of its subtle nature. Privilege accrues, according to proponents of the term, without the holders of the assumed privilege necessarily being aware of it. As in the case of white supremacy and rape culture, debating the use of the term forces us to track disparities in society and figure out ways to increase justice and fairness. The discussion, in other words, at least gets us thinking about fundamental structural issues.

Zionism

One term that occupies a lot of space in my writings and social media travels is "Zionism." According to its proponents, it is the belief in the rightness and justness of a Jewish (and, as liberal Zionists would stress, a democratic) state. Zionism has always had its critics, who define it as a system that privileges Jews over non-Jews; a system of ethnic oppression. But lately, there's been a new twist in the debate over Zionism, as a much-maligned activist, white nationalist Richard Spencer (see the white supremacy discussion, above), has weighed in on Zionism favorably, calling himself a "white Zionist."[18]

Some anti-Zionist activists, in this case, Naomi Dann, who at the time was a Jewish Voice for Peace staffer, seized the opportunity Spencer presented to get American Jews thinking about Zionism in a much more critical way. "Richard Spencer Might Be The Worst Person In America. But He Might Also Be Right About Israel," read the headline of Dann's op-ed in the *Forward*, where she said Spencer's comparison between Zionism and white nationalism had a "kernel of truth." As Dann wrote, "Richard Spencer, whose racist views are rightfully abhorred by the majority of the Jewish community, is holding a mirror up to Zionism and the reflection isn't pretty." Dann continues:

> Looking at Israel today, we can see a state premised on the privileging of one group, and all too often perpetuating the erasure and displacement of another. We also see an obsession with demographics and the maintenance of an ethnic majority.
>
> Then you have the demolition of Palestinian homes in East Jerusalem, the state sanctioning of Jewish settlers who seize Palestinian homes in Hebron, and the policy of seizing the property of "present absentees" after Palestinians were displaced during the war to establish the state of Israel are [*sic*] just some examples.[19]

Many of Zionism's supporters believe that the ideology, at its core, supporting Jewish self-determination through what is today the State of Israel, was being misunderstood and unfairly maligned. Responding to Dann's piece, Jane Eisner, the *Forward*'s editor in chief, wrote, "It was offensive enough when, in the aftermath of the deadly events in Charlottesville, Virginia last weekend, the white supremacist leader Richard Spencer called himself a 'white Zionist,' comparing his form of Nazism to the belief in a homeland for the Jews. It was even more distressing to read on these pages a supportive rendering of that assertion by Naomi Dann of the radical group Jewish Voice for Peace." Eisner continued:

> We work hard to reflect a range of American Jewish opinion, which is why the piece and reaction to it was published. The free flow of ideas is to be cherished. But when a Jew even hints at comparing Israel to Nazis, it must be denounced.[20]

The debate about the meaning of Zionism has migrated from the op-ed pages onto the streets of social justice marches. After a controversy at the Chicago Dyke March in June 2017 where participants carrying Pride flags emblazoned with a star of David were confronted and, according to some reports, kicked out, defining Zionism became an especially contentious issue within the social justice community.[21] At the New York March for Racial Justice in October 2017, a contingent called Zioness received some heat. Women's March co-organizer Linda Sarsour, a Palestinian American political organizer and social justice advocate who attended the New York March, later said, "I'm going to be honest, there are instances of things that happened to me at this space [meaning in the march] that made me feel unsafe." Some took that to be a reference to the group Zioness.[22]

Months earlier, much ink had been spilled over the role of Zionism in the feminist movement, including the op-ed in the *New York Times*, "Does Feminism Have Room for Zionists?" written by Emily Shire. Shire writes:

> Although I hope for a two-state solution and am critical of certain Israeli government policies, I identify as a Zionist because I support Israel's right to exist as a Jewish state. Increasingly, I worry that my support for Israel will bar me from the feminist movement that, in aiming to be inclusive, has come to insist that feminism is connected to a wide variety of political causes.[23]

In an interview in the *Nation*, Linda Sarsour responded to Shire's point by saying, "It just doesn't make any sense for someone to say, 'Is there room for people who support the state of Israel and do not criticize it in the [feminist] movement?'"[24] Some interpreted

Sarsour's statement as impugning all of Zionism, while others saw her as impugning only the kind of Zionism that omits criticism of Israel, in other words, only right-wing Zionism.

It didn't help that the *Nation* headlined its piece "Can You Be a Zionist Feminist? Linda Sarsour Says No." After all, Sarsour had specifically said—or seemed to say—that those Zionists who didn't criticize Israel at all were the ones not welcome, in her view. There are many Zionists who do criticize Israeli policy. Still, this debate remains a point of confusion and contention for many.

Owing to the tortuous attempts to infer what exactly is being debated when it comes to Zionism, it is helpful to think about how different expressions of Zionism (or Palestinian political identity, for that matter) track to particular policy positions. That way, policies, rather than ideologies, can be debated more effectively. Some obvious policy issues that lend themselves to direct discussion are: should Israel grant the Palestinian refugees a "right to return?" Should settlements be removed? Is there a conflict, in practice, between the idea of a Jewish state and a democracy? Is BDS (boycott, divestment, and sanctions) against Israel an ethical response to human rights breaches? Is the two-state solution the best solution to bring about peace and justice? Are there viable alternatives? Many of these discussions should be grounded in international law and in transparent frameworks of rights and justice in order to yield the most effective and translatable arguments.

Islamophobia

The term "Islamophobia" has taken on particular significance in recent years. The attacks of 9/11 had already led Muslim-Americans to experience new and intensified forms of Islamophobia. And now Trump's immigration restrictions, or his "Muslim Ban," seem to many to be an extension of anti-Muslim racism. In Canada, on 29 January 2017, a gunman entered a Quebec City mosque, killing six and injuring 19. Muslim Canadians now had the tragic distinction of being the only people murdered in their house of worship in Canadian history. Soon after, a fierce debate ensued in Canada over the term "Islamophobia." Parliamentary motion M-103, passed in 2017, sought to draw attention to, and combat, Islamophobia. As debates over the motion took place, some critics drew attention to what they saw as a problematic term.

Whatever their motivations—and I suspect that many of those who seek to criticize the use of the term "Islamophobia" are themselves motivated by the very dynamic they seek to critique—the critiques deserve to be aired and addressed. First, there is the problem that the term employs the suffix "phobia" rather than the prefix "anti." Using "phobia" suggests that people are fearful rather than hateful. Seen in this light, it would be easier if all terms used to describe bigotry used the "anti" prefix. But like homophobia, Islamophobia is the term we have.

A second critique levied by opponents of the parliamentary motion on Islamophobia was that the motion would chill speech, meaning that those who sought to issue theological critiques about Islam would be prohibited from doing so. I have written four op-eds (two of which are coauthored) about this very issue, responding to the critics. What I and my coauthor argued was that in the case of the motion, and like all parliamentary motions, which simply express the will of parliament, the criminal code remains unchanged. Canada's existing broad speech protections remain in place.[25]

In sum, discussions about Islamophobia in the public sphere have been as much about the term as they have been about the phenomenon. Knowing this, and being aware of the linguistic dynamics, can help move the conversation forward.

Ableism

Another term that is used only by those who seek to criticize a particular practice is "ableism." A more recent addition to popular discourse, ableism refers to discrimination against people with disabilities, whether direct and interpersonal, whether intended or not, and whether more structural or specific.[26]

Social media activists also label as "ableist" one person's correcting of another's spelling or grammar, particular if the correction is done in the context of a heated social media debate about something else entirely. Recent years have seen a move to identify and oppose "ableist" terms, which is to say, words that carry a pejorative message about disabilities. Words identified as "ableist" by some social activists, depending on their context, include stupid, dumb, moronic, lame, lunatic, manic, idiot, crazy, and insane.[27] Readers need to decide whether they want to adapt their language out of respect for those who hear what were once everyday terms as insulting toward people with disabilities. For my part, I have tried to eliminate the term "crazy" by replacing it with the term I hear a lot these days on podcasts, "bananas." Others may think that this is all too much language policing. Critics of that approach, however, might point to a realization of how often the phrase "that's so gay" was thrown around as a thoughtless statement in previous generations. It took a concerted effort to rid ourselves of that practice, and I suspect that most of us are glad we did.

Practice Exercise

Using a term discussed in the chapter (or another related term you can think of), identify ten online uses of the word or phrase in a variety of sources. Now write an op-ed pitch addressing the following questions. Are the terms being used in an identical way in each instance, or do you see patterns of difference? How would the author's or speaker's explicit attempt to define the term before writing about it have affected their argument? How would having an explicit definition affect the ensuing conversation, including around policies and practices?

chapter nine

Sharpening Your Public Engagement

The previous chapter discussed how labels in contemporary social and political debates can easily become flashpoints. Social media is not only a place to engage in debate for its own sake, but is also increasingly a platform from which to pursue multiple types of public engagement, including social and political activism. This chapter discusses various engagement strategies and analyzes the dilemmas and dynamics around activism that play out on social media, even when you may not intend your contributions to be viewed in an activist light. These include the dynamics of outrage culture, the tendency toward "slacktivism," the practices of "virtue signaling," shaming, the debate over "calling out" versus "calling in," "tone policing," and the charge of "white fragility." The chapter concludes with a discussion of best practices for those who are helping an organization enhance its social media presence.

Outrage Culture

A key component of political culture these days is what's become known as "outrage culture." Digital spaces facilitate this, both by being a convenient place for people to express anger and frustration about social and political events and the place where people are most likely to learn about outrageous things in the first place.[1]

But there's a cost to all this. O'Carroll notes that because of social media's business model, "it is in the interest of the social media companies to encourage sharing of moral outrage in a way that fosters amplification rather than action."[2] In other words, social media–fueled outrage takes place more often than not in its own, hermetically sealed system. Scholars and experts can tap into particular waves of outrage to clarify issues and point societies forward in productive ways.

In this system, social media is a place where the expression of outrage manifests itself as performance and spectacle. I will discuss the idea of performance later on this chapter when I get to the issue of "virtue signaling." But there is also the tendency by some to post politically or socially provocative material to stoke debate. People like to watch a good fight unfold, after all. Before getting to these dynamics in more detail, I will turn to a discussion of some hashtag campaigns directed at instances of injustice.

Hashtag Campaigns: The Cases of #StopKony and #MeToo

One of the ways outrage is expressed on social media is through hashtag campaigns. This section will look at two such campaigns, #StopKony and #MeToo. In 2012, a video circulated to raise awareness of the terrible deeds of a Ugandan warlord named Joseph Kony. Titled "Kony 2012," the video quickly received over 100 million views.[3] In just two days, Invisible Children, the NGO that produced the video, garnered $5 million in donations.[4] But the video soon came under attack for flattening the complexity of the situation involving Kony and his Lord's Resistance Army. And then, when the campaign produced a second, more nuanced video, viewer interest in the issue waned.[5] The incident gave rise to criticisms of "slacktivism," "clicktivism" and "white savior complex." Kony remains at large, and in 2017 Uganda ended its pursuit of the warlord.[6]

The #MeToo campaign that took off in the fall of 2017 to draw attention to the phenomenon of sexual harassment and sexual assault was a different sort of campaign, aimed at changing ongoing behavior by spreading awareness.[7] The campaign erupted following a cascade of sexual assault allegations against

Hollywood mogul Harvey Weinstein that quickly spread to other industries and professions. Soon allegations against many other celebrities and media figures appeared, and film, theater, and television idols began falling, among them Kevin Spacey, Dustin Hoffman, and Jeffrey Tambor.[8] Using the hashtag #MeToo, women used social media to indicate that they, too, had been the victims of sexual harassment or assault, either by posting the hashtag with no accompanying commentary or by recounting a personal episode. The hashtag quickly gained momentum, raising consciousness, allowing people to receive emotional support and validation—something very important in post-trauma healing—and leading to more people coming forward.[9] To accompany the #MeToo campaign, I re-posted an op-ed I had written a year prior about my own past experience with sexual harassment.[10]

But not everyone was enamored with the power of the #MeToo campaign. In thinking about the phenomenon of outrage culture, Jessi Hempel had a different take on #MeToo. She argued that #MeToo "is everything that's wrong with social media," in that it "harnesses social media's mechanisms to drive users … into escalating states of outrage while exhausting us to the point where we cannot meaningfully act."[11]

Outrage culture also gives rise to virtue signaling, meaning posting something or commenting or clicking "like" on a post, to indicate to a given audience that you possess a certain set of moral virtues. Virtue signaling is an efficient way of expressing a moral position, in that one can post something to indicate one's agreement with the public outrage about an issue without necessarily taking any costly action. That agreement, in turn, can serve two functions: helping a cause along (at low cost), while also shoring up increased amounts of social capital from one's target audience. Keep in mind that people have multiple audiences on social media though, and what might win them social capital from one audience might lose them social capital from another.

David Shariatmadari traces the origins of the contemporary use of the term "virtue signaling," describing it as "making a statement because you reckon it will garner approval, rather than because you actually believe it. It's a form of vanity, all the worse because it's dressed up as selfless conviction."[12] Of course, signalling one's moral approval and taking more direct political action are not necessarily mutually exclusive activities.

The case of #MeToo has another built-in tension. With a few exceptions, it is meant to identify women's experiences at the hands of men. Where does this leave men, aside from those who have been victimized at the hands of other men? Some men have opted to pledge that they will do whatever they can to be part of the solution. And a few have acknowledged being perpetrators. Of these, some have used the hashtag #IDid. Some have even taken to the op-ed pages to model personal accountability.[13]

The Dynamics of Shaming

With outrage culture has evolved the practice of shaming. The most conventional kind of shaming is name-calling. In my social media travels, I've seen people being called racist, misogynist, bigot, prick, and asshole. Others have told me they've been called a cultural appropriator and a kapo (a Jew who collaborated with the Nazis). Readers will likely have different views about whether this kind of name-calling is within the bounds of fair discourse or whether it's akin to playing dirty. For some, nasty names bounce off their back and are easily forgotten.

My personal preference is to avoid names and labels and to stick to debating the ethics, morality, and evidence behind the ideas presented, though sometimes identifying a post as being beyond the pale, whether as racist or misogynist, etc., is warranted. When deciding whether to chastise a user for a problematic statement, it's helpful to keep in mind that there's a difference between being insensitive or unaware on one hand, and being deliberately inflammatory on another. While some in the social justice community advance the idea that the impact of a speaker's words is more relevant than the speaker's intent when adjudicating problematic speech, I think it is helpful to consider the entire discursive system as an interdependent whole. People are more likely to learn and internalize how their speech impacts others if they are not unduly attacked for something they did not intend. This is where calling in can be helpful. (See the next section.)

Attacks on a perceived perpetrator of some offense often quickly multiply since the act of shaming someone can cause others to pile on. To the recipient, this can feel like cyberbullying. For those doing the piling on, this can either feel authentic or serve as a form of social solidarity with the group expressing themselves as aggrieved. Piling on can also be another form of virtue signaling.

Writing in *Wired*, Laura Hudson cautions against shaming: "At its best, social media has given a voice to the disenfranchised, allowing them to bypass the gatekeepers of power and publicize injustices that might otherwise remain invisible. At its worst, it's a weapon of mass reputation destruction, capable of amplifying slander, bullying, and casual idiocy on a scale never before possible."[14] Hudson likens shaming to bullying: "even if you think your bullying is serving a greater good, the fact remains that you're still just a bully."

In a *New York Times* op-ed, philosophy professor Kelly Oliver lays out the benefits and dangers of public shaming:

> The problematic effects of public shaming are many—among them, silencing "allies," blaming individuals rather than examining social context, fostering intolerance and divisiveness, creating a "with-us-or-against-us" ethos, and reducing identity politics to a version of "oppression Olympics." In cases where pain and suffering are equated with moral authority, calling out injustice can operate as a form of signaling virtue.[15]

Jon Ronson, who recounted the tale of Justine Sacco (an episode discussed below under "risky tweeting") reflects on the feeling he would get when he piled on:

> In those early days, the collective fury felt righteous, powerful and effective. It felt as if hierarchies were being dismantled, as if justice were being democratized. As time passed, though, I watched these shame campaigns multiply, to the point that they targeted not just powerful institutions and public figures but really anyone perceived to have done

something offensive. I also began to marvel at the disconnect between the severity of the crime and the gleeful savagery of the punishment. It almost felt as if shamings were now happening for their own sake, as if they were following a script.[16]

Ronson elaborates on the theme of internet shaming in his book *So You've Been Publicly Shamed*:

I think our natural disposition as humans is to plod along until we get old and stop. But with social media, we've created a stage for constant artificial high drama. Every day a new person emerges as a magnificent hero or a sickening villain. It's all very sweeping, and not the way we actually are as people.[17]

There is one area in which shaming takes on a different quality, that is, in public campaigns attempting to shame corporations and governments into action. Despite the same use of the word, we should realize there are different ethical implications. Given the power context, shaming governments and corporations is not a form of bullying. This kind of shaming can be an effective tool for changing policy and business practices in such areas as humanitarian aid, debt relief, cigarette labeling, labor conditions, and environmental responsibility.[18]

Ronson opens his book by discussing individual and corporate shaming nearly in the same breath, but I would argue that the two types of shaming should be kept analytically distinct. Shaming directed at large organizations, whether corporations or government, has different ethical implications. In short, large organizations are accountable to the public in ways that individuals are not.

Calling Out

Though some will disagree, my observations on social media have led me to see call outs as frequently taking the form of shaming. One must be aware that, if not done very carefully, calling out a friend can lead to the rupture of the friendship. Doing it to a stranger can lead to a hardening of alliances that feels satisfying in the short term, but can also lead to an atrophying of productive conversation across a wide swath of people and perspectives. This is why some people have opted for a "call in" strategy (see next section).

In an essay titled "Why I've Started to Fear My Fellow Social Justice Activists," Frances Lee expresses concern over call outs:

> Shutting down racist, sexist, and similar conversations protects vulnerable participants. But has it devolved into simply shutting down all dissenting ideas? When these tactics are liberally applied, without limit, inside marginalized groups, I believe they hold back movements by alienating both potential allies and their own members.[19]

Ruti Regan, in her blog *Real Social Skills*, adds that the rules for how to react to call outs "aren't working." She writes:

> "Shut up and listen to marginalized people" isn't quite the right rule, because it objectifies marginalized people, leaves us open to sabotage, enables abuse, and prevents us from working through conflicts in a substantive way. We need to do better by each other, and start listening for real.[20]

(I touched on this from a different angle in chapter 8 in the section on privilege.)

One example of how calling out has spiraled out of control is the case of the 28,000-member Facebook group "Upper East Side (UES) Mommas." (This is the same group around which I constructed the op-ed I examined in chapter 4.) Two members sent cease and desist letters in August 2017 to four other members. A dispute had arisen over the term "white supremacy" (which one group member called a "fantasy") and Black Lives Matter (which she claimed had no "purpose").

As the lawyer's letter said:

> The repeated reference to my clients as "racists" "a racist," "the racists" "Nazis" "white supremacists" "white supremacy" "a bully" "real racists

of the upper east side" and threatening to add my clients to a Twitter account that "outs racists" are all statements which are actionable under New York State Law for Tortious Interference, libel and slander [punctuation original].[21]

Sometimes pushing back on specific high-octane interventions or criticizing call-out culture in general may feel like the right thing to do. If you do so, though, be prepared for the accusation of "tone policing." This is a term that originated in social justice circles to critique the phenomenon of someone inappropriately trying to control the way a marginalized person relays their experience of oppression. Social justice activists who draw attention to tone policing accuse tone police of focusing on oppressed people's emotional intensity to deflect from the actual message in order to avoid doing something about oppression and marginalization.

A single comic strip called "No We Won't Calm Down: Tone Policing Is Just Another Way to Protect Privilege" by Robot Hugs describes this dynamic. As the cartoon states, "A key part of tone policing is that it allows privileged people to define the terms of a conversation about oppression in order for that discussion to continue." This argument rests on the assumption that, in the words of the cartoon, "some topics don't have two equal sides and don't have to be met neutrally."[22]

If you think that "conversations are 'debates,' with two or more sides presented calmly, equally and neutrally," as the cartoon describes the worldview of those who tone police, and if you place a high value on civility as a guiding ethic for productive conversations, a concept the cartoonist also skewers, the logic of the tone-policing charge will be tough to swallow. Alternately, if you think that many political and social issues don't have two equal sides, but rather rest on a dynamic of oppression versus privilege, the tone-policing charge may resonate.

One final dynamic to consider if you participate in or observe escalating debates on social media about racism and oppression where at least one of the interlocutors is white is this: sometimes a white person who takes umbrage at something their interlocutor says to them in one of these debates gets accused of exhibiting "white fragility." Robin DiAngelo, who coined the term, explains it this way:

> White Fragility is a state in which even a minimum amount of racial stress becomes intolerable, triggering a range of defensive moves. These moves include the outward display of emotions such as anger, fear, and guilt, and behaviors such as argumentation, silence, and leaving the stress-inducing situation. These behaviors, in turn, function to reinstate white racial equilibrium.[23]

Some readers may feel demoralized by this analysis. Managing social justice debates in light of accusations of white fragility and the charge of tone policing, while wanting to uphold and encourage some optimal practices of discussion, can be a delicate balancing act. Being aware of these debates is an important first step in developing your social media voice and using it in the most effective and ethical way.

Calling In: An Alternative to Call-Out Culture

The tone-policing debate points to the social justice risks in opposing call outs. On the other hand, call outs can quickly devolve into shaming and pile-ons. Given the perils of call-out culture, if you do want to issue a direct critique, does private correspondence work better?

Since calling out can so often lead to shaming, some have advocated the alternative of "calling in," approaching someone privately to challenge a statement they've made or an action they've taken, or to gently point out how it may be heard by others. Social activist Ngọc Loan Trần writes about calling in as an alternative to calling out under some circumstances. However, Trần notes that the essay is aimed at "people who we want to be in community with, people who we have reason to trust or with whom we have common ground," rather than "a fuckery free-for-all for those with privilege to demand we put their hurt feelings first regardless of the harm they cause."[24] If you do hope to get called in by social justice allies rather than called out, be sure to have established that you share common social, political, and philosophical goals. In the case of close friendships, even calling in can be risky, particularly if the person being called in already feels pounced upon by others. Timing may be everything. (I discuss personal relationships further in chapter 11.)

High-Risk Tweeting

We should also consider the impact of jokes, metaphors, or offhanded remarks intended to entertain, provide social commentary, or even to express outrage. If done too pithily and without context, these types of remarks can spiral out of control. Two cases, both of which took place on Twitter, are instructive here. One is the case of Justine Sacco, who Ronson was referring to above when he wrote about shaming. On her way to board an international flight, Sacco tweeted this to her meager 170 followers: "Going to Africa. Hope I don't get AIDS. Just kidding. I'm white!" By the time she landed, she had received tens of thousands of angry responses and her job was in jeopardy, with her employer tweeting that Sacco's post was "an outrageous, offensive comment." Sacco later explained her thinking behind the tweet, telling a *New York Times* journalist that "Living in America puts us in a bit of a bubble when it comes to what is going on in the third world. I was making fun of that bubble."[25]

Another example is the case of scholar Steven Salaita. During the 2014 Israel-Gaza conflict, Salaita issued a series of tweets condemning Israeli actions. Perhaps the most cutting was this one: "Zionism: transforming 'antisemitism' from something horrible into something honorable since 1948." From this tweet alone, it seemed to some that Salaita was baldly promoting antisemitism. I inferred as much at first and went head-to-head on Twitter with some of his supporters.[26] Then my colleague Brent Sasley and I decided to investigate further. We ended up publishing a short essay on the London School of Economics blog where we argued that the tweets that came before and after the apparently inflammatory one in question clarified Salaita's meaning, and it was, in our estimation, not antisemitic. What it was, given the separate URL that accompanies a given tweet (especially back then when people were more likely to share single tweets than full threads), was highly risky tweeting behavior on Salaita's part.

Indeed, Salaita lost his promise of employment: he was due to be hired at University of Illinois Urbana-Champaign. That summer, in a highly controversial and widely debated move, the president rescinded the offer at the eleventh hour.[27] In one sense, Salaita was a victim of a then-140-character medium that limited his scope for expression.

Leveraging Social Media for Your Organization

In addition to #MeToo and #StopKony, many other powerful social media campaigns have emerged in recent years, including health-related philanthropic ones (#IceBucketChallenge), anti-racism awareness (#BlackLivesMatter and #IStandWithAhmed), opposition to gun violence and calls for gun control (#NotOne-More and #NeverAgain), protesting of deportation (#Not-1More), demanding more refugee intake (#RefugeesWelcome), and free speech mixed with opposition to terrorism (#JeSuis-Charlie). Some, like #LoveWins, are used to mark a momentous decision, in this case, the US Supreme Court overturning a state ban on same-sex marriage.

Many of these address large, diffuse issues, making success hard to measure. Some campaigns are more focused so that change, if it happens, is easier to spot. One recent example is the #NoConfederate campaign. In 2017, the showrunners of *Game of Thrones* were planning a new, speculative-fiction show with HBO called *Confederate*. The show sought to examine what would have happened had the Confederacy won the Civil War. Many black media critics took offense. April Reign, who helped launch the campaign (and had launched the #OscarsSoWhite campaign), said, "We don't need a TV show [to show us what racism is like]. We have, you know, our daily existence and stuff."[28] After a concentrated hashtag campaign reaching #1 in the US and #2 worldwide, reports emerged that HBO had stalled work on the production.[29]

What about hashtags for political campaign purposes? Charles Lenchner, co-founder of "People for Bernie," a grassroots social media initiative founded to support Bernie Sanders's bid for president (but independent of the formal campaign) that reached a million Facebook followers, noted in a short essay that when pushing a hashtag initiative in political races, "it's best conducted through a semi-hidden network of influencers who would be responsive to the campaign, but not accountable to the campaign."[30] His article was actually a lengthy Facebook note, rather than an article hosted by an independent news outlet or a separate website. That in and of itself is notable in revealing how nimble one can be in spreading ideas using only social media.

Getting Your Organization's Message Out

As a scholar or related expert, you may be in the position of running your organization's social media presence or advising others on how to do it. You might be helping a university department or research center increase its public profile. You may be overseeing the social media presence for a conference you're organizing, or you may be supporting an NGO you advise on how to sharpen its message. Elana Levin is Director of Trainings at Netroots Nation/ New Media Mentors. I spoke with her to find out how she advises her clients when it comes to getting their message out on social media. She stressed two things: the first is getting client organizations to articulate what she calls their "theory of change." How many signatures will they need to get on a given online petition, for example, to make a difference? If 4,000 people show up at a rally, will the city councillor change his or her vote? A good way to determine meaningful targets is to consult with an elected official who is already on your side. They know better than anyone how many signatures or rally participants would sway them.

The second concept is what Levin calls the "ladder of engagement." This means thinking about how to get people to move from online activity to offline, in-person involvement. Signing a petition will get the person onto the organization's email list. Being on their email list may in turn lead them to respond to a request to make a phone call to their elected official, and, in this way, potentially move up the ladder to a position of leadership in the organization. Digital engagement makes it easy to track how many people open an email message or click "like," "share," or "retweet" on a given social media post.

Facebook advertisements, Levin explained, are a great way to reach your target lay audience. Twitter, on the other hand, is a good way to reach journalists and celebrities who would be able to amplify your message. If you are running your organization's social media page, make sure the group's social media policy is clearly in place so you don't need to seek permission every time you post.

Audra Lawler and Sara Hook echo this in their research on successful social media practices. They point out that the policy should be well documented and that the number of people who run the social media page should be kept small. They add that content should be "fresh, sincere and purposeful" and "never arbitrary or perfunctory."[31] Establish a following so that you are prepared for any breaking event or public crisis that requires response and action. And don't post more than once per hour.

To all this, I would add a few more points gleaned from talking with other social media professionals. When building up a support base, you'll have more success targeting people who are already linked to related causes. If they have joined one thing, it may be easier to get them to join something else than it is to recruit people who are totally unaffiliated. Images can be powerful. Faces, in particular, can grab people's attention and keep it: they're a way of creating empathy and connection. Finally, the most important thing is mastering the one-sentence story. Give people something short and rich to grab on to. What is the problem? What are you asking people to do to help solve it?

Some organizations distinguish themselves on social media as being particularly effective. Many observers have noted the increasing relevance of the Southern Poverty Law Center (SPLC), especially in the wake of the election of Donald Trump. Jeff Rum lauds the SPLC's successful use of tone, which he describes as "straight forward and logical. It reads as evenhanded and unambiguous, but it's also accessible." By way of example, Rum cites this SPLC post: "[Detainees] desperately need access to the law library to put together their cases. Failure to provide this access blatantly disregards their rights to fair legal representation and due process." SPLC makes sure that followers don't just wring their hands in despair. Instead, the group posts short articles (hosted on their website and then shared on social media), showing what people can do. "Ten Ways to Fight Hate: A Community Response Guide" is one example. Through judicious use of videos showing "real people in distress and victims of injustice," the group manages to elicit emotion. All this points to an organization that is able to remain relevant in the crowded market of social justice and civil rights advocacy.[32]

I've talked about the importance of grabbing people's attention through stories of people in distress or focused, factual accounts of injustice. Timing is everything. Linking to a particular news story helps keep people's attention focused on the issue. But are there times when one should remain silent? One difficult case is the death of a famous person. Some say that this is a good opportunity to expose additional nuance about the person and discuss related issues of injustice that need more attention. Particularly controversial are people who were widely admired but have had a lesser-known, problematic side. Is it your job to expose these unsavory qualities if you think it would help your cause? Others may take offense at this tactic, thinking that a person's memory should be allowed to stand unsullied, at least in the days and weeks following the person's death.

One such person was Elie Wiesel, a Holocaust survivor and human rights activist. Soon after his death in 2016, some Israel-Palestine watchers noted with displeasure his involvement with the board of Elad, an Israeli settler organization. When I shared this information on social media in the wake of Wiesel's death, I received pushback from some Facebook friends. It is, admittedly, a dilemma. If you are representing an organization's Facebook page rather than running your own personal account, err on the side of caution. Be careful not to lose supporters who are otherwise sympathetic to the cause because they feel the organization has stepped over the line of good taste.

Practice Exercise

Think of a cause. Imagine that you are running an organization's social media page in the service of that cause. What is the story you want your followers to grab on to? Try composing a 15-words-or-less message that captures what you want your followers to understand about the issue. Now write another message, this one under seven words, that describes what you want your followers to do.

chapter ten

Dealing with Social Media Blowback

Many of us have participated in online conversations that become toxic. In an essay in the *New York Times*, Nick Bilton recalls a debate he got into about Trayvon Martin, the Florida teen who, in 2012, was shot and killed by George Zimmerman, who was later acquitted for murder in a trial widely seen to be a referendum on racial justice. "I know, how could I be so stupid? To think that I could have a constructive conversation about something on social media," he wrote. "Luckily, my part in the Twitter fight didn't last long. A friend saw my tweets and instantly sent me the text message: 'ABORT! ABORT! ABORT!'"[1]

While Bilton's short piece is tongue in cheek, it is important to know when to step away from social media debates. But I wouldn't have written this book if I thought that engaging in social media conversations didn't have a certain value for enhancing democratic discourse and thus bolstering civil society. This chapter will help you navigate some of the waters of tone and tenor. Should you ever get angry? When should you kill with kindness? When should you step away from a conversation? When should you block someone? The chapter will go on to analyze doxxing, the frightening phenomenon of publishing private information about someone to harass them; the risk of employer pushback; and the phenomenon of taking a social media "detox."

If You Get Angry

As I've discussed, social media can give rise to intense emotions. Whenever possible, try not to lose your cool. It's more professional to keep a calm and studied demeanor; getting angry can shut down the conversation, risks having an interlocutor block you, and can jeopardize an actual friendship (see chapter 11). But it's not always possible to remain calm, and sometimes a dose of anger helps to get a point across. If you do get angry, avoid name-calling. If the person takes offense at your sharp words, consider apologizing for your tone. (Though note the discussion of tone policing in chapter 9.) Many interlocutors will appreciate an attempt to redirect the conversation.

Dealing with Pushback

If you have published a post or written an op-ed or related analytical essay that generates lots of hostility, and you manage to keep calm, one strategy is to deploy some good old-fashioned sweetness, or what I call killing your critics with kindness. This can help establish the upper hand in the debate and reminds the interlocutors that you are a person, after all. However, I would *not* advise doing this if what your critics are complaining about is racism or some other structural offense that they have inferred from your writing (whatever your intention), especially if you are perceived to be a writer possessing some sort of privilege. In those cases, it's important to listen to how your critics hear your work. Killing with kindness, in those cases, is too easily interpreted as mocking and can readily backfire. Defending something you've written that is interpreted as racist, especially if you are baffled by the critique and particularly if you are white, can end up leading critics to assume that you don't understand or are unwilling to acknowledge your racial privilege. White Nonsense Roundup is a group with a social media account that was established by white people to respond to other white people who don't appear to see their part in structural racism. Commenters might tag White Nonsense Roundup, which results in a volunteer from the group paying your social media account a visit to reiterate the message your critics are trying to convey. Even if you did not intend what your critics are hearing, consider issuing an apology for the impact.

In a similar move, the hashtag #SettlerCollector was created in 2018 to provide allyship to Indigenous people. As Elaine Corden explained in a tweet:

> If you're an Indigenous person getting harassed or if you encounter racists harassing our grieving Indigenous brothers and sisters on Twitter, hashtag the conversation #settlercollector to have someone come collect the garbage. UNTAG THE PERSON BEING HARASSED IN YOUR REPLY, PLS.[2]

It's one thing to be misunderstood in an act of public engagement or for your words to be seen as contributing to a culture of racism, and another thing to be perceived as an outright racist, inciter, harasser, or troll. The line can appear to be fine, though, especially if your defensiveness gives rise to an impression that you are deepening the hurt.

Stepping Away from a Conversation

There's nothing wrong with taking a break from a heated conversation. If you want to extend an olive branch while you do so, you can let your interlocutor know that you have to step away and that you look forward to continuing the dialogue when you get back. In my Jewish social media travels, I see some folks on a Friday afternoon mention that they have to prepare for the Sabbath, a 25-hour forced media, work, and labor break, which happens to be helpful for defusing these kinds of arguments.[3] This sort of announcement often leads to the conventional "shabbat shalom" (good Sabbath) greeting from those who have just seconds before been in a virtual headlock. If you don't have the excuse of a religiously legislated media break, make up some other reason.

When to Block

If you are feeling at all unsafe, use the "block" feature. The blocked person will no longer be able to see any of your activity on social media, though neither will you be able to see theirs. The downside to blocking is that you can no longer keep tabs on the person's activity, and they will know you blocked them if they seek to look at your activity. On Facebook, specifically on pages where you both interact, you will not see the other person's interventions. This means that some mutual friends' conversation threads may become hard to follow. Twitter provides an antidote to this: if you want to see a blocked person's tweet (assuming you are the one who blocked them), you can click on their profile; Twitter will remind you that you've blocked the user while giving you the option to see the tweets, without having to unblock the person.

More generally, there is an effectiveness drawback to blocking, as well as a built-in tension if the goal is public engagement. As sociologist Kieran Healy notes,

> Calls to simply ignore abuse—to not feed the trolls, and to block or avoid pests—are intrinsically limited in their effectiveness. This is especially the case when this outcome is itself the flip-side of the "engagement" or "impact" that the whole enterprise is geared toward generating, and a built-in feature of the sharing network.[4]

Social Media: From Being Doxxed and Bullied to Being Fired

Occasionally people are driven out of social media spaces by those attempting to bully and expose them by publishing personal data and encouraging others to harass the person. This phenomenon is known as "doxxing" (or "doxing"). The term "doxxing" is derived from "docs," as in various documents that early doxxers revealed publicly. How you feel about the practice may depend on who you see as being on the receiving end of the mob's pitchfork.

Doxxing was thrust into the spotlight after the neo-Nazi marches in Charlottesville. Fallon (her chosen pseudonym), a member of the antifa (a network of anti-fascist activists) that works to dox and thus expose neo-Nazis, calls doxxing a "digital brick through the window."[5] Doxxing can get out of hand, though. In at least one case, a professor at the University of Arkansas was harassed after being mistaken for someone else who had marched.[6]

On the other hand are journalists who get doxxed for doing the hard work, essential in any free society, of exposing unsavory truths. Rose Eveleth suggests that freelancers, who are more financially and legally vulnerable, should ask their outlet to lend them their in-house counsel in the event that they are on the receiving end of doxxing.[7] As op-ed writers, this advice might well apply to scholar-freelancers as well. A provocative opinion piece can place writers in the crosshairs of all sorts of negative forces, including doxxing.

Another increasingly publicized phenomenon is pressure from employers resulting from particular social media posts, including the threat of job loss. Academia has seen several high-profile cases of social media use leading to doxxing, bullying, or job insecurity. In the previous chapter, I discussed the case of Steven Salaita, whose employment offer at the University of Illinois Urbana-Champaign was rescinded after a series of tweets during the 2014 Israel-Hamas war in Gaza.

Another is the case of Drexel University professor George Ciccariello-Maher. The spark was a tweet in December 2016 where the professor of politics and global studies wrote "All I Want for Christmas Is White Genocide." The university responded by issuing this statement: "While the university recognizes the right of its faculty to freely express their thoughts and opinions in public debate, Professor Ciccariello-Maher's comments are utterly reprehensible, deeply disturbing and do not in any way reflect the values of the university."[8] The university went on to say that they would be meeting with the professor.

For his part, Ciccariello-Maher later explained the meaning of the tweet:

On Christmas Eve, I sent a satirical tweet about an imaginary concept, "white genocide." For those who haven't bothered to do their research, "white genocide" is an idea invented by white supremacists and used to denounce everything from interracial relationships to multicultural policies (and, most recently, against a tweet by State Farm Insurance). It is a figment of the racist imagination, it should be mocked, and I'm glad to have mocked it.[9]

For a year, Ciccariello-Maher received death threats. Two other tweets of his added to the controversy, one about the military and another about the 2017 Las Vegas shooting. After that one, in October 2017, the university placed him on administrative leave, claiming it was for his own safety. In December 2017, he resigned.[10]

Another is the case of Joy Karega, who was an assistant professor of rhetoric and composition at Oberlin College. After the university launched an investigation into a series of Facebook posts that were interpreted as antisemitic, the university fired her. In their words, Karega had "fail[ed] to meet the academic standards that Oberlin requires of its faculty and fail[ed] to demonstrate intellectual honesty."[11] Most Oberlin faculty had signed a statement in which they condemned her statements as being antisemitic.[12]

A Canadian case involving a student is also instructive. During the summer of 2017, as Canada was marking its 150th anniversary, Dalhousie University's student union voted not to participate in the celebrations. Masuma Khan, a student union vice president, wrote on Facebook, presumably in a nod to Indigenous awareness, that "white fragility can kiss my ass. Your white tears aren't sacred, this land is." Khan received harassing messages, and the university announced it would be formally disciplining her. After a public backlash, the university backed down.[13]

These cases point to a complex web of issues around academic freedom; perceived racism and bigotry; the quest by some to use strong language, outrage, and evocative metaphors to advance their view of justice; and the question of civility, which is itself a highly contested term among academics and activists.

The Social Media Detox

Every once in a while, I see a Facebook friend announce that they are taking a break from social media. Others, no doubt, do the same thing without announcing it. If you search the phrase "social media detox," blogs will appear, touting a Facebook or Twitter vacation like the latest fad diet.

The blogger behind *Jason Does Stuff* says that from his 30-day social media detox, his "productivity, attention span and clarity of thought all increased greatly" and that he appreciated having a break from "being under the knife of criticism."[14] *Lifehack* blog warns about social media increasing feelings of anxiety and depression related to incessant social-comparison impulses and the "fear of missing out" (something known by its FOMO acronym) that social media can engender. These writers suggest reducing the time per day spent on sites.[15] Chou and Edge have found that "the longer people have used Facebook, the stronger was their belief that others were happier than themselves, and the less they agreed that life is fair." Interestingly, "the more 'friends' people included on their Facebook whom they did not know personally, the stronger they believed that others had better lives."[16]

The incessant impulse to enact social comparisons spurred by social media is a powerful force. Consider how young Iranians in the protests of 2017–18 cited social media comparison as motivating their action, something that came at considerable risk. At the time of writing, 21 people have been killed in protests drawing thousands to the streets. And social media's role in all of this? For one thing, the social media platform called Telegram proved particularly germane.[17] But social media could also be argued to have fuelled the initial resentment in the first place. One 33-year-old Iranian citizen told CNN that "a lot of the kids in the smaller cities have gotten a taste for a better life through social media."[18] Iranian authorities responded by shutting down access to social media sites.

On *Vice*, Allison Tierney writes that her break from social media, which was complicated by social media being something she relies on for work, was

> "bliss." I was alone with my thoughts, at peace, without the pressure of getting into stressful discussions with strangers on the internet. I saw more friends. I took more photos with no intention of posting them anywhere to be validated. I took trips to waterfalls, spent time with the person I love.

When she eventually returned to social media, she described it this way:

> Though I've replugged, I do so with my own personal boundaries intact. I usually don't get on Twitter except during business hours; I don't get as personal in my posts (for now); the Twitter app is not on my phone; I have muted all social media notifications; I do my best to use email and text message over communicating on social media. I have plenty of words muted, I unfollowed some people, and I opted to turn my quality filter on.[19]

I spoke to one theater professional for whom Facebook was taking too much of an emotional toll. She was alternating between feelings of "petty jealousy," she told me, and being overwhelmed by the state of the world. What's more, she felt she was addicted, mindlessly scrolling through her feed from the time her wake-up alarm rang. When she saw a Facebook friend, also in the theater industry, announce that along with one other person, he was looking for other friends to commit to a six-month break from the social media site, she jumped at the chance. They created an email group for some basic accountability, and she announced the move to her Facebook friends with an alternate way of reaching her.

She realizes that she has lost an important platform for spreading the word about productions she's involved in. And her whole extended family lives overseas, and sharing photos and updates has been an important way to keep in touch. But she feels it is worth it. To keep in touch with family, she Skypes or emails. For news, she reads the newspaper. As she emphasized, while she's leaving social media behind, she still has the internet. As for the social media break, she'll re-evaluate in six months.

In the *Forward*, Lisa Goldman writes boldly about needing to exercise caution with social media. Facebook and Twitter, she says,

> seem huge and invulnerable at the moment, but who remembers AOL and Yahoo these days? And the anxiety people are feeling at having their data collected and their thoughts made into a commodity is palpable, which also makes one feel as though we are near a tipping point. But after the death of Facebook and Twitter there will be other avaricious corporations standing by, waiting to market our thoughts and feelings for money. It is not realistic to think that we can just disconnect our decade-old network of connection; it is an entire lifestyle.
>
> The solution, I think, lies in reimagining how we connect online, via platforms that are not for profit and which are open source.[20]

If you rely on social media as a main news source, as many do, and you want to engage in a social media detox, follow the news through direct visits to several news outlets that publish from a variety of perspectives. If you rely on social media for a sense of self-affirmation, as many do, taking a break can sever that unhealthy cycle. If you rely on it as I do to understand the zeitgeist of what people are talking about and caring about, and *how* they are talking about it, then a break will be more costly. On the other hand, for the trends are that powerful, missing one week or more of the debates won't hurt your data collection significantly. The most enduring trends will continue.

As I was writing this section on social media detox and toggling between internet tabs to source the articles that are quoted here, I noticed my Facebook tab alight with three notifications. That alert drew me like a siren call. I succumbed, clicking onto Facebook to discover that a colleague had formed a new Facebook group relevant to my research interests, which I joined. I then started receiving notifications of others wanting to join, which meant I felt I had to go back to click accept. Discussion in the group turned to an upcoming conference initiative that led me to fire off an email to the program chair to inquire about something I needed confirmation on. This was all relevant and productive but took me away from the flow of writing this chapter and spurred a wave of low-level anxiety that washed over me, as I now was aware of new deadlines and initiatives. When I completed this sentence, I returned to Facebook to see if any other notifications required my attention. None did, but I pressed "refresh" just to be sure. Finally, a song I like came on my music streaming channel and I tried to relax, grateful for the aesthetic distraction as I managed not to click on Facebook for another few minutes. But then, I rewarded myself for completing this last paragraph by clicking on Facebook yet again. One of my Facebook friends was in search of restaurant recommendations in Boca Raton. I have never been to Boca and I know no one and no restaurants there. Still, for some reason, I lingered on that post, staring at it blankly. Facebook can be a time suck, clearly. On the other hand, staring at those words took me back to one of my most memorable meals. It was at a Cuban restaurant in a Miami strip mall when I was a doctoral student and was attending one of my first academic conferences along with my husband and some good friends from graduate school. It was before I developed a severe shellfish allergy and could therefore enjoy a plate of strip-mall Cuban paella. Had it not been for that Boca restaurant Facebook post, I would not have enjoyed that short reverie. Social media, like most things, is a mixed blessing.

Practice Exercise

Research the case of Steven Salaita, Masuma Khan, Joy Karega, George Ciccariello-Maher, or another similar person of your choosing and develop an op-ed pitch using that as a news peg. Make an argument weighing the values of decency or civility (as you define it; critique those concepts too, if you wish) and academic freedom. In your argument, make reference to speech laws in your country as well.

chapter eleven

Navigating Personal Relationships through Political Debate

The social networking platform Facebook originated as a way to meet college classmates and keep in touch with existing friends. For a while it was a medium intended mostly for idle socializing. But now that not only cat photos and vintage summer camp reunion pictures, but also political and social debate, have become a significant part of the medium, what is the best way to engage constructively with a multitude of people and personalities while maintaining existing relationships? What if friends' posts bother you? And what if what you want to say carries social risk?

This chapter will discuss social media engagement and, relatedly, advancing unpopular ideas via op-ed and related writing in the context of intellectual and philosophical integrity, while being aware of concerns about maintaining social capital, as well as emotional equanimity. I will draw on personal examples to illustrate these challenges and suggest some strategies.

A disclaimer: I wish I could tell you simply not to care what other people think. And I would agree that you should aim to be respected more than to be liked necessarily. Though I am not always successful, I try to heed this advice. But I am also aware that many of us are keenly affected by the vagaries of social dynamics, especially as they play out on social media, and so I believe this issue is worth giving some attention to. The alternative is to leave social media behind altogether. And I think that would be a loss for many of the reasons outlined in this book.

How Social Media Has Shifted

Watching social media platforms shift over time is a fascinating study in observing how designers respond to shifting user preferences and how evolving technology enables new functionality. When Facebook first launched, "posts" were called status updates and were preceded with a locked-in "is." This meant that you were forced to describe what you were doing or where you were. I joined near the end of 2006, not long after it had expanded outward from its initial college campus focus. My early status updates included references to books I was reading, movies I was watching, or food that was being cooked for me by my husband while I fed my social media habit. Most of the time, partly—but only partly—owing to the forced "is," my wording was cryptic. Looking back, my posting style seems a bit silly, as if being enigmatic signaled some form of coolness.

At that time, there was still no comment feature. While a user could respond to someone's status by going over to their "wall" to write something, it was not always obvious what the person was responding to. That there was no comment function and no famous "like" feature meant that my posts about my husband's fluffy pita bread were tossed into the Facebook universe without any expectation of dialogue or reaction. The forced brevity, the reference to "status updates" and the absence of a comment feature meant that people weren't so much having conversations as they were gesturing to something vague, and, let's face it, often posturing. It was so many messages in a bottle being cast out to sea.

Everything changed when the built-in "is" was removed. Users could now write in any tense and use any verb, and not necessarily have to refer to themselves at all. Soon Facebook asked users to tell others "what's on your mind," and people could ask a question or post links to articles. While the posting box initially had limited space, you could write something longer via a Facebook note, which I initially relied on for sharing my earliest columns in hard-copy-only community newspapers. Once the comment function was introduced, Facebook became a space for wide-ranging conversations across broad networks of people.[1] Status updates were soon replaced by posts. Social media was, increasingly, becoming a platform for political organizing and for debating issues of social and political relevance.

While Twitter had already been a place where people were discussing current events, there too, the response feature became more automatic and intuitive. Eventually, users no longer needed to remember to precede their response to another user's tweet with a period in order for the response to be widely viewable, and eventually Twitter doubled the posting limit to 280 characters.

Making—and Keeping—Friends

Facebook has now enabled and even encouraged us to debate politics and idly socialize all in one place, and while it's a great place for keeping in touch with friends, it isn't always easy on friendships. I wouldn't be surprised if some old friends who I had friended (or who had friended me) as a way of keeping in touch have since "unfollowed" me or even de-friended me after being inundated by my political posts. On the other hand, many more additional people have friended me for the express purpose of keeping up with my writing, whether they agree or not with my perspectives, or to read or participate in the political discussions I host. Similarly, Twitter has a mute function allowing you to still follow someone's tweets without having them appear on your timeline. Like being unfollowed on Facebook, Twitter users who have been muted by someone are unaware of having been muted.[2]

There was a short phase where some professionals kept two Facebook accounts, one ordinary "friends" account for social purposes and a second account called a "like page" for those who wanted to follow the person's professional activities. Though some of these dual accounts remain, the trend has fallen out of favor. Facebook has become a mixed-motive platform. People are expected to be able to write about whatever they want, to seek advice, connection, or to self-promote, all in one place. The added feature of being able to customize any given post to be visible to friends, the public, acquaintances, or a specific group facilitates this. The added function of being able to create and join various groups, including closed and secret ones, helps target conversations to relevant users even further.

The types of "friends" one amassed in the early days meant that Facebook posts gravitated toward certain topics and away from others, at least in my recollection. In-person social life naturally has a way of regulating political and religious talk; consider the old adage of what topics not to bring up when socializing. Though even on this, researchers have shown that happiness is associated with more meaningful conversation than with small talk.[3] Kristen Berman and Dan Ariely point to the purpose of laying out rules, say, at a dinner party, to encourage maximum happiness and to override the temptation to maintain superficial conversations on topics such as the weather.[4]

Does, or can, social media have such rules? Social media is notable for being both a nearly anarchic space and one governed by all sorts of partially hidden codes. It's partly anarchic in that there's no such thing as an inappropriate non sequitur. Through standalone posts, users can toss out whatever thought they are thinking without regard for what came before. Even if you attempted to remain in sync with what your friends are posting, each user has a distinct network which means that what seems like a clear linkage in your mind may appear to come out of nowhere when a friend reads it. There are some exceptions, though. On a day devoted to collective grieving over a terrorist attack or natural disaster, for example, you might feel squeamish about posting something lighthearted. Others might disagree, though, arguing that it's one thing to be lighthearted on the day of a somber event, and it's another thing to be lighthearted about that somber event.

Another unspoken but not-totally-agreed-upon code is whether it is important to be clear and direct in your Facebook posts, so as to avoid the charge of "vaguebooking." Other codes relate to promoting a particular self-image. As I discussed in chapter 9 about virtue signaling, certain posts help advance a certain type of self-presentation. That impulse in and of itself can feel emotionally draining too.

In bringing together multiple roles onto a single platform—social, professional, family, recreational, etc.—social media has erased many of the old boundaries that helped us negotiate our "presentation of self in everyday life," a phrase that Erving Goffman used to frame his sociological treatise on the subject of interpersonal relations.[5] Long before the emergence of social media, Goffman pointed to the ways we cultivate public images, what he called being "onstage," which may or may not accord with our private selves, the selves that we keep hidden in our "backstage" lives. Backstage, Goffman wrote, "the performer can relax; he can drop his front, forego speaking his lines, and step out of character."[6] Though owing to the idea that Facebook interactions take place through a screen, rather than actually in person, one's presentation of self is a hybrid between "onstage" and "backstage" selves. Through careful curating, participating in these forums can be exciting and liberating; we can try on different selves. Though curating can also take a toll. Trying too hard to project a certain image is exhausting, it can chip away at one's self-esteem, and it can stunt the growth of many interpersonal relationships that rely on authenticity to feel fulfilling.

Facebook already is a place where, as Gwendolyn Seidman has noted, users engage in various strategies to build connection and enhance the performance of various role identities. Key aspects of social media engagement include the search for social connection (and thus "coping with the feeling of social disconnection"), "peer acceptance," self-esteem "boosts," "strategic self-presentation," "acceptance-seeking," and "connection/caring."[7] While the social comparisons that social media users make among one another have mixed effects in that they are emotionally taxing and politically motivating (see my discussion of the role of social media in political protest in chapter 10), there is some evidence to suggest that image-based platforms like Instagram reduce loneliness among users.[8]

All these dynamics become that much more challenging the more complex one's networks become, and because regular Facebook users are becoming increasingly networked in complex ways, users have to contend with multiple audiences. Among actual friends, one may wish to portray oneself as fun loving, among one's colleagues one may want to be perceived as smart and capable, and among one's family members one might try to put forth a responsible, loving, and generous image.

And then there's the matter of politics.

Facebook is an incredibly efficient way of sharing information and perspectives with any number of people. I wrote in chapter 7 about the risk of echo chambers. But there is an additional risk: the loss of social capital that one works hard to accrue on social media in the first place. These can be tricky waters to navigate; you might want to post or comment on an issue about which you feel passionate, but where there can be risky fallout, whether verbalized or cloaked in silence.

At its most neutral, users can develop social capital by engaging with Facebook friends through "relationship-maintenance activities": clicking "like" on a post, commenting, or posting "happy birthday" on the friend's wall.[9] This dynamic is not particularly puzzling or complex. But what of the risk of sharing an opinion that is unpopular in some circles or by commenting on another user's post in a way that invites disagreement?

If you are a public figure, whether a scholar or some other expert or professional who is widely known in your area of specialty, your perspectives on social or political issues are already well-known. As such, you may feel somewhat inured from the fallout that can result from participating in vigorous debate. Your social networks may already be well organized along lines that are ideologically demarcated. Of course, this is far from an optimal way of expanding one's intellectual horizons, as I've already discussed. Then again, you may have professional communities where agreement coalesces around certain topics and where other issues are less often discussed. Revealing these views to your peers may still carry some risk. And there's the everyday social risk of expressing an unpopular view.

One recent personal example captures some of these tensions. With a vote over an academic boycott resolution against Israel taking place at the Modern Language Association conference, the debate over the boycott was at an all-time high in my professional network in January 2017. (I am not part of the MLA, but some users in my network are.) As with most issues related to Israel-Palestine and North American political dynamics around those issues, I had a lot of thoughts about the boycott resolution and BDS (boycott, divestment, and sanctions) more generally.

There were two problems. Though I had a lot of thoughts, my ideas didn't coalesce around one side of the issue. Second, I was concerned that expressing my views would alienate peers and allies. I experienced a strange mix of feeling prudent and feeling cowardly. On the one hand, it was prudent to be reticent in that my activism would have very little impact on this vote since I was not a member of the MLA, and I might lose allies with little to show for it. That position pointed to being circumspect. But I was also cowardly in that I was scared of being judged by friends and colleagues for whatever position I would articulate.

Eventually, I worked through this quandary by taking to *Duck of Minerva*, an international relations blog. *The Duck*, as it's known, is more forgiving about not coming down on a single side than are op-ed pages that require writers to be definitive in taking a stand. Take *New York Times* columnist Bret Stephens's admonition that opinion editors want "one-handed" writers, not those who equivocate.[10]

On *Duck of Minerva*, I wrote a piece critiquing both sides of the boycott debate. Even though it was probably naive on my part, I hoped that my appearance of being fair-minded would gird me against criticisms that I hadn't fully taken a stand and against criticisms from those on either side. In drafting the piece, I approached a well-respected peer who held a similar middle-ground position. To shore up my credibility, I included more extensive quotations from her than I would otherwise have done from a strictly stylistic perspective in an ordinary op-ed, where I would have kept my own voice front and center. I concluded with a point I grabbed from, and attributed to, another well-respected blogger from the left as a counter to my more middle-ground position. (The careful reader may now realize from which side I was more frightened of being judged.) The result was a piece I titled "Thoughts for (Both Sides) on the Academic Boycott."[11] When I read it over some time later, it struck me as too tepid. But that was what I could manage emotionally at the time, and at the very least it engendered some productive discussion on social media.

Nearly a year later, I was itching to contribute again to the academic boycott debate. I had proposed a paper on the topic for an academic conference, so the issue was at the top of my mind. Then a new professional crisis broke out: the executive committee of the American Academy of Religion canceled a round table on the topic of BDS slated to take place at its annual conference in Boston. Tempers flared on Facebook as different versions of events circulated. Not being part of that academic association either, I was seeing descriptions of events second- and thirdhand. So I took to Facebook late one night to post this:

> If we can't even get a common narrative around why a BDS-debate panel at an upcoming scholarly association meeting was cancelled at the 11th hour, how will there ever be hope for getting to a common narrative around 1948? I am offering my page as a brokering space for getting to that narrative—at least around the American Academy of Religion panel. And now I will step away and leave y'all to it.[12]

I had already been a vocal critic on a colleague's page of his attempt to target another colleague about the issue, considered by some to be doxxing. (See a discussion of doxxing in chapter 10.) But in this other post of mine, I wanted to depersonalize things and encourage a broader level of debate. By the next morning, various principal figures had weighed in, and we succeeded in gaining some clarity about the circumstances of the panel (though still not enough) and issues around how best to understand the events of 1948 and whether a joint narrative on that was attainable or even desirable.[13] (That had not been the primary purpose of my post, so its discussion was a happy bonus.)

In the post, I had managed to bring opposing sides together, enabling some clarity to emerge and leading to some important issues being discussed. The post even resulted in two journalists approaching me for further links and contacts. And I saved myself having to take a stand on BDS, as this is an issue on which my views continue to shift.

The Value of Crowdsourcing on Social Media

What I did in that BDS thread is what's called crowdsourcing, or asking your followers for ideas, suggestions, and opinions. As I was writing the manuscript for this book, my Facebook followers became used to seeing "hive mind" requests from me on topics I was writing about: op-ed writers who have a distinctive style, podcasts that span the academic-popular divide, favorite academic blogs, personal reflections on using the "block" function, navigating personal relationships through political debates on social media, witnessing or experiencing social media shaming, confirmation bias, words that are often misunderstood in social media debates, the appropriateness of using the f-bomb in social media debates, running a Facebook page for a nonprofit organization, and taking a Facebook break. Sometimes Facebook friends would reference my forthcoming book if it came up in a relevant topical thread or send me articles relevant to my project. In short, for scholars Facebook can be both a laboratory and a collection of research assistants.

Crowdsourcing is useful not only for gathering more information than you would otherwise have, but also for taking society's temperature on an issue. On the latter, be aware that one's social media network is not necessarily a representative sample. Be aware of what kinds of people are answering. Do they skew older? Younger? Are they scholars? Professionals? Students? Is there a gender, religious, racial, or ethnic difference? This will help you put the collection of replies into context. It also helps to offer some examples first, so that readers don't think you're asking them to do your work for you. Make sure to thank your followers for answering the call, and return the favor often.

Practice Exercise

Identify a question to pose to a large set of hypothetical social media followers whose crowdsourced answer could form the backdrop to an idea for an op-ed.

How to Debate and Not Lose Friends

You might think that some friends, once you learn of your wide political disagreements, are worth losing. But there's a reason you became friends in the first place: you clearly had a bond or affection that was worth maintaining for as long as you did. Plus, these friends might be part of a wider social circle, making it awkward to cut ties. Add to the mix family members, with whom political debates can be even more acrimonious and where cutting ties is nearly impossible or deeply undesirable, and how can you show your political stripes, engage in robust debate, and keep existing relationships intact?

When it comes to debating politics with actual friends, start by treading carefully. You might want to steer away from responding to a political post of a friend altogether. But if you do think your friendship can sustain it, start by posing a question. See if some mutually respectful exchange can occur. If it can, try again. If it doesn't, consider letting it go. Some people find that debating politics with close friends comes more easily than doing so with casual friends or acquaintances, that the scaffolding of a close friendship can handle the weight of some disagreement. Others find that it's too uncomfortable. Keep in mind that any intervention on a friend's thread can be useful for reaching others who may be following along.

Asking questions rather than making pronouncements can help draw out a hesitant interlocutor. Show some lack of certainty (the opposite of being a know-it-all); pose the kinds of questions you yourself wonder about. Use humor but never at the expense of another person. Self-deprecating remarks or general jokes may help lower the temperature. Snark may be okay; mocking is not. In a pinch, try emojis to soften the tone. As political scientist Joshua Busby has suggested, draw from sources that you think the other person will respect. A liberal who is debating a conservative, for example, could look for data from the *Wall Street Journal* in trying to build a case.[14]

Busby also writes about how he took to social media to try to correct misinformation he saw circulating around the time of the 2016 US election, especially among friends and family:

> In the aftermath of the election, I have reflected on whether my time was well spent. On one level, my approach was informed by my work on framing and social movements, in which I found that persuasive appeals are more effective when attached to value commitments in which target actors already believe.... In my online engagement, I relied on shared history and a respectful tone as a way to foster openness to my messages.
>
> However, I often appealed to facts by hyperlinking articles based on news sources that I believed to be accurate. To my dismay, findings from political psychology suggest that fact-based argumentation potentially can backfire and reinforce misperceptions.... Insights like these have increasingly led me to believe that appeals to reason alone are not likely to work. Going forward, values-based and emotional arguments rooted in faith and democratic norms may be as potent, if not more so, [as other] forms of engagement. [15]

When engaging in political debate on Facebook, avoid ad hominem attacks. I've already discussed name-calling. Another thing to avoid is bringing up information about the person to discredit their position. A position should be debated on its merits.

The Problem of Social Capital and Social Reputation

Sometimes airing a particular view will result in falling out with friends or colleagues. It can be painful to receive harsh disagreement from certain corners, especially if those are folks you consider allies. The commonly heard advice "find your people" is a mixed bag. Once you've found a group of people who "get you," should you risk alienating them with a post that goes against an article of faith in that group? Or can you rely on the security of having that group to buffer you through whatever the upshot is of stating your mind on the issue? It can help to ensure that you have some friendships that transcend politics altogether, friendships where you share political musings over drinks but that aren't defined by political outlooks—and most of all, friendships that allow space to explore ideas together, bringing a sense of shared vulnerability and desire for personal intellectual and social growth. Nurturing friendships like these in real life can serve, to some extent, as a buffer against the vagaries of social media, although, as I have learned the hard way, even knowing friends IRL does not ensure ultimate protection from feeling shamed, judged, and attacked on social media.

Back to that on-the-one-hand-on-the-other-hand blog post of mine on BDS. When I published that post on *Duck of Minerva*, I prefaced the piece by saying that this post "will win me no friends." Yet one Facebook friend, after reading the piece, responded by saying "if we weren't already friends, you would have made a friend out of me with this post." The lesson: buffer your anxiety of negative reaction with the positive reactions that will inevitably come when things get testy.

chapter twelve

Conclusion

This concluding chapter tackles a couple of additional issues: I discuss whether academia does—and should—value public engagement for tenure and promotion decisions, and I examine what happens when a conversation with one's readership starts to feel unproductive.

Does Academia Value Public Engagement and Should It?

This short section concerns a debate that is internal to academia, but given that academia is about the promotion of ideas for the public good, the question has broader relevance.

Over a decade ago, when academic blogging pioneers like Daniel Drezner hit the scene, a fierce debate ensued as to whether blogging could hurt a scholar's career. The debate intensified when Drezner was denied tenure at University of Chicago. (He later landed at the Fletcher School at Tufts, where by all accounts he's had a stellar career. As for his public-commentary efforts, Drezner also moved on from his personal blog to being a regular contributor at *Foreign Policy* and now at the *Washington Post*.) Writing in *Slate* back in 2005, Robert Boynton put it this way: "although his department claimed that blogging hadn't been a factor in the decision, junior academics across the blogosphere were traumatized."[1]

More recently, the field has pluralized. Academics are now writing scholarly books updating the conversation about what it means to be a public intellectual by including discussions of contemporary forms of engagement, like blogging.[2] And the book you're holding in your hand was published by a university press! More and more professors are translating their expertise into various forms of public commentary.

There are a few questions that need to be asked though. Drawing on a guiding theme of the book, which is how op-eds and other forms of public commentary capture the range of questions that guide academia, one is a descriptive question: are academics appearing in op-ed and related public-commentary pages more frequently than before? The other is a prescriptive question: should academics blog, write op-eds, and engage in social media? A third question is this: should this kind of public intellectual activity count toward a university's view of faculty productivity, including for tenure and promotion? As an individual academic, I am not the holder of the purse of norms and values of the profession. But asking these questions, I hope, will get my peers thinking more deeply and constructively about these issues. For now, I will make three brief points.

First, I see the target of public engagement, at its most basic, as representing a potentially broader audience with which to share one's scholarly expertise. While the academic vocation has long entailed writing for one's peers almost exclusively, this need not be so. Second, if one believes that, in their mission to search for knowledge and train students to do the same, universities and colleges intrinsically serve a public good, then it would follow that part of fulfilling this value would be to share knowledge more widely. Kieran Healy teases out the tensions between public engagement and doing research "in public."

> It is a mistake to think that there is a research phase and a publicity phase.... From a first-personal [sic] point of view it is much better ... to think of yourself as routinely doing your work "slightly in public." You write about it as you go, you are in regular conversation with other like-minded researchers or interested parties, and some of those people may have or be connected to larger audiences with a periodic interest in what you are up to.[3]

Third, the more that academics engage in these broad-reaching activities, the more norms will loosen and pluralize. Alternately, one might decide that strategically, or even ethically, one should stick to traditional forms of publishing to get tenure, and after that, engage in blogging, op-ed writing, and the like. Relatedly, one could make the argument that those who wish to focus on public engagement at the expense of more traditional academic publishing after tenure and one's first promotion should be willing to forego the final promotion, in North American terms, from associate professor to full professor. One could embrace a tacit agreement that full professors are those who dedicate themselves to traditional academic publishing, while those who want to make a difference in other ways accept not being promoted beyond associate professor. However, for my part, and I accept that there is a self-serving aspect to this argument, I would rather see the standards of tenure and especially promotion pluralized so as to recognize the range of contributions academics can and do make to the profession.

Already, scholars are noting the utility of social media to boost the visibility of their academic work and of their scholarly persona through metrics known as "altmetrics."[4] The next step, I'd argue, is to encourage productivity indicators to include alternative venues, such as op-eds and related public-commentary pieces. At a minimum, complementing more traditional scholarly publishing with public-engagement writing and social media engagement is something that can energize the scholarly task (see chapter 3).

When It All Becomes Too Much

As I discussed in the previous chapter, sometimes the fallout from a particular op-ed or other public-commentary piece can be too much. Part of girding for this is first determining to what extent you share the guiding assumptions of the audience or whether you are seeking, in your public engagement, to challenge some of their assumptions. Doing the former is simpler, but you might make less of a difference. If you are trying to challenge assumptions frequently and often, you might find that that task is intellectually and ethically sustaining. But at times it may feel overwhelming.

In one case, an op-ed I wrote ended up being the subject of more heated debate than I had anticipated. When the attacks turned personal, I tried to engage with my Twitter critics but that engagement, in turn, led to more attacks. The result was what I can only describe as an internet pile-on on both Twitter and Facebook. And I, in turn, crumpled. My social media network saw me at my worst. A lot of what I've shared in this book derives from dynamics I've learned and observed in intense and difficult periods like this. I have tried to help you avoid some of the most stinging aspects of public engagement, while helping you advance the conversation in constructive ways.

Another personal example is instructive here: the story of my regular column, a monthly op-ed, at the *Canadian Jewish News*. While I held that column for several years, I was aware that the most vocal segment of my readership and I shared common values on some issues and differed on others. In an early piece, I wrote a short tribute to my late father-in-law, who had been a Holocaust survivor. In that piece, I highlighted the more unusual and poignant messages he aimed to deliver to his loved ones and to the various groups of high school students he spoke to throughout his adult life. Another was a piece I wrote about how to make Bar and Bat Mitzvah coming-of-age ceremonies meaningful. A third piece I wrote talked about sexual harassment. On all these issues, I assumed my audience and I shared a common baseline of values, and judging from the response, I think I was right in that assumption.

But around the topic of Israel—my primary scholarly expertise—a vocal segment of my readership saw things differently. One piece on which I received pushback was when I challenged the idea that a program of Israel advocacy was useful for young minds, either intellectually or from a social justice perspective.[5] That resulted in a column being published from an opposing view. That is all good and fine, and is part of the legitimate exchange of ideas. But things came to a head when, in another piece, many readers took umbrage at my use of the term "occupation" to describe Israel's rule of the West Bank and, to an extent, Gaza. This state of affairs, as I understand it as a scholar, is such a fundamental component of analyzing and understanding Israel-Palestine relations that part of my mission as a columnist was to emphasize and explain how the occupation must be addressed directly.

However, continually challenging the assumptions of one's readers does not always end well. I resigned my column at the *Canadian Jewish News* because I felt that my task had become Sisyphean and that my readership, at least the most vocal segment, didn't agree with me on what I considered basic scholarly and legal terminology. Ultimately, I felt that the implicit dialogue between writer and reader was no longer productive. I resigned with an exit column in which I expressed my frustration. That column, in turn, garnered some additional media and scholarly attention.[6]

So what's the takeaway? Not only do you need a thick skin for challenging conventional community understandings, you also need more patience than I had at that juncture. The downside, of course, to walking away in a huff is that I ended up cutting off my own voice to that audience. It's a complicated matter, and I would hesitate to write a book about public engagement and close it by urging you to exit when you get frustrated. (Though if you do find yourself in a similar situation, we could commiserate.) What I can say for now is try not to internalize these debates in a way that makes them personal. Keep your intellectual and ethical tools sharp and use your scholarly tools to elevate the discourse through public commentary and on social media. Keeping those ideals front and centre means that the work, if it is guided by the standards of logic, evidence, and compassion, will ultimately be able to withstand the critics.

How to Assign Op-Eds in a Research-Oriented Course (with Practice Exercises)

This final section is aimed at course instructors who want to assign op-ed writing in their courses while ensuring that students are sharpening their research skills. All the practice exercises that appear in the book are reprinted at the end of the appendix.

When I assign op-eds in my courses, which I do in all my courses, I use a hybrid model assignment: like any ordinary academic research paper, students are required to have extensive footnotes in their assignments. (I ask that they provide me with a pre-footnoted word count at the bottom of the text so I can ensure that they are adhering to the basic op-ed form, not counting the footnotes.) These footnotes serve to do three things: indicate the source of their ideas, embed their arguments in scholarly literature, and provide additional data, background, and context through my encouragement of extensive annotation. This is also why I insist they use footnotes rather than parenthetical citation style.

To make this assignment come alive for them in the weeks leading up to the due date, I teach what is often called "the ladder of abstraction," a metaphor that encourages students to make conceptual links between concrete concerns and more thematic, scholarly concepts. This helps them learn how to embed the specifics of their op-ed topics in scholarly literature. It also helps them spot an academic discipline behind their everyday interests.

Many of the op-ed topics my students have chosen have clustered around the news of the day. One semester, there were multiple assignments about Quebec's face-covering ban. Moving up the ladder of abstraction, I encouraged students to mine the scholarly literature on the relationship between religion and state. For op-eds on NATO, I suggest that they should discuss burden-sharing, buck-passing, and security communities. And so on. Sometimes students can work these higher-order concepts into the text itself; at other times they choose to leave these more abstract concerns for the footnotes. Either way, I urge them to ensure that the argument they present in the piece is sufficiently supported through logic and empirical evidence right in the text.

Aside from the more obvious headline issues, I've had students pitch op-ed ideas on rock climbing, where I encouraged them to investigate questions about the role of publicly funded parks and state regulation around personal risk. An op-ed assignment about online sports gambling led one student to investigate the psychological literature on addiction. The possibilities in animating abstract concepts through students' everyday interests come alive through the prescriptive argument and the concise style demanded by the op-ed form. Students are not required to peg their op-ed to a current news item, but showing them how to do so helps transform the piece from evergreen (discussed in chapter 3) to current.

In terms of course mechanics, I ask students to submit a pitch that forms part of their course grade. On the pitch, I give the kind of feedback an editor would, suggesting directions they might pursue in crafting the actual op-ed. I allow them to continue with the pitch idea for the actual op-ed or else switch to a new idea. (If we had more time, I would require a pitch before each op-ed.)

I also require that one or more of the required course op-eds are submitted a week before the due-date for a required "pre-read." On this pre-read I again give the kinds of comments and editing suggestions that an editor would, urging them to take the comments into account in their next draft. This serves to simulate the kind of writer-editor relationship they will experience in the world of actual op-ed publishing. Still, it's good to remind them that if they want to increase the chances that their editor will accept a subsequent pitch from them, their pre-submission should be as copy-ready as they can make it. To eliminate too heavy a grading glut so that I can give pre-read feedback in a timely manner, I assign three possible due dates for each of the assignments, in the hope that assignments will arrive throughout the term. This works better in theory than in practice, with most students selecting the latest possible date each time. (Recalling my many all-nighters as an undergraduate, I can't honestly say I don't relate.)

Whatever research area your students are interested in is usually suitable for an op-ed. Students should be encouraged to tackle unfamiliar topics, even for a prescriptive assignment like this. Pointing areas out to students where they already possess expertise is also helpful, particularly if they would like to consider submitting an op-ed to a campus newspaper. If they've researched a topic for a course assignment they may already have more specialized knowledge about that topic than does the average op-ed reader. Even having conducted an academic literature review provides them with insights about the state of the field. If they've researched a historical topic, they should consider how their research has led them to understand contemporary events in a new way.

If they have conducted an experiment for a course, then they have new data to share. Ideally, they should try to then find a news peg. Being a university student gives them a host of special knowledge: perhaps they have insights they want to share on what it's like to live away from home for the first time, a topic that incoming students and their families might be eager to read about. Perhaps they have advice on how universities can better serve students in the area of mental health. Perhaps they have some thoughts about the value of a liberal arts education in the age of apparent waning interest in BA degrees. Maybe they are humanities students with a different perspective on an issue current in STEM (science, technology, engineering, and math) scholarship. Perhaps they have something to say about the perceptions of the millennial generation (this is more likely to apply to graduate students) or Generation Z. Or maybe they've been involved in a particular club or cause on campus that gives them knowledge into what to do, and what not to do, when it comes to social activism and political organizing. Part of the goal of university education is to encourage students to shift from being consumers of knowledge and ideas to consumers *and* producers of knowledge and ideas. Pointing out areas where they already possess expertise can increase their confidence in believing they have something to contribute.

Practice Exercises

From Chapter 2:

Practice Exercise

Identify a controversial issue and consider what the two existing prominent sides of the debate are (I will call them argument A and argument B). Find at least one op-ed that advances argument A and another that advances argument B. Write a paragraph outlining the debate, indicating what the writer or writers on side A argue and what those on side B argue. Now tell the audience what's missing. Your argument C could be the basis of an op-ed.

From Chapter 3:

Practice Exercise

Develop a pitch email to a hypothetical editor. The pitch should address the following questions: a) What is the issue to be discussed? b) Why now? What is the news peg? Is there something in the news or some upcoming event or anniversary that makes discussion of this particular event timely? c) What is your argument? d) How will you support and illustrate your argument? d) Why should readers care? What is at stake? e) Why are you the right person to write the piece?

From Chapter 6:

Practice Exercise A: Conversational Voice

FRIEND: What's your opinion about x?
YOU: I think y about x.
FRIEND: Really, huh? Why do you think that?
YOU: Because of z, a, and b.
FRIEND: But what about c? Doesn't that change things?
YOU: Yeah, I can see why you'd think c would make a difference, but it actually doesn't. Here's why.

Use the above six-line script to write a persuasive paragraph that brings a conversational voice directly to the reader. Replace the variables with ideas, remove your friend's dialogue, and smooth out the transitions.

Practice Exercise B: Urgent Voice

Take the paragraph you wrote above, and rewrite it in a blunter and more urgent voice. Which of the two paragraphs feels like a better fit for you?

From Chapter 7:

Practice Exercise

Find an online debate on social media, and read through the comment thread. Consider the points of agreement and the points of disagreement. Are people disagreeing on evidence, interpretation of evidence, or on basic values? Write a comment to add to that thread hypothetically that describes and illuminates the nature of the debate.

From Chapter 8:

Practice Exercise

Using a term discussed in the chapter (or another related term you can think of), identify ten online uses of the word or phrase in a variety of sources. Now write an op-ed pitch addressing the following questions. Are the terms being used in an identical way in each instance, or do you see patterns of difference? How would the author's or speaker's explicit attempt to define the term before writing about it have affected their argument? How would having an explicit definition affect the ensuing conversation, including around policies and practices?

From Chapter 9:

Practice Exercise

Think of a cause. Imagine that you are running an organization's social media page in the service of that cause. What is the story you want your followers to grab on to? Try composing a 15-words-or-less message that captures what you want your followers to understand about the issue. Now write another message, this one under seven words, that describes what you want your followers to do.

From Chapter 10:

Practice Exercise

Research the case of Steven Salaita, Masuma Khan, Joy Karega, George Ciccariello-Maher, or another similar person of your choosing and develop an op-ed pitch using that as a news peg. Make an argument weighing the values of decency or civility (as you define it; critique those concepts too, if you wish) and academic freedom. In your argument, make reference to speech laws in your country as well.

From Chapter 11:

Practice Exercise

Identify a question to pose to a large set of hypothetical social media followers whose crowdsourced answer could form the backdrop to an idea for an op-ed.

Notes

1 Introduction

1 This anecdote is recounted in Michael J. Socolow, "A Profitable Public Sphere: The Creation of the *New York Times* Op-Ed Page," *Journalism and Mass Communication Quarterly* 87, no. 2 (Summer 2010): 285. See also Jack Shafer, "The Op-Ed Page's Back Pages," *Slate,* September 27, 2010, http://www.slate.com/articles/news_and_politics/press_box/2010/09/the_oped_pages_back_pages.html.

2 Nicholas Kristof, "Professors, We Need You!" *New York Times,* February 15, 2014, https://www.nytimes.com/2014/02/16/opinion/sunday/kristof-professors-we-need-you.html?smid=tw-share.

3 Erik Voeten, "Dear Nicholas Kristof: We Are Right Here!" *Washington Post,* February 15, 2014, https://www.washingtonpost.com/news/monkey-cage/wp/2014/02/15/dear-nicholas-kristof-we-are-right-here/?utm_term=.754dc7ffa3c7&noredirect=on. For additional responses to Kristof, see Jessie Daniels, "Roundup of Responses to Kristof's Call for Professors in the Public Sphere," *Just Publics @365,* accessed August 6, 2018, https://justpublics365.commons.gc.cuny.edu/02/2014/roundup-kristof-professors-public-sphere.

2 Saying What You Want to the Right Audience

1 Mira Sucharov, "Values, Identity and Israel Advocacy," *Foreign Policy Analysis* 7, no. 4 (2011): 361–62, doi:https://doi.org/10.1111/j.1743-8594.2011.00145.x.

2 Mira Sucharov, "Anti-Occupation Jews: Time to Do Some Bible Thumping of Your Own," *Haaretz,* November 27, 2016, https://www.haaretz

.com/opinion/.premium-anti-occupation-jews-time-to-do-some-bible
-thumping-of-your-own-1.5466232.

3 Helen Young, "Game of Thrones: Race, Racism, and the Middle Ages,"
  Public Medievalist, July 21, 2017, https://www.publicmedievalist.com/
  game-thrones-racism-problem.
4 Brent Bambury, "Medieval History Scholars Are Suddenly on the Front
  Lines in the Fight Against White Supremacists," *Day 6*, CBC Radio,
  September 29, 2017, http://www.cbc.ca/player/play/1058212419968.
5 Stephanie Coontz, "Do Millennial Men Want Stay-at-Home Wives?" *New
  York Times*, March 31, 2017, https://www.nytimes.com/2017/03/31/
  opinion/sunday/do-millennial-men-want-stay-at-home-wives
  .html?mcubz=0.

3 Developing Ideas and Pitching an Op-Ed

1 Sung-Yoon Lee, "The Way to Make North Korea Back Down," *New York
  Times*, September, 6, 2017, https://www.nytimes.com/2017/09/06/
  opinion/the-way-to-make-north-korea-back-down.html.
2 Mohammed Hanif, "Not All Attacks Are Created Equal," *New York Times*,
  June 9, 2017, https://www.nytimes.com/2017/06/09/opinion/london
  -kabul-terrorist-attack.html.
3 Mira Sucharov, "Peres's Vision for Peace Reached Too Far, and Not
  Far Enough," *Globe and Mail*, September 28, 2016, https://www
  .theglobeandmail.com/opinion/peress-vision-for-peace-reached-too-far
  -and-not-far-enough/article32102765.
4 Mira Sucharov, "Why Jews Must Defend Muslim Women's Right to
  Wear the Burqa," *Haaretz*, October 19, 2017, https://www.haaretz
  .com/opinion/.premium-why-jews-must-defend-muslim-women
  -s-right-to-wear-the-burqa-1.5458940; Farhana Khera and Jonathan J.
  Smith, "How Trump Is Stealthily Carrying Out His Muslim Ban," *New
  York Times*, July 18, 2017, https://www.nytimes.com/2017/07/18/
  opinion/trump-muslim-ban-supreme-court.html; Mira Sucharov,
  "Israel's Travel Ban: How Banning Settlement Boycotters Is Driving
  Me into the Arms of BDS," *Haaretz*, March 7, 2017, https://www
  .haaretz.com/opinion/.premium-how-israel-s-travel-ban-is-driving
  -me-into-the-arms-of-bds-1.5445758.
5 Anshel Pfeffer, "What Kerry's Speech Says about the Obama
  Administration's Israel Strategy," *Los Angeles Times*, December 29, 2016,
  http://www.latimes.com/opinion/op-ed/la-oe-pfeffer-kerry-speech
  -20161228-story.html.

6 Richard Moon, "Pope's Refusal to Apologize for Residential Schools
   Evokes a Past Tragedy," *Ottawa Citizen*, April 4, 2018, https://
   ottawacitizen.com/opinion/columnists/moon-popes-refusal-to
   -apologize-for-residential-schools-evokes-a-past-tragedy.
7 Jon Wiener, "A Forgotten Hero Stopped the My Lai Massacre 50 Years
   Ago Today," *Los Angeles Times*, March 16, 2018, http://www.latimes.
   com/opinion/op-ed/la-oe-wiener-my-lai-hugh-thompson-20180316
   -story.html.
8 Bernie M. Farber and Mira Sucharov, "We Must Overcome Islamophobia
   in 2018," *Toronto Star*, January 2, 2018, https://www.thestar.com/opinion/
   contributors/2018/01/02/we-must-overcome-islamophobia-in-2018.html.
9 Jonathan Malloy, "How Ontario's NDP Is Setting Itself up to Repeat
   History," *Globe and Mail*, May 31, 2018, https://www.theglobeandmail.
   com/opinion/article-how-ontarios-ndp-is-setting-itself-up-to-repeat
   -history; Arnold Barnett and Edward Kaplan, "How to Cure the Electoral
   College," *Los Angeles Times*, December 16, 2016, http://www
   .latimes.com/opinion/op-ed/la-oe-barnett-kaplan-cure-electoral-college
   -20161216-story.html.
10 Daniel C. Kurtzer, "Donald Trump's Israel Ambassador Pick Is Hazardous
   to Peace," *New York Times*, December 16, 2016, https://www.nytimes
   .com/2016/12/16/opinion/donald-trumps-israel-ambassador-pick-is
   -hazardous-to-peace.html.
11 Ronald Niezen, "Inquiry into Violence against Indigenous Women Needs
   Teeth," *Toronto Star*, December 23, 2015, https://www.thestar
   .com/opinion/commentary/2015/12/23/inquiry-into-violence-against
   -indigenous-women-needs-teeth.html.
12 Bree Akesson, "Respond to Aleppo by Sponsoring a Syrian family,"
   Toronto Star, December 20, 2016, https://www.thestar.com/opinion/
   commentary/2016/12/20/respond-to-aleppo-by-sponsoring-a-syrian
   -family.html.
13 Bernie M. Farber and Mira Sucharov, "Ottawa Must Seek Justice for Hassan
   Diab," *Toronto Star*, July 10, 2017, https://www.thestar.com/opinion/
   commentary/2017/07/10/ottawa-must-seek-justice-for-hassan-diab.html.
14 Jake Sullivan and Victor Cha, "The Right Way to Play the China
   Card on North Korea," *Washington Post*, July 5, 2017, https://www
   .washingtonpost.com/opinions/the-right-way-to-play-the-china-card-on
   -north-korea/2017/07/05/6d223aa0-6187-11e7-a4f7-af34fc1d9d39_story
   .html?utm_term=.625cd6ef8cf9.
15 Elise Labott, Kevin Liptak, and Nicole Gaouette, "Ambassador Candidate
   Dropped over Stark Warning on North Korea," *CNN*, January 30, 2018,

https://www.cnn.com/2018/01/30/politics/victor-cha-ambassador-to
-south-korea/index.html.

16 Joshua Schreier and Mira Sucharov, "If Israel Lets in Palestinian
Refugees, Will It Lose Its Jewish Character?" *Forward*, October 17, 2016,
https://forward.com/opinion/352075/if-israel-lets-in-palestinian
-refugees-will-it-lose-its-jewish-character/?attribution=author-article
-listing-2-headline.

17 See, for example, Jamil Zaki and Paul Bloom, "Does Empathy Guide
or Hinder Moral Action?" *New York Times*, December 29, 2016, https://
www.nytimes.com/roomfordebate/2016/12/29/does-empathy-guide
-or-hinder-moral-action.

18 Roland Paris and Thomas Juneau, "Read and Vote: Has Canada
Drifted into a Combat Mission in Iraq?" *Globe and Mail*, January 29,
2015; updated June 19, 2017, https://www.theglobeandmail.com/
opinion/read-and-vote-has-canada-drifted-into-all-out-combat-in-iraq/
article22696704.

19 Mira Sucharov, "Upper East Side Moms Facebook Group in Turmoil—Over
Israel and the Palestinians," *Forward*, November 20, 2017, https://forward
.com/life/tech/387997/upper-east-side-mothers-facebook-group-in-turmoil
-over-israeli-palestinian/?utm_content=sisterhood_Newsletter_MainList
_Title_Position-1&utm_source=Sailthru&utm_medium=email&utm_campaign
=Sisterhood+Redesign+2017-11-21&utm_term=Sisterhood.

20 See, for example, Mira Sucharov, "Anti-Occupation Jews: Time to Do
Some Bible Thumping of Your Own," *Haaretz*, November 27, 2016,
https://www.haaretz.com/opinion/.premium-anti-occupation-jews
-time-to-do-some-bible-thumping-of-your-own-1.5466232.

21 An op-ed written by the head of the Centre for Israel and Jewish Affairs
in response to a piece I had written in *Haaretz*. Shimon Koffler Fogel,
"How Anti-Zionism and Anti-Semitism Are Converging," *Haaretz*, March
24, 2016, https://www.haaretz.com/opinion/.premium-how-anti
-zionism-and-anti-semitism-are-converging-1.5422096.

22 Zeynep Tufekci, "Does a Protest's Size Matter?" *New York Times*, January
27, 2017, https://www.nytimes.com/2017/01/27/opinion/does-a
-protests-size-matter.html.

23 James Loeffler, "The Zionist Founders of the Human Rights Movement,"
New York Times, May 14, 2018, https://www.nytimes.com/2018/05/14/
opinion/zionism-israel-human-rights.html.

24 There are so many pieces growing out of personal experience. Here are a
few: Roxane Gay, "Dear Men: It's You, Too," *New York Times*, October 19,
2017, https://www.nytimes.com/2017/10/19/opinion/metoo-sexual

-harassment-men.html; Victoria Breckwich Vásquez, Phyllis Gutiérrez Kenney, and Guadalupe Gamboa, "Where is the #MeToo for Sexual Harassment against Immigrant Workers?" *Seattle Times*, November 13, 2017, https://www.seattletimes.com/opinion/where-is-the-metoo-for -sexual-harassment-against-immigrant-workers; Vanessa Grigoriadis, "What the Weinstein Effect Can Teach Us about Campus Sexual Assault," *New York Times*, November 15, 2017, https://www.nytimes .com/2017/11/15/opinion/campus-sexual-assault-weinstein.html.

25 Mira Sucharov, "The Trouble with the King Who Was Cosby," *Haaretz*, December 4, 2014, https://www.haaretz.com/.premium-the-trouble -with-cosby-1.5340462; Mira Sucharov, "The Shavit Story Is, Sadly, All Too Familiar," *Canadian Jewish News*, November 10, 2016, http://www .cjnews.com/perspectives/opinions/shavit-story-sadly-familiar.

26 Mira Sucharov, "Hashtag Protests against IDF Sexual Assault Case Inspire Backlash," *Forward*, December 7, 2016, https://forward.com/ sisterhood/356383/hashtag-protests-against-idf-sexual-assault-case -inspire-backlash.

27 Raed Jarrar, "Why Won't Israel Let Me Mourn My Father?" *New York Times*, November 23, 2017, https://www.nytimes.com/2017/11/23/ opinion/why-wont-israel-let-me-mourn-my-father.html?_r=0.

28 Charles M. Blow, "Library Visit, then Held at Gunpoint," *New York Times*, January 26, 2015, https://www.nytimes.com/2015/01/26/opinion/ charles-blow-at-yale-the-police-detained-my-son.html.

29 Paul J. Zak, "Why Inspiring Stories Make Us React: The Neuroscience of Narrative," *Cerebrum* (January–February 2015), https://www.ncbi.nlm .nih.gov/pmc/articles/PMC4445577.

30 Mira Sucharov, "Uncovering the Lost Palestinian Villages underneath Glitzy Tel Aviv," *Forward*, July 19, 2017, https://forward.com/ opinion/345430/uncovering-the-lost-palestinian-villages-underneath -glitzy-tel-aviv.

31 Mira Sucharov, "Are Israel's Jewish-Arab Coexistence Schools Setting Kids Up for a Cruel Fall?" *Haaretz*, September 8, 2016, https://www .haaretz.com/opinion/.premium-are-jewish-arab-schools-setting-kids -up-for-a-cruel-fall-1.5438547.

32 Dean Obeidallah, "'Black Panther' Inspires More than African Americans," *CNN*, February 18, 2018, https://www.cnn.com/ 2018/02/18/opinions/black-panther-minorities-opinion-obeidallah/ index.html.

33 Mira Sucharov, "How Can Israel End 'Jewish Privilege' When Most Citizens Believe They Deserve It?" *Forward*, March 28, 2016, https://

forward.com/opinion/337152/how-can-israel-end-jewish-privilege
-when-most-citizens-believe-they-deserve.

34 See, for example, Mira Sucharov, "In Diaspora Jewish Communities, Just
Don't Call It the 'Occupation,'" *Haaretz*, May 10, 2017, https://www
.haaretz.com/opinion/.premium-in-diaspora-jewish-communities-just
-don-t-call-it-the-occupation-1.5470414.

35 Mira Sucharov, "Parental Involvement," *Ottawa Citizen*, October 27, 2008:
A12.

36 Stephen Marche, "Canada Doesn't Know How to Party," *New York
Times*, June 23, 2017, https://www.nytimes.com/2017/06/23/opinion/
sunday/canada-doesnt-know-how-to-party.html.

37 This is the acceptance rate at *International Studies Quarterly* for 2016.
Daniel H. Nexon, "*ISQ* Annual Report, 2016," December 12, 2016,
https://www.isanet.org/Portals/0/Documents/ISQ/ISQ%20
Annual%20Report%202016.pdf.

4 Writing an Effective Op-Ed and Managing the Ensuing Conversation

1 Mira Sucharov, "Can Jewish Institutions Survive without Mega-Donors?"
Haaretz, October 11, 2015, https://www.haaretz.com/blogs/the-fifth
-question/.premium-1.679802.

2 Email correspondence, Thomas Juneau with author, January 31, 2018.

3 Sucharov, "Upper East Side Moms."

4 Sucharov, "In Diaspora Communities."

5 Lisa Respers France, "Mayim Bialik Responds to 'Victim Blaming' Backlash,"
CNN, October 16, 2017, https://www.cnn.com/2017/10/16/entertainment/
mayim-bialik-weinstein-backlash/index.html.

6 Kieran Healy, "Public Sociology in the Age of Social Media," *Perspectives
on Politics* 15, no. 3 (2017): 776.

7 Quoted in Tolly Wright, "Mayim Bialik Apologizes for her Controversial
Harvey Weinstein Op-Ed," *Vulture*, October 18, 2017, http://www.vulture
.com/2017/10/mayim-bialik-apologizes-for-controversial-weinstein-op-ed.
html.

8 Email correspondence, Thomas Juneau with author, January 31, 2018.

9 Cornel West, "Ta-Nehisi Coates Is the Neoliberal Face of the Black
Freedom Struggle," *Guardian*, December 17, 2017, https://www.
theguardian.com/commentisfree/2017/dec/17/ta-nehisi-coates
-neoliberal-black-struggle-cornel-west.

10 Jennifer Schuessler, "Ta-Nehisi Coates Deletes Twitter Account Amid
Feud with Cornel West," *New York Times*, December 19, 2017, https://
www.nytimes.com/2017/12/19/arts/ta-nehisi-coates-deletes-twitter
-account-cornel-west.html?_r=0; Jamiles Larty, "Ta-Nehisi Coates Quits

Twitter after Public Row with Cornel West," *Guardian*, December 20, 2017, https://www.theguardian.com/books/2017/dec/20/ta-nehisi -coates-quits-twitter-after-public-row-with-cornel-west.

5 Finding the Right Platform: Op-Eds, Blogs, Social Media, Podcasts, and Other Outlets

1 Bret Stephens, "Tips for Aspiring Op-Ed Writers," *New York Times*, August 25, 2017, https://www.nytimes.com/2017/08/25/opinion/tips-for -aspiring-op-ed-writers.html?_r=0.
2 Rebecca Greenfield, "Judge Upholds *Huffington Post*'s Right Not to Pay Bloggers," *Atlantic*, March 30, 2012, https://www.theatlantic.com/ business/archive/2012/03/judge-upholds-huffington-posts-right-not -pay-bloggers/329891/?utm_source=twb.
3 Todd Spangler, "HuffPost Shuts Down Unpaid Contributor Blogger Program," *Variety*, January 18, 2018, https://variety.com/2018/digital/ news/huffington-post-ends-unpaid-contributor-blogger-program -1202668053; Chloe Angyal and Emily McCombs, "How To Pitch To HuffPost Opinion And HuffPost Personal," *Huffington Post*, January 18, 2018, https://www.huffingtonpost.com/entry/how-to-pitch-huffpost -opinion-personal_us_5a5e0726e4b0fcbc3a1388f0.
4 Blog Directory, *New York Times*, accessed August 6, 2018, https://archive. nytimes.com/www.nytimes.com/interactive/blogs/directory.html ?mcubz=00.
5 John Sides, "Why this Blog?" Monkey Cage, November 20, 2007, http:// themonkeycage.org/2007/11/why_this_blog/; John Sides, "About the Monkey Cage," *Washington Post*, January 1, 2014, http://www .washingtonpost.com/news/monkey-cage/wp/2014/01/01/about-the -monkey-cage/?utm_term=.e7e7beb3d15a.
6 Eugene Volokh, "Who Are We?" *Washington Post*, January 16, 2014, https://www.washingtonpost.com/news/volokh-conspiracy/who-are -we/?utm_term=.cb76145e8c26.
7 Office of the Associate Vice-President (Teaching and Learning), (Blog), accessed August 6, 2018, https://carleton.ca/teachinglearning/blog.
8 Brookings Blogs, *Brookings*, accessed August 6, 2018, https://www .brookings.edu/blogs.
9 Daniel Drezner, "So Friday Was a Pretty Bad Day," October 8, 2005, http://www.danieldrezner.com/archives/002353.html. Six years later he reflected on it here: Daniel W. Drezner, "A Professor and His Wife on Absorbing the Shock of Tenure Denial," *Chronicle of Higher Education*, July 3, 2011, https://www.chronicle.com/article/A-ProfessorHis-Wife- on/128077.

10 Chris Blattman, *International Development, Economics, Politics, and Policy* (Blog), accessed August 6, 2018, https://chrisblattman.com/about; Tom Pepinsky, Blog, accessed August 6, 2018, https://tompepinsky.com/blog.

11 Craig Forcese, *National Security Law: Canadian Practice in Comparative Perspective* (Blog), accessed August 6, 2018, http://craigforcese .squarespace.com/national-security-law-blog.

12 Dwayne Winseck, *Mediamorphis: Network Media Industries and the Forces of Change and Conservation* (Blog), accessed August 6, 2018, https://dwmw .wordpress.com/about.

13 Stephen M. Saideman, *Saideman's Semi-Spew: International Relations, Ethnic Conflict, Civil-Military Relations, Academia, Politics in General, Selected Silliness* (Blog), accessed August 6, 2018, http://saideman. blogspot.com.

14 Nervana Mahmoud, *From the Middle East to the British Isles* (Blog), accessed August 8, 2018, https://nervana1.org.

15 Cheryl Rofer, *Nuclear Diner* (Blog), accessed August 8, 2018, https:// nucleardiner.wordpress.com.

16 John Marshall, *Talking Points Memo* (Blog), accessed August 8, 2018, https://talkingpointsmemo.com.

17 Frances Woolley, *WorthWhile Canadian Initiative: A Mainly Canadian Economics Blog*, accessed August 6, 2018, http://worthwhile.typepad .com/worthwhile_canadian_initi/about-frances-woolley.html.

18 Benjamin Wittes (editor in chief), *Lawfare* (Blog), accessed August 6, 2018, https://www.lawfareblog.com/masthead.

19 Dan Markel et al., *PrawfsBlawg* (Blog), accessed August 8, 2018, http:// prawfsblawg.blogs.com.

20 Dan Nexon et al., *Duck of Minerva* (Blog), accessed August 8, 2018, http://duckofminerva.com; Ryan Goodman and Steve Vladeck, editors in chief, *Just Security* (Blog), accessed August 8, 2018, https:// www.justsecurity.org; Erica Chenoweth et al., *Political Violence @ a Glance: Expert Analysis of Violence and its Alternatives* (Blog), accessed August 9, 2018, http://politicalviolenceataglance.org; Farley, *Lawyers, Guns and Money*; Chris Bertram et al., *Crooked Timber* (Blog), accessed August 8, 2018, http://crookedtimber.org; Judd Legam, editor in chief, *ThinkProgress* (Blog), accessed August 8, 2018, https://thinkprogress.org; Shannon Tiezzi, editor in chief, *The Diplomat* (Blog), accessed August 8, 2018, https://thediplomat.com/category/blogs; Taylor Owen, founder, *OpenCanada* (Blog), accessed August 8, 2018, https://www.opencanada .org; Stephen McGlinchey, editor in chief, *E-International Relations* (Blog), accessed August 8, 2018, https://www.e-ir.info.

21 Mira Sucharov and Brent E. Sasley, "Blogging Identities on Israel/ Palestine: Public Intellectuals and Their Audiences," *PS: Political Science and Politics* 47, no. 1 (2014): 177–81. Our article built on this one by Robert Farley: "Complicating the Political Scientist as Blogger," *PS: Political Science and Politics* 46, no. 2 (2013): 383–86. Farley blogs at *Lawyers, Guns and Money*.

22 Andrea Doucet, "Scholarly Reflections on Blogging: Once a Tortoise, Never a Hare," *Chronicle of Higher Education*, January 3, 2012, https:// www.chronicle.com/article/Scholarly-Reflections-on/130191.

23 Taylor Marvin and Barbara F. Walter, "Where Are All the Female Bloggers?" *Political Violence @ a Glance: Expert Analysis on Violence and Its Alternatives* (Blog), June 28, 2013, http://politicalviolenceataglance .org/2013/06/28/where-are-all-the-female-bloggers.

24 Olivia Crellin, "Only Men at Your Event? This Blog Will Shame You," *BBC Trending*, May 27, 2015, https://www.bbc.com/news/blogs -trending-32789580; Elmira Bayrasli and Lauren Bohn, *FPInterrupted* (Website), accessed August 6, 2018, http://www.fpinterrupted.com; Amber Boydstun et al., *#WomenAlsoKnowStuff* (Website), accessed August 6, 2018, https://womenalsoknowstuff.com; *POCAlsoKnowStuff* (Twitter Account), accessed August 6, 2018, https://twitter.com/ pocalsoknow?lang=en; People of Color Also Know Stuff (Website) . https://sites.google.com/view/pocexperts/home?authuser=2.

25 Benjamin Walker, *Theory of Everything* (Podcast), accessed on August 8, 2018, https://theoryofeverythingpodcast.com; Paul Kennedy, *Ideas* (Podcast), CBC, accessed on August 8, 2018, http://www.cbc.ca/radio/ ideas; Melvyn Bragg, *In Our Time* (Podcast), BBC, accessed on August 8, 2018, https://www.bbc.co.uk/programmes/b006qykl/episodes/ downloads; Laurie Taylor, *Thinking Allowed* (Podcast), BBC, accessed on August 8, 2018, https://www.bbc.co.uk/programmes/b006qy05; Christine Becker and Michael Kackman, *Aca-Media* (Podcast), accessed on August 8. 2018, http://www.aca-media.org; *Tel Aviv Review* (Podcast), accessed on August 8, 2018, https://tlv1.fm/podcasts/tel-aviv-review -show; *Cited* (Podcast), accessed on August 8, 2018, http://citedpodcast .com; *The Scholarly Kitchen Podcast*, accessed on August 8, 2018, https:// scholarlykitchen.sspnet.org/category/podcast.

26 Jason M. Kelly, *Practicing History* (Podcast), accessed on August 8, 2018, https://www.jasonmkelly.com/jason-m-kelly/2016/08/03/practicing -history-podcast-episode-5-primary-sources; Nate DiMeo, *The Memory Palace* (Podcast), accessed on August 8, 2018, http://thememorypalace .us; Sean Guillory, *Sean's Russia Blog Podcast*, accessed on August 8, 2018,

https://seansrussiablog.org; Gary Brecher, *Radio War Nerd* (Podcast), accessed on August 8, 2018, https://www.patreon.com/radiowarnerd; *Uncivil* (Podcast), accessed on August 8, 2018, http://www.gimletmedia .com/uncivil; Stephanie Carvin and Craig Forcese, *Intrepid* (Podcast), accessed on August 8, 2018, https://www.intrepidpodcast.com.

27 Frankely Judaic Podcasts, University of Michigan, accessed August 6, 2018, https://lsa.umich.edu/judaic/resources/frankely-judaic-podcasts .html.

28 John Biewen, *Scene on Radio* (Podcast), accessed on August 8, 2018, http://www.sceneonradio.org; Cynthia Graber and Nicola Twilley, *Gastropod* (Podcast), accessed on August 8, 2018, https://gastropod .com; *The Nostalgia Trap* (Podcast), accessed on August 8, 2018, https:// nostalgiatrap.libsyn.com; *Ottoman History* (Podcast), accessed on August 8, 2018, http://www.ottomanhistorypodcast.com; Shane Harris, Susan Hennessey, Benjamin Wittes, and Tamara Cofman Wittes, *Rational Security* (Podcast), accessed on August 8, 2018, https://www .lawfareblog.com/topic/rational-security; *War on the Rocks* (Podcast), accessed on August 8, 2018, https://warontherocks.com/podcasts; Bobby Chesney and Steve Vladeck, *The National Security Law Podcast*, accessed on August 8, 2018, https://www.nationalsecuritylawpodcast .com; Jeffrey Lewis and Aaron Stein, *Arms Control Wonk* (Podcast), accessed on August 8, 2018, https://www.armscontrolwonk.com/ archive/author/podcast; Sam Bick and David Zinman, *Treyf* (Podcast), accessed on August 8, 2018, https://treyfpodcast.wordpress.com; Daniel Libenson and Lex Rofeberg, *Judaism Unbound* (Podcast), accessed on August 8, 2018, http://www.judaismunbound.com; *Frankely Judaic* (Podcast), accessed on August 8, 2018, https://lsa.umich.edu/judaic/ resources/frankely-judaic-podcasts.html; *Hot and Bothered* (Podcast), accessed on August 8, 2018, https://www.hotandbotheredrompod .com/the-podcast; Sarah Jaffe and Michelle Chen, *Belabored* (Podcast), accessed on August 8, 2018, https://www.dissentmagazine.org/tag/ belabored; Gretchen McCulloch and Lauren Gawne, *Lingthusiasm* (Podcast), accessed on August 8, 2018, https://lingthusiasm.com; John H. McWhorter, *Lexicon Valley* (Podcast), accessed on August 8, 2018, http://www.slate.com/articles/podcasts/lexicon_valley.html; Malcolm Gladwell, *Revisionist History* (Podcast), accessed on August 8, 2018, http://revisionisthistory.com; Stephen D. Levitt and Stephen J. Dubner, *Freakonomics Radio* (Podcast), accessed on August 8, 2018, http:// freakonomics.com; *Dan Carlin's Hardcore History* (Podcast), accessed on August 8, 2018, https://www.dancarlin.com/hardcore-history

-series. For additional suggestions, see H-Podcast, "Academic Podcast Roundup," accessed August 6, 2018, https://networks.h-net.org/node/84048/pages/111820/academic-podcast-roundup.

29 Patrick Allan, "How to Start Your Own Podcast," *Lifehacker*, August 9, 2017, https://lifehacker.com/how-to-start-your-own-podcast-1709798447; Tee Morris and Chuck Tomasi, *Podcasting for Dummies* (Hoboken, NJ: John Wiley & Sons, 2017).

30 Peter Beinart, "Republican Is Not a Synonym for Racist," *Atlantic*, December 2017, https://www.theatlantic.com/magazine/archive/2017/12/conservatism-without-bigotry/544128.

31 For an example of such a crossover piece, see Callie Marie Rennison, "I'm the Professor Who Made Brock Turner the 'Textbook Definition' of a Rapist," *Vox*, November 17, 2017, https://www.vox.com/first-person/2017/11/17/16666290/brock-turner-rape.

32 Brent E. Sasley and Mira Sucharov, "Scholarly versus Activist Identities: What Standards Should Govern Academic Engagement in the Public Sphere?" *LSE Impact Blog*, accessed August 6, 2018, http://blogs.lse.ac.uk/impactofsocialsciences/2014/08/18/scholarly-versus-activist-identities-standards.

33 Sarah Perez, "Twitter Officially Launches 'Threads,' a New Feature for Easily Posting Tweetstorms," *Tech Crunch*, December 12, 2017, https://techcrunch.com/2017/12/12/twitter-officially-launches-threads-a-new-feature-for-easily-writing-tweetstorms.

34 Healy, "Public Sociology," 777.

35 Nicholas Thompson, "Exclusive: Facebook Opens Up about False News," *Wired*, May 23, 2018, https://www.wired.com/story/exclusive-facebook-opens-up-about-false-news.

6 Striking an Effective Online Voice

1 Thomas L. Friedman, "Folks, We're Home Alone," *New York Times*, September 27, 2017, https://www.nytimes.com/2017/09/27/opinion/globalization-trump-american-progress.html?smid=tw-share.

2 Jade Schiff Facebook thread, September 23, 2017 (quoted with permission).

3 Michael Ward, "Create Your Own Theme Friedman Op-ed Column," April 28, 2004, https://www.mcsweeneys.net/articles/create-your-own-thomas-friedman-op-ed-column; NYO Staff, "Write Your Own Thomas Friedman Column!" *Observer*, May 5, 2014, http://observer.com/2004/05/write-your-own-thomas-friedman-column; Brian Mayer,

"Thomas Friedman Op/Ed Generator," accessed August 6, 2018, http://thomasfriedmanopedgenerator.com/about.php.

4 Hamilton Nolan, "Thomas Friedman Writes His Only Column Again," *Gawker*, June 25, 2012, http://gawker.com/5921030/thomas-friedman-writes-his-only-column-again.

5 Margaret Wente, "Why Treat University Students Like Fragile Flowers?" *Globe and Mail*, September 19, 2017; updated September 20, 2017, https://www.theglobeandmail.com/opinion/why-treat-university-students-like-fragile-flowers/article36292886.

6 Heather Mallick, "Agree or disagree, I deserve an A+ for this column," *Toronto Star*, September 8, 2017, *https://www.thestar.com/opinion/2017/09/08/agree-or-disagree-i-deserve-an-a-for-this-column-mallick.html*.

7 Ranen Omer-Sherman Facebook thread, September 23, 2017 (quoted with permission).

8 Charles M. Blow, "Dispatch from the Resistance," *New York Times*, September 14, 2017, https://www.nytimes.com/2017/09/14/opinion/dispatch-from-the-resistance.html.

9 David Brooks, "How We Are Ruining America," *New York Times*, July 11, 2017, https://www.nytimes.com/2017/07/11/opinion/how-we-are-ruining-america.html?smid=tw-share.

10 Caitlin Dewey, "The Real Problem with David Brooks's Sandwich Column," *Washington Post*, July 11, 2017, http://www.washingtonpost.com/blogs/wonkblog/wp/2017/07/11/the-real-problem-with-david-brooks-sandwich-column/?tid=ss_tw&utm_term=.745f62e28300; Ester Bloom and Caroline Moss, "*New York Times* Columnist David Brooks Says Rich People and Their Fancy Sandwich Shops Are 'Ruining America,'" *CNBC.com*, July 11, 2017, https://www.cnbc.com/2017/07/11/david-brooks-column-about-italian-sandwiches-is-causing-an-uproar.html; Ben Mathis-Lilley, "Times Columnist Says Confusing Sandwich Menus, Not Structural Inequality, Killed the American Dream," *Slate*, July 11, 2017, http://www.slate.com/blogs/the_slatest/2017/07/11/david_brooks_cites_foreign_ingredients_as_barrier_to_social_mobility.html; Jill Filipovic, "David Brooks' Fancy Sandwich Story Misses Point on America's Divide," *CNN.com*, July 13, 2017, http://www.cnn.com/2017/07/13/opinions/david-brooks-sandwich-misses-the-point-filipovic/index.html. *New York Times* also ran a subsequent piece, *New York Times*, "'It's Not the Fault of the Sandwich Shop': Readers Debate David Brooks's Column," July 13, 2017, https://www.nytimes.com/2017/07/13/opinion/its-not-the-fault-of-the-sandwich-shop-readers-debate-david-brookss-column.html?smid=tw-share.

11 Rex Murphy, "Thinking of Dishing Out for Hillary's Book? I'll Save You the Expense," *National Post*, September 8, 2017, https://nationalpost .com/opinion/rex-murphy-thinking-of-dishing-out-for-hillarys-book-ill -save-you-the-expense.

12 Anthony Burke Facebook thread, September 23, 2017 (quoted with permission).

13 George Monbiot, "Why Are the Crucial Questions about Hurricane Harvey Not Being Asked?" *Guardian*, August 29, 2017, https://www .theguardian.com/commentisfree/2017/aug/29/hurricane-harvey -manmade-climate-disaster-world-catastrophe.

14 Lisa Pryor, "Heterosexual Couples Deserve Our Support," *New York Times*, September 28, 2017, https://www.nytimes.com/2017/09/28/ opinion/heterosexuals-deserve-our-support.html?_r=0.

15 Trish Hall, "Op-Ed and You," *New York Times*, October 13, 2013, https:// www.nytimes.com/2013/10/14/opinion/op-ed-and-you.html?mcubz=0.

16 Bruce Y. Lee, "Use Emojis in Work Emails? You May Be Tainting Your Colleagues' Opinion of You," *Forbes*, August 15, 2017, https://www .forbes.com/sites/brucelee/2017/08/15/using-emojis-at-work-beware -of-this-risk/#1cbaa5113eca.

17 See John Baldoni, "Is It Okay to Show Vulnerability?" *Forbes*, April 23, 2013, https://www.forbes.com/sites/johnbaldoni/2013/04/23/is-it-okay-to -show-vulnerability/#50d7f2945189; Tiffany Page, "Vulnerable Writing as a Feminist Methodological Practice," *Feminist Review* 115, no. 1 (2017): 13–29; Frank Bruni, "Oversharing in Admissions Essays," *New York Times*, June 14, 2014, https://www.nytimes.com/2014/06/15/opinion/sunday/frank -bruni-oversharing-in-admissions-essays.html?mcubz=0&_r=0.

18 Sucharov, "Israel's Travel Ban."

19 Jordan Schneider, "Why I Curse in Class," *Chronicle of Higher Education*, October 26, 2016, https://www.chronicle.com/article/Why-I-Curse-in -Class/238164.

7 Avoiding the Echo Chamber and Communicating Your Ideas to an Evidence-Resistant Audience

1 Daniel Chandler and Rod Munday, "Confirmation Bias," in *A Dictionary of Social Media* (Oxford: Oxford University Press, 2016).

2 Maeve Duggan and Aaron Smith, "The Political Environment on Social Media," *Pew Research Center*, October 25, 2016, http://www.pewinternet .org/2016/10/25/the-political-environment-on-social-media.

3 "About." Black Lives Matter, accessed January 10, 2018, https:// blacklivesmatter.com/about.

4 Kia Makarechi, "What the Data Really Says about Police and Racial Bias," *Vanity Fair*, July 14, 2016, https://www.vanityfair.com/news/2016/07/data-police-racial-bias.

5 Vivian Wang, "Erica Garner, Activist and Daughter of Eric Garner, Dies at 27," *New York Times*, December 30, 2017, https://www.nytimes.com/2017/12/30/nyregion/erica-garner-dead.html?smid=tw-share.

6 Henri Tajfel, M.G. Billig, R.P. Bundy, and Claude Flament, "Social Categorization and Intergroup Behaviour," *European Journal of Social Psychology* 1, no. 2 (1971): 149–78.

7 Caitlin Dewey, "98 Personal Data Points that Facebook Uses to Target Ads to You," *Washington Post*, August 19, 2016, http://www.washingtonpost.com/news/the-intersect/wp/2016/08/19/98-personal-data-points-that-facebook-uses-to-target-ads-to-you/?tid=ss_tw&utm_term=.39353cd30f9f.

8 Julia Carrie Wong, "Facebook Overhauls News Feed in Favor of 'Meaningful Social Interactions,'" *Guardian* (international edition), January 12, 2018, https://www.theguardian.com/p/7qeaf/stw.

9 Cass R. Sunstein, *#Republic: Divided Democracy in the Age of Social Media* (Princeton: Princeton University Press, 2017), 5.

10 Rune Karlsen, Kari Steen-Johnsen, Dag Wollebaek, and Bernard Enjolras, "Echo Chamber and Trench Warfare Dynamics in Online Debates," *European Journal of Communication* 32, no. 3 (2017): 257–73.

11 Jack Karsten and Darrell M. West, "Inside the Social Media Echo Chamber," *Brookings*, December 9, 2016, https://www.brookings.edu/blog/techtank/2016/12/09/inside-the-social-media-echo-chamber.

12 Eytan Bakshy, Solomon Messing, and Lada A. Adamic, "Exposure to Ideologically Diverse News and Opinion on Facebook," *Science* (June 5, 2015): 1130.

13 Ibid., 1131.

14 Ibid., 1132.

15 Robert B. Cialdini, "If You Want to Influence People Don't Try to Persuade Them. Use 'Pre-Suasion' Instead," *Los Angeles Times*, October 23, 2016, http://www.latimes.com/opinion/op-ed/la-oe-cialdini-presuasion-20161023-snap-story.html. Cialdini's book-length treatment is *Pre-Suasion: A Revolutionary Way to Influence and Persuade* (New York: Simon & Schuster, 2016).

16 June West, "Strategic Communication to Inform or Persuade," *Darden Ideas to Action*, February 12, 2015, https://ideas.darden.virginia.edu/2015/02/strategic-communication-to-inform-or-persuade.

17 Michael F. Dahlstrom, "Using Narratives and Storytelling to Communicate Science with Nonexpert Audiences," *Proceedings of the*

National Academy of Sciences of the United States of America 111, no. 4 (2014): 13614.

18 Ibid., 13615.

19 Joanne O'Connell, "How to Stop Arguing and Actually Change Someone's Mind on Social Media," *Guardian*, January 28, 2017, https://www.theguardian.com/media/2017/jan/28/how-to-stop-arguing-and-actually-change-someones-mind-on-social-media.

20 Amanda Robb, "Anatomy of a Fake News Scandal," *Rolling Stone*, November 16, 2017, http://www.rollingstone.com/politics/news/pizzagate-anatomy-of-a-fake-news-scandal-w511904.

21 Scott Shane and Vindu Goel, "Fake Russian Facebook Accounts Bought $100,000 in Political Ads," *New York Times*, September 6, 2017, https://www.nytimes.com/2017/09/06/technology/facebook-russian-political-ads.html.

22 Associated Press, "Russian Hacking Went Far beyond US Election, Digital Hitlist Reveals," *Guardian*, November 2, 2017, https://www.theguardian.com/technology/2017/nov/02/russian-hacking-beyond-us-election-digital-hitlist.

23 Sheera Frenkel and Daisuke Wakabayashi, "After Florida School Shooting, Russian 'Bot' Army Pounced," *New York Times*, February 19, 2018, https://www.nytimes.com/2018/02/19/technology/russian-bots-school-shooting.html.

24 Quoted in Bob Abeshouse, "Troll Factories, Bots and Fake News: Inside the Wild West of Social Media," *Al Jazeera*, February 8, 2018, https://www.aljazeera.com/blogs/americas/2018/02/troll-factories-bots-fake-news-wild-west-social-media-180207061815575.html.

25 Yair Rosenberg, "Confessions of a Digital Nazi Hunter," *New York Times*, December 27, 2017, https://nyti.ms/2pLYdEQ.

26 Bob Moser, "How Twitter's Alt-Right Purge Fell Short," *Rolling Stone*, December 19, 2017, http://www.rollingstone.com/politics/news/how-twitters-alt-right-purge-fell-short-w514444.

27 Ibid.

28 Claire Wardle and Hossein Derakhshan, "Information Disorder: Toward an Interdisciplinary Framework for Research and Policy Making," Council of Europe Report DGI(2017)09, September 27, 2017, https://firstdraftnews.org/wp-content/uploads/2017/11/PREMS-162317-GBR-2018-Report-désinformation-1.pdf.

29 David Uberti, "The Real History of Fake News," *Columbia Journalism Review*, (December 15, 2016), https://www.cjr.org/special_report/fake_news_history.php.

30 http://washingtonredhawks.com/press_release.pdf.

31 Michael Barthel, Amy Mitchell, and Jesse Holcomb, "Many Americans Believe Fake News Is Sowing Confusion," *Pew Research Centre*, December 15, 2016, http://www.journalism.org/2016/12/15/many-americans -believe-fake-news-is-sowing-confusion.

32 Benedict Carey, "How Fiction Becomes Fact on Social Media," *New York Times*, October 20, 2017, https://www.nytimes.com/2017/10/20/health/ social-media-fake-news.html?hp&action=click&pgtype=Homepage&clic kSource=story-heading&module=second-column-region&region=top -news&WT.nav=top-news&_r=1.

33 Wardle and Derakhshan, "Information Disorder," 13.

34 Evan Annett, "What Is 'Fake News,' and How Can You Spot It? Try Our Quiz," *Globe and Mail*, February 1, 2017, https://www.theglobeandmail .com/community/digital-lab/fake-news-quiz-how-to-spot/ article33821986.

35 Gleb Tsipursky, "The Pro-Truth Pledge: An Effective Strategy for Skeptics to Fight Fake News and Post-Truth Politics," *Skeptic*, accessed August 6, 2018, https://www.skeptic.com/reading_room/take-pro-truth-pledge- fight-fake-news/?utm_source=eSkeptic&utm_campaign=7bf26f20da -EMAIL_CAMPAIGN_2017_11_28&utm_medium=email&utm_ term=0_8c0a740eb4-7bf26f20da-73259197&mc_cid=7bf26f20da&mc _eid=cc296fe2ae. For the accountability mechanism, see *ProTruthPledge*, "How Are Pledge-Takers Held Accountable?" *ProTruthPledge*, accessed August 6, 2018, https://www.protruthpledge.org/how-are-pledge -takers-held-accountable.

36 Ta-Nehisi Coates, "The Lost Cause Rides Again," *Atlantic*, August 4, 2017, https://www.theatlantic.com/entertainment/archive/2017/08/ no-confederate/535512/?utm_source=atlfb.

8 What You Need to Know about Political Labels

1 Charles M. Blow, "Is Trump a White Supremacist?" *New York Times*, September 18, 2017, https://www.nytimes.com/2017/09/18/opinion/ trump-white-supremacist.html?_r=0.

2 N.D.B. Connolly, "Charlottesville Showed That Liberalism Can't Defeat White Supremacy. Only Direct Action Can." *Washington Post*, August 15, 2017, https://www.washingtonpost.com/news/made -by-history/wp/2017/08/15/charlottesville-showed-that-liberalism -cant-defeat-white-supremacy-only-direct-action-can/?utm_term =.e6f479ff0db7.

3 Lauren Duca, "How 'Nice White People' Benefit from Charlottesville and White Supremacy," *Teen Vogue*, August 14, 2017, https://www .teenvogue.com/story/complacency-racism-white-supremacy -charlottesville-thigh-high-politics-lauren-duca.

4 Maya Oppenheim, "Alt-Right Leader Richard Spencer Worries Getting Punched Will Become 'Meme to End All Memes,'" *Independent*, January 23, 2017, https://www.independent.co.uk/news/world/americas/alt -right-richard-spencer-punched-anti-donald-trump-protest-meme-pepe -the-frog-inauguration-day-a7541461.html.

5 For more on identity politics, see German Lopez, "The Battle over Identity Politics, Explained," *Vox*, August 17, 2017, https://www.vox .com/identities/2016/12/2/13718770/identity-politics.

6 A useful multi-part podcast on the subject of whiteness is "Seeing White," *Scene on Radio*, accessed August 6, 2018, http://www .sceneonradio.org/seeing-white.

7 Robert Sibley, "Do We Really Think Our Universities Are Full of Sexual Attackers?" *Ottawa Citizen*, August 29, 2016, https://ottawacitizen.com/ opinion/columnists/sibley-do-we-really-think-our-universities-are-full -of-sexual-attacker.

8 Madeline Ashby, "Carleton University Must Acknowledge Rape Culture," *Ottawa Citizen*, August 23, 2016, https://ottawacitizen.com/ opinion/columnists/ashby-carleton-must-acknowledge-rape-culture.

9 For Carleton University's Sexual Violence Policy, see https:// carleton.ca/secretariat/wp-content/uploads/Sexual-Violence-Policy -December-1-2016.pdf. Disclosure: I was in attendance at the University senate meeting (having served on Carleton's senate) when the matter was debated briefly and I spoke via a comment. I was not part of the drafting committee or policy committee for the document or policy.

10 See for example, Jamie Utt, "Income versus Wealth: How Privilege Is Passed Down from Generation to Generation," *Everyday Feminism* (May 26, 2014), https://everydayfeminism.com/2014/05/income-vs-wealth; Raj Chetty, Nathaniel Hendren, Patrick Kline, Emmanuel Saez, and Nicholas Turner, "Is the United States Still a Land of Opportunity? Recent Trends in Intergenerational Mobility," *American Economic Review: Papers & Proceedings* 104, no. 5 (2014): 141–47; Fabian Pfeffer, "Multigenerational Approaches to Social Mobility: A Multifaceted Research Agenda," *Research in Social Stratification and Mobility* 35 (2014): 1–12.

11 Maisha Z. Johnson, "160+ Examples of Male Privilege in All Areas of Life," *Everyday Feminism*, February 25, 2016, https://everydayfeminism .com/2016/02/160-examples-of-male-privilege.

12 Kimberlé Crenshaw, "Mapping the Margins: Intersectionality, Identity Politics, and Violence against Women of Color," *Stanford Law Review* 43, no. 6 (July 1991): 1252.

13 Peggy McIntosh, "White Privilege and Male Privilege: A Personal Account of Coming to See Correspondences through Work in Women's Studies," Working Paper 189, (Wellesley, MA: Wellesley College, Center for Research on Women, 1988). See also Joshua Rothman, "The Origins of 'Privilege,'" *New Yorker*, May 12, 2014, https://www.newyorker.com/books/page-turner/the-origins-of-privilege.

14 Paul F. Campos, "White Economic Privilege Is Alive and Well," *New York Times*, July 29, 2017, https://www.nytimes.com/2017/07/29/opinion/sunday/black-income-white-privilege.html.

15 Brendan O'Neill, "I Hate to Break it to Feminists, but 'White Male Privilege' is a Myth," *Spectator*, January 5, 2016, https://blogs.spectator.co.uk/2016/01/i-hate-to-break-it-to-feminists-but-white-male-privilege-is-a-myth.

16 Tal Fortgang, "Checking My Privilege: Character as the Basis of Privilege," *Princeton Tory*, April 2, 2014, http://theprincetontory.com/checking-my-privilege-character-as-the-basis-of-privilege. Thanks to Rothman, "Origins" for pointing me to this.

17 See for example Eric L. Goldstein, *The Price of Whiteness: Jews, Race, and American Identity* (Princeton, NJ: Princeton University Press, 2008); Emma Green, "Are Jews White?" *Atlantic*, December 5, 2016, https://www.theatlantic.com/politics/archive/2016/12/are-jews-white/509453/?utm_source=twb.

18 Sam Kestenbaum, "Richard Spencer Touts Himself as 'White Zionist' in Israeli Interview," *Forward*, August 17, 2017, https://forward.com/fast-forward/380235/richard-spencer-touts-himself-as-white-zionist-in-israeli-interview.

19 Naomi Dann, "Richard Spencer Might Be the Worst Person in America. But He Might Also Be Right about Israel," *Forward*, August 17, 2017, https://forward.com/opinion/380384/richard-spencer-israel.

20 Jane Eisner, "Zionism Cannot Be Compared to Nazism—Even if Spencer and JVP Say So," http://forward.com/opinion/380526/zionism-nazism-richard-spencer-jvp.

21 Emily Shire, "We Were Kicked Off Chicago's Dyke March For Not Being 'the Right Kind of Jew,'" *Daily Beast*, July 2, 2017, https://www.thedailybeast.com/we-were-kicked-off-chicagos-dyke-march-for-not-being-the-right-kind-of-jew.

22 Taly Krupkin, "Linda Sarsour at Racial Justice March: 'It Is Not My Job to Educate Jewish People That Palestinians Deserve Dignity,'" *Haaretz*,

October 2, 2017, https://www.haaretz.com/us-news/.premium-sarsour
-not-my-job-to-teach-jews-that-palestinians-deserve-dignity-1.5454882.

23 Emily Shire, "Does Feminism Have Room for Zionists?" *New York Times*,
March 7, 2017, https://www.nytimes.com/2017/03/07/opinion/does
-feminism-have-room-for-zionists.html?_r=0.

24 Collier Meyerson, "Can You Be a Zionist Feminist? Linda Sarsour Says
No," *Nation*, March 13, 2017, https://www.thenation.com/article/can
-you-be-a-zionist-feminist-linda-sarsour-says-no.

25 Mira Sucharov, "Why Would Jews Have a Problem with the Term
'Islamophobia'?" *Haaretz*, February 20, 2017, https://www.haaretz
.com/opinion/.premium-why-would-jews-have-a-problem-with-the
-term-islamophobia-1.5439026; Mira Sucharov, "Poison by PowerPoint:
Reading between the Lines of Islamophobic Emails," *Haaretz*, July 31,
2013, https://www.haaretz.com/.premium-poison-by-powerpoint
-reading-between-the-lines-of-islamophobic-emails-1.5315039; Bernie M.
Farber and Mira Sucharov, "Why We Need a Parliamentary Motion to
Fight Islamophobia," *Toronto Star*, October 5, 2017, https://www.thestar.
com/opinion/commentary/2017/10/05/why-we-need-a-parliamentary
-motion-to-fight-islamophobia.html; Farber and Sucharov, "We Must
Overcome Islamophobia."

26 Ouchlets, "First There Was Racism and Sexism, Now There's Ableism,"
Ouch (Blog), June 16, 2014, https://www.bbc.com/news/blogs
-ouch-27840472.

27 A longer list with alternatives is available at *Ableism/Language* (Blog),
accessed August 6, 2018, http://www.autistichoya.com/p/ableist
-words-and-terms-to-avoid.html?m=1.

9 Sharpening Your Public Engagement

1 Eoin O'Carroll, "How Digital Media Fuels Moral Outrage—And What
To Do about It," *Christian Science Monitor*, September 22, 2017, https://
www.csmonitor.com/Technology/2017/0922/How-digital-media-fuels
-moral-outrage-and-what-to-do-about-it.

2 Ibid.

3 *Invisible Children*, "Kony 2012," YouTube, March 5, 2012, https://www.
youtube.com/watch?v=Y4MnpzG5Sqc&feature=youtu.be&noredirect=1.

4 Christina Cauterucci, "The Lessons of Kony 2012," *Slate*, September 16,
2016, http://www.slate.com/articles/news_and_politics/the
_next_20/2016/09/kony_2012_quickly_became_a_punch_line_but_what
_if_it_did_more_good_than.html.

5 Joshua Keating, "The Less You Know," *Slate*, May 20, 2014, http://www
   .slate.com/blogs/the_world_/2014/05/20/the_depressing_reason
   _why_hashtag_campaigns_like_stopkony_and_bringbackourgirls.html.
6 Zack Baddorf, "Uganda Ends Its Hunt for Joseph Kony Empty-Handed,"
   New York Times, April 20, 2017, https://www.nytimes.com/2017/04/20/
   world/africa/uganda-joseph-kony-lra.html.
7 On the origins of the campaign and hashtag, see "#MeToo: How a
   Hashtag Became a Rally Cry against Sexual Harassment," *Guardian*,
   accessed August 8, 2018, https://www.theguardian.com/world/2017/
   oct/20/women-worldwide-use-hashtag-metoo-against-sexual
   -harassment.
8 Laura Bradley, "Jeffrey Tambor 'Profoundly Disappointed' with Amazon
   Following *Transparent* Firing," *Vanity Fair*, February 15, 2018, https://
   www.vanityfair.com/hollywood/2018/02/jeffrey-tambor-leaving
   -transparent-amazon-investigation-sexual-harassment; Lisa Respers
   France, "Anthony Rapp 'Gratified' by Response to His Allegations
   against Kevin Spacey," *CNN.com*, December 5, 2017, https://www
   .cnn.com/2017/12/05/entertainment/anthony-rapp-kevin-spacey
   -response/index.html; Anna Graham Hunter, "Dustin Hoffman Sexually
   Harassed Me When I was Seventeen," *Hollywood Reporter*, November 1,
   2017, https://www.hollywoodreporter.com/features/dustin-hoffman
   -sexually-harassed-me-i-was-17-guest-column-1053466; Lisa Respers
   France, "Dustin Hoffman Accused of Sexual Assault," *CNN*, December
   16, 2017, https://www.cnn.com/2017/12/15/entertainment/dustin
   -hoffman-sexual-allegations/index.html. The accusations against
   Hoffman are serious, though his fall from grace has been less sharp than
   that of Spacey, who was suspended from his role in the Netflix series
   House of Cards.
9 In one study, trauma survivor participants "consistently identified
   attention to the trauma, listening, and being believed as instrumental
   in their healing." Jeffrey L. Todahl, Elaine Walters, Deepa Bharwdi, and
   Shanta R. Dube, "Trauma Healing: A Mixed Methods Study of Personal
   and Community-Based Healing," *Journal of Aggression, Maltreatment &
   Trauma* 23, no. 6 (2014): 622.
10 Mira Sucharov, "The Shavit Story, Sadly, Hits Too Very Close to Home,"
   Canadian Jewish News, November 10, 2016, http://www.cjnews.com/
   perspectives/opinions/shavit-story-sadly-familiar.
11 Jessi Hempel, "The Problem with #MeToo and Viral Outrage," *Wired*,
   October 18, 2017, https://www.wired.com/story/the-problem-with-me
   -too-and-viral-outrage/?mbid=nl_101817_daily_list3_p.

12 David Shariatmadari, "'Virtue-Signalling'—The Putdown That Has Passed Its Sell-By Date, *Guardian*, January 20, 2016, https://www.theguardian.com/commentisfree/2016/jan/20/virtue-signalling-putdown-passed-sell-by-date?CMP=share_btn_link.

13 Tom Pessah, "Men Who Are Silent after #MeToo: It's Time to Speak Up," *Guardian*, October 2017, https://www.theguardian.com/commentisfree/2017/oct/20/men-silent-me-too-sexism?CMP=share_btn_link.

14 Laura Hudson, "Why You Should Think Twice before Shaming Anyone on Social Media," *Wired*, July 24, 2013, https://www.wired.com/2013/07/ap_argshaming/?mbid=email_onsiteshare.

15 Kelly Oliver, "Education in the Age of Outrage," *New York Times*, October 16, 2017, https://www.nytimes.com/2017/10/16/opinion/education-outrage-morality-shaming.html?smid=fb-share.

16 Jon Ronson, "How One Stupid Tweet Blew Up Justine Sacco's Life," *New York Times*, February 12, 2015, https://www.nytimes.com/2015/02/15/magazine/how-one-stupid-tweet-ruined-justine-saccos-life.html.

17 Jon Ronson, *So You've Been Publicly Shamed* (New York: Riverhead Books, Penguin, 2015), 78–79.

18 Joshua William Busby, "Bono Made Jesse Helms Cry: Jubilee 2000, Debt Relief, and Moral Action in International Politics," *International Studies Quarterly* 51 (2007): 247–75; Brent J. Steele, "Making Words Matter: The Asian Tsunami, Darfur, and 'Reflexive Discourse' in International Politics," *International Studies Quarterly* 51, no. 4 (2007): 901–25; Jennifer Jacquet, *Is Shame Necessary? New Uses for an Old Tool* (New York: Vintage, 2015).

19 Frances Lee, "Why I've Started to Fear My Fellow Social Justice Activists," *YES! Magazine*, October 13, 2017, http://www.yesmagazine.org/people-power/why-ive-started-to-fear-my-fellow-social-justice-activists-20171013.

20 Ruti Regan, "The Rules for Responding to Call Outs Aren't Working," *Real Social Skills* (Blog), October 24, 2017, https://www.realsocialskills.org/blog/the-rules-about-responding-to-call-outs-arent.

21 Ellie Shechet, "Members of 'UES Mommas' Facebook Group Threaten Legal Action after Being Called Racist," *Jezebel*, August 23, 2017, https://jezebel.com/members-of-ues-mommas-facebook-group-threaten-legal-act-1798309160.

22 "No, We Won't 'Calm Down': Tone Policing Is Just Another Way to Protect Privilege," *Robot Hugs* (Webcomic), accessed August 6, 2018, http://www.robot-hugs.com/tone-policing.

23 Robin DiAngelo, "White Fragility," *International Journal of Critical Pedagogy*, 3, no. 3 (2011): 54, https://libjournal.uncg.edu/ijcp/article/viewFile/249/116. See also Robin DiAngelo, *White Fragility: Why It's So Hard for White People to Talk about Racism* (Boston: Beacon Press, 2018).

24 Ngọc Loan Trần, "Calling In: A Less Disposable Way of Holding Each Other Accountable," *BGD*, December 18, 2013, http://www.bgdblog.org/2013/12/calling-less-disposable-way-holding-accountable.

25 Ronson, "How One Stupid Tweet Blew Up."

26 Phan Nguyen, "Reading Salaita in Illinois," *Mondoweiss*, August 13, 2014, http://mondoweiss.net/2014/08/reading-salaita-illinois-1.

27 Sasley and Sucharov, "Scholarly versus Activist Identities."

28 Hope Reese, "Meet the Activist Who Wants to Stop HBO's *Confederate* from Getting Made," *Vox*, August 4, 2017, https://www.vox.com/conversations/2017/8/4/16098256/no-confederate-hbo-game-of-thrones?.

29 "HBO's Controversial 'Confederate' Series Is 'Not Actively' Being Worked On," *Shadow and Act*, November 30, 2017, https://shadowandact.com/hbos-controversial-confederate-series-is-not-actively-being-worked-on#shadowAndAct.

30 Charles Lenchner, "People for Bernie: An Answer to Some of Our Persistent Critics" (Facebook note), December 3, 2017, https://www.facebook.com/notes/charles-lenchner/people-for-bernie-an-answer-to-some-of-our-persistent-critics/10155982863849758.

31 Audra J. Lawler and Sara Ann Hook, "Developing a Social Media Strategy for a Small Non-Profit Organization: More Conversation, Less Marketing" (Poster), 23rd Indiana University Undergraduate Research Conference, Indianapolis, Indiana, November 17, 2017.

32 Jeff Rum, "A Civil Rights Organization That Does Social Media Right," *Social Media Today*, August 24, 2017, https://www.socialmediatoday.com/news/a-civil-rights-organization-that-does-social-media-right/504245.

10 Dealing with Social Media Blowback

1 Nick Bilton, "Don't Fight Flames with Flames," *New York Times*, August 6, 2014, https://www.nytimes.com/2014/08/07/fashion/social-media-arguments-cant-win-propositions.html?smid=tw-share.

2 CBC Radio, "#SettlerCollector: Hashtag Helps Redirect Racist Attacks on Social Media," February 16, 2018, http://www.cbc.ca/radio/unreserved/after-colten-boushie-where-do-we-go-from-here-1.4535052/

settlercollector-hashtag-helps-redirect-racist-attacks-on-social-media
-1.4537594.

3 The Sabbath ritual is one that neurologist Oliver Sacks wrote about in
a moving op-ed in the *New York Times* as he was nearing death. Oliver
Sacks, "Sabbath," *New York Times*, August 14, 2015, https://www
.nytimes.com/2015/08/16/opinion/sunday/oliver-sacks-sabbath
.html?smid=tw-share.

4 Healy, "Public Sociology," 779.

5 Decca Muldowney, "Info Wars: Inside the Left's Online Efforts to Out
White Supremacists," *ProPublica*, October 30, 2017, https://www
.propublica.org/article/inside-the-lefts-online-efforts-to-out-white
-supremacists. I first learned about Muldowney and her research and
writing on doxxing from the December 22, 2017, "Fire with Fire" episode
of the podcast *On the Media*.

6 Nellie Bowles, "How Doxxing Became a Mainstream Tool in the
Culture Wars," *New York Times*, August 30, 2017, https://www.nytimes
.com/2017/08/30/technology/doxxing-protests.html?_r=0.

7 Rose Eveleth, "How to Deter Doxxing: Newsroom Strategies to Prevent
the Harassment That Follows the Public Posting of Home Addresses,
Phone Number and Journalists' Other Personal Information," *Nieman
Reports*, June 1, 2015, http://niemanreports.org/articles/how-to-deter
-doxxing.

8 Quoted in Scott Jaschik, "Drexel Condemns Professor's Tweet," *Inside
Higher Ed*, December 26, 2016, https://www.insidehighered.com/
news/2016/12/26/drexel-condemns-professors-tweet-about-white
-genocide#.Wke3W4V0sc0.link.

9 Quoted in ibid.

10 Marwa Eltagouri, "Professor Who Tweeted, 'All I Want for Christmas
Is White Genocide,' Resigns after Year of Threats," *Washington Post*,
December 29, 2017, https://www.insidehighered.com/news/2016/12/26/
drexel-condemns-professors-tweet-about-white-genocide.

11 Quoted in Colleen Flaherty, "Oberlin Ousts Professor," *Inside
Higher Ed*, November 16, 2016, https://www.insidehighered.com/
news/2016/11/16/oberlin-fires-joy-karega-following-investigation-her
-anti-semitic-statements-social#.Wke6sbe-Ck4.link.

12 Ibid.

13 Anjuli Patil, "Dalhousie Withdraws Disciplinary Action against Masuma
Kham over 'White Fragility' Facebook Post," *CBC News*, October 25, 2017,
https://www.cbc.ca/news/canada/nova-scotia/dalhousie-withdraws
-complaint-against-masuma-khan-1.4371332.

14 Jason Zook, "Do a Social Media Detox," *Jason Does Stuff* (Blog), accessed August 6, 2018, https://jasondoesstuff.com/social-media-detox-recap.

15 Holly Chavez, "Nine Positive Benefits of a Social Media Detox," *Lifehack*, accessed August 6, 2018, https://www.lifehack.org/483829/9-positive -benefits-of-a-social-media-detox.

16 Hui-Tzu Grace Chou and Nicholas Edge, "'They Are Happier and Having Better Lives than I Am': The Impact of Using Facebook on Perceptions of Others' Lives," *CyberPsychology, Behavior and Social Networking* 15, no. 2 (2012): 119.

17 CBC News, "Social Media Plays 'Extremely Important' Role in Iranian Protests Despite Censorship," *CBC*, January 4, 2018, https://www.cbc .ca/news/technology/iran-protests-social-media-telegram-1.4471226.

18 Amanda Erickson, "Iran's Protests Are Fading, but Iranians Are Still Angry," *Washington Post*, January 4, 2018, http://www.washingtonpost .com/blogs/worldviews/wp/2018/01/04/irans-protests-are-fading-but -iranians-are-still-angry/?tid=ss_tw&utm_term=.5236ea2f4d30.

19 Allison Tierney, "I Took a Social Media Break and You Should Too." *Vice*, October 5, 2017, https://www.vice.com/en_us/article/43a55j/i-took-a -social-media-break-and-you-should-too.

20 Lisa Goldman, "Social Media Is Dangerously Undermining Our Democratic Values," *Forward*, December 27, 2017, https://forward .com/opinion/391029/social-media-is-dangerously-undermining-our -democratic-values.

11 Navigating Personal Relationships through Political Debate

1 For a more detailed history of the evolution of Facebook in its first nine years, see Niels Brügger, "A Brief History of Facebook as a Media Text: The Development of an Empty Structure," *First Monday: Peer-Reviewed Journal on the Internet* 20, no. 5 (2015), doi:https://doi.org/10.5210/ fm.v20i5.5423.

2 Twitter, "How to Mute Accounts on Twitter," accessed August 6, 2018, https://help.twitter.com/en/using-twitter/twitter-mute.

3 Matthias R. Mehl, Simine Vazire, Shannon E. Holleran, and C. Shelby Clark, "Eavesdropping on Happiness: Well-Being Is Related to Having Less Small Talk and More Substantive Conversations," *Psychological Science* 21, no. 4 (2010): 539–41.

4 Kristen Berman and Dan Ariely, "Small Talk Should Be Banned—Here's Why," *Wired*, September 21, 2016, http://www.wired.co.uk/article/ banning-small-talk.

5 Erving Goffman, *The Presentation of Self in Everyday Life* (New York: Doubleday, 1959).
6 Ibid., 112.
7 Gwendolyn Seidman, "Self-Presentation and Belonging on Facebook: How Personality Influences Social Media Use and Motivations," *Personality and Individual Differences* 54, no. 3 (2013): 402–403.
8 Matthew Pittman and Brandon Reich, "Social Media and Loneliness: Why an Instagram Picture May Be Worth More Than a Thousand Twitter Words," *Computers in Human Behavior* 62 (September 2016): 155–67.
9 Nicole B. Ellison, Jessica Vitak, Rebecca Gray, and Cliff Lampe, "Cultivating Social Resources on Social Network Sites: Facebook Relationship Maintenance Behaviors and Their Role in Social Capital Processes," *Journal of Computer-Mediated Communication* 19 (2014): 855–70.
10 Bret Stephens, "Tips for Aspiring Op-Ed Writers," *New York Times*, August 25, 2017, https://www.nytimes.com/2017/08/25/opinion/tips -for-aspiring-op-ed-writers.html?_r=0.
11 Mira Sucharov, "Thoughts (for 'Both Sides') on the Academic Boycott," *Duck of Minerva*, January 12, 2017, http://duckofminerva.com/2017/01/ thoughts-for-both-sides-on-the-academic-boycott.html.
12 Mira Sucharov Facebook post, https://www.facebook.com/sucharov/ posts/10155584474125266?pnref=story.
13 One op-ed I've written on this question is Mira Sucharov, "As They Celebrate Independence, Israelis Should Remember the Nakba," *Haaretz*, May 11, 2016, https://www.haaretz.com/opinion/.premium-israelis -remember-the-nakba-on-independence-day-1.5382192.
14 Facebook correspondence, Joshua Busby with author, November 14, 2017.
15 Joshua Busby, "Social Media and the Scholar in an Era of Hyper -Nationalism and Fake News," *PS: Political Science and Politics* 50, no. 4 (2017): 1004–1007. doi:https://doi.org/10.1017/S1049096517001160.

12 Conclusion

1 Robert Boynton, "Attack of the Career-Killing Blogs," *Slate*, November 16, 2005, http://www.slate.com/articles/news_and_politics/college _week/2005/11/attack_of_the_careerkilling_blogs.html.
2 Michael C. Desch, ed., *Public Intellectuals in the Global Arena: Professors or Pundits?* (Notre Dame: University of Notre Dame Press, 2016) and especially the chapter by Paul Horwitz, "Of Mirrors and Media: The Blogger as Public Intellectual," in *Public Intellectuals in the Global Arena: Professors or Pundits?* ed. Michael C. Desch, 214–46 (Notre Dame: University of Notre Dame Press, 2016).

3 Healy, "Public Sociology," 775.
4 Amy Atchison, "Metrics, Metrics, (Alt)metrics," *The New West: Official Blog of the Western Political Science Association*, June 16, 2017, https:// thewpsa.wordpress.com/2017/06/16/metrics-metrics-altmetrics.
5 Mira Sucharov, "Canada 150 and 50 Years of Israel's Occupation Need Sober Reflection," *Canadian Jewish News*, May 3, 2017, http://www .cjnews.com/perspectives/opinions/this-year-deserves-sober-reflection -in-canada-and-israel; Mira Sucharov, "A Shoah Survivor Who Found Kindness in Unexpected Places," *Canadian Jewish News*, February 11, 2015, http://www.cjnews.com/perspectives/opinions/guest-voice-shoah -survivor-found-kindness-unexpected-places; Mira Sucharov, "Let's Keep Israel Lobbying Out of Jewish Youth Groups," *Canadian Jewish News*, April 3, 2017, http://www.cjnews.com/perspectives/opinions/keep -lobbying-israel-out-jewish-youth-groups.
6 Mira Sucharov, "Why I'm Resigning my CJN Column," *Canadian Jewish News*, June 2, 2017, http://www.cjnews.com/perspectives/mira -sucharov-cjn-column. I discussed the process on the TREYF Podcast, "Short: Mira Sucharov," June 7, 2017, https://soundcloud .com/treyfpodcast/short-mira-sucharov. For other coverage of the story of my resignation, see Alex Verman, "Canadian Jewish News Loses Last Regular Left-Leaning Columnist over Word 'Occupation,'" *Canadaland*, June 30, 2017, http://www.canadalandshow.com/cjn-loses -mira-sucharov; David S. Koffman, "Suffering and Sovereignty: Recent Canadian Jewish Interest in Indigenous Peoples and Issues," *Canadian Jewish Studies* 25 (2017): 47.

Bibliography

Abeshouse, Bob. "Troll Factories, Bots and Fake News: Inside the Wild West of Social Media." *Al Jazeera*, February 8, 2018. https://www.aljazeera.com/blogs/americas/2018/02/troll-factories-bots-fake-news-wild-west-social-media-180207061815575.html.

Ableism/Language (Blog), accessed on August 6, 2018. http://www.autistichoya.com/p/ableist-words-and-terms-to-avoid.html?m=1.

Akesson, Bree. "Respond to Aleppo by Sponsoring a Syrian family." *Toronto Star*, December 20, 2016. https://www.thestar.com/opinion/commentary/2016/12/20/respond-to-aleppo-by-sponsoring-a-syrian-family.html.

Allan, Patrick. "How to Start Your Own Podcast." *Lifehacker*, August 9, 2017. https://lifehacker.com/how-to-start-your-own-podcast-1709798447.

Annett, Evan. "What Is 'Fake News,' and How Can You Spot It? Try Our Quiz." *Globe and Mail*, February 1, 2017. https://www.theglobeandmail.com/community/digital-lab/fake-news-quiz-how-to-spot/article33821986.

Ashby, Madeline. "Carleton University Must Acknowledge Rape Culture." *Ottawa Citizen*, August 23, 2016. https://ottawacitizen.com/opinion/columnists/ashby-carleton-must-acknowledge-rape-culture.

Associated Press. "Russian Hacking Went Far beyond US Election, Digital Hitlist Reveals." *Guardian*, November 2, 2017. https://www.theguardian.com/technology/2017/nov/02/russian-hacking-beyond-us-election-digital-hitlist.

Atchison, Amy. "Metrics, Metrics, (Alt)metrics." *The New West: Official Blog of the Western Political Science Association*, June 16, 2017. https://thewpsa.wordpress.com/2017/06/16/metrics-metrics-altmetrics.

Baddorf, Zack. "Uganda Ends Its Hunt for Joseph Kony Empty-Handed," *New York Times*, April 20, 2017. https://www.nytimes.com/2017/04/20/world/africa/uganda-joseph-kony-lra.html.

Bakshy, Eytan, Solomon Messing, and Lada A. Adamic. "Exposure to Ideologically Diverse News and Opinion on Facebook." *Science* (June 5, 2015): 1130–32.

Baldoni, John. "Is It Okay to Show Vulnerability?" *Forbes*, April 23, 2013. https://www.forbes.com/sites/johnbaldoni/2013/04/23/is-it-okay-to-show-vulnerability/#50d7f2945189.

Bambury, Brent. "Medieval History Scholars Are Suddenly on the Front Lines in the Fight against White Supremacists." *Day 6*, CBC Radio, September 29, 2017. http://www.cbc.ca/player/play/1058212419968.

Barnett, Arnold, and Edward Kaplan. "How to Cure the Electoral College," *Los Angeles Times*, December 16, 2016. http://www.latimes.com/opinion/op-ed/la-oe-barnett-kaplan-cure-electoral-college-20161216-story.html.

Barthel, Michael, Amy Mitchell, and Jesse Holcomb. "Many Americans Believe Fake News Is Sowing Confusion." Pew Research Center, December 15, 2016. http://www.journalism.org/2016/12/15/many-americans-believe-fake-news-is-sowing-confusion.

Bayrasli, Elmira, and Lauren Bohn. *FPInterrupted* (Website), accessed on August 6, 2018. http://www.fpinterrupted.com.

Becker, Christine, and Michael Kackman. *Aca-Media* (Podcast), accessed on August 8, 2018. http://www.aca-media.org.

Beinart, Peter. "'Republican Is Not a Synonym for Racist.'" *Atlantic*, December 2017. https://www.theatlantic.com/magazine/archive/2017/12/conservatism-without-bigotry/544128.

Berman, Kristen, and Dan Ariely. "Small Talk Should Be Banned—Here's Why." *Wired*, September 21, 2016. http://www.wired.co.uk/article/banning-small-talk.

Bertram, Chris, et al., *Crooked Timber* (Blog), accessed on August 8, 2018. http://crookedtimber.org

Bick, Sam, and David Zinman. *Treyf* (Podcast), accessed on August 8, 2018. https://treyfpodcast.wordpress.com.

Biewen, John. *Scene on Radio* (Podcast), accessed on August 8, 2018. http://www.sceneonradio.org.

Bilton, Nick. "Don't Fight Flames with Flames." *New York Times*, August 6, 2014. https://www.nytimes.com/2014/08/07/fashion/social-media-arguments-cant-win-propositions.html?smid=tw-share.

Black Lives Matter. "About." Black Lives Matter, accessed on January 10, 2018. https://blacklivesmatter.com/about.

Blattman, Chris. *International Development, Economics, Politics, and Policy* (Blog), accessed on August 6, 2018. https://chrisblattman.com/about.

Blog Directory. *New York Times*, accessed on August 6, 2018. https://
archive.nytimes.com/www.nytimes.com/interactive/blogs/directory
.html?mcubz=00.

Bloom, Ester, and Caroline Moss. "New York Times Columnist David
Brooks Says Rich People and Their Fancy Sandwich Shops Are 'Ruining
America.'" *CNBC.com*, July 11, 2017. https://www.cnbc.com/2017/07/11/
david-brooks-column-about-italian-sandwiches-is-causing-an-uproar.html.

Blow, Charles M. "Dispatch from the Resistance." *New York Times*, September 14,
2017. https://www.nytimes.com/2017/09/14/opinion/dispatch-from
-the-resistance.html.

Blow, Charles M. "Is Trump a White Supremacist?" *New York Times*,
September 18, 2017. https://www.nytimes.com/2017/09/18/opinion/
trump-white-supremacist.html?_r=0.

Blow, Charles M. "Library Visit, Then Held at Gunpoint." *New York Times*,
January 26, 2015. https://www.nytimes.com/2015/01/26/opinion/
charles-blow-at-yale-the-police-detained-my-son.html.

Bowles, Nellie. "How Doxxing Became a Mainstream Tool in the Culture
Wars." *New York Times*, August 30, 2017. https://www.nytimes
.com/2017/08/30/technology/doxxing-protests.html?_r=0.

Boydstun, Amber, et al. #WomenAlsoKnowStuff (Website), accessed on
August 6, 2018. https://womenalsoknowstuff.com.

Boynton, Robert. "Attack of the Career-Killing Blogs." *Slate*, November 16,
2005. http://www.slate.com/articles/news_and_politics/college
_week/2005/11/attack_of_the_careerkilling_blogs.html.

Bradley, Laura. "Jeffrey Tambor 'Profoundly Disappointed' with Amazon
Following Transparent Firing." *Vanity Fair*, February 15, 2018. https://
www.vanityfair.com/hollywood/2018/02/jeffrey-tambor-leaving
-transparent-amazon-investigation-sexual-harassment.

Bragg, Melvyn. *In Our Time* (Podcast), accessed on August 8, 2018. https://
www.bbc.co.uk/programmes/b006qykl/episodes/downloads.

Brecher, Gary. *Radio War Nerd* (Podcast), accessed on August 8, 2018.
https://www.patreon.com/radiowarnerd.

Breckwich Vásquez, Victoria, Phyllis Gutiérrez Kenney, and Guadalupe
Gamboa. "Where Is the #MeToo for Sexual Harassment against
Immigrant Workers?" *Seattle Times*, November 13, 2017. https://www
.seattletimes.com/opinion/where-is-the-metoo-for-sexual-harassment
-against-immigrant-workers.

Brookings Blogs. Brookings, accessed on August 6, 2018. https://www.brookings
.edu/blogs.

Brooks, David. "How We Are Ruining America." *New York Times*, July 11, 2017. https://www.nytimes.com/2017/07/11/opinion/how-we-are-ruining-america.html?smid=tw-share.

Brügger, Niels. "A Brief History of Facebook as a Media Text: The Development of an Empty Structure," *First Monday: Peer-Reviewed Journal on the Internet* 20, no. 5 (2015). doi:https://doi.org/10.5210/fm.v20i5.5423.

Bruni, Frank. "Oversharing in Admissions Essays." *New York Times*, June 14, 2014. https://www.nytimes.com/2014/06/15/opinion/sunday/frank-bruni-oversharing-in-admissions-essays.html?mcubz=0&_r=0.

Busby, Joshua William. "Bono Made Jesse Helms Cry: Jubilee 2000, Debt Relief, and Moral Action in International Politics." *International Studies Quarterly* 51 (2007): 247–75.

Busby, Joshua William. "Social Media and the Scholar in an Era of Hyper-Nationalism and Fake News." *PS: Political Science and Politics* 50, no. 4 (2017): 1004–1007. doi: https://doi.org/10.1017/S1049096517001160.

Campos, Paul F. "White Economic Privilege Is Alive and Well." *New York Times*, July 29, 2017. https://www.nytimes.com/2017/07/29/opinion/sunday/black-income-white-privilege.html.

Carey, Benedict. "How Fiction Becomes Fact on Social Media." *New York Times*, October 20, 2017. https://www.nytimes.com/2017/10/20/health/social-media-fake-news.html?hp&action=click&pgtype=Homepage&clickSource=story-heading&module=second-column-region&region=top-news&WT.nav=top-news&_r=1.

Carleton University's Sexual Violence Policy. https://carleton.ca/secretariat/wp-content/uploads/Sexual-Violence-Policy-December-1-2016.pdf.

Carlin, Dan. *Hardcore History* (Podcast), accessed on August 8, 2018. https://www.dancarlin.com/hardcore-history-series.

Carvin, Stephanie, and Craig Forcese. *Intrepid* (Podcast), accessed on August 8, 2018. https://www.intrepidpodcast.com.

Cauterucci, Christina. "The Lessons of Kony 2012." *Slate*, September 16, 2016. http://www.slate.com/articles/news_and_politics/the_next_20/2016/09/kony_2012_quickly_became_a_punch_line_but_what_if_it_did_more_good_than.html.

CBC News. "Social Media Plays 'Extremely Important' Role in Iranian Protests Despite Censorship." *CBC*, January 4, 2018. https://www.cbc.ca/news/technology/iran-protests-social-media-telegram-1.4471226.

CBC Radio. "#SettlerCollector: Hashtag Helps Redirect Racist Attacks on Social Media." February 16, 2018. http://www.cbc.ca/radio/unreserved/after-colten-boushie-where-do-we-go-from-here-1.4535052/

settlercollector-hashtag-helps-redirect-racist-attacks-on-social-media
-1.4537594.

Chandler, Daniel, and Rod Munday. "Confirmation Bias." *A Dictionary of Social Media*. Oxford: Oxford University Press, 2016.

Chavez, Holly. "Nine Positive Benefits of a Social Media Detox." *Lifehack*, accessed on August 6, 2018. https://www.lifehack.org/483829/9-positive -benefits-of-a-social-media-detox.

Chenoweth, Erica, et al., *Political Violence at a Glance: Expert Analysis of Violence and its Alternatives* (Blog), accessed on August 9, 2018. http:// politicalviolenceataglance.org.

Chesney, Bobby, and Steve Vladeck. *The National Security Law Podcast*, accessed on August 8, 2018. https://www.nationalsecuritylawpodcast.com.

Chetty, Raj, Nathaniel Hendren, Patrick Kline, Emmanuel Saez, and Nicholas Turner. "Is the United States Still a Land of Opportunity? Recent Trends in Intergenerational Mobility." *American Economic Review: Papers and Proceedings* 104, no. 5 (2014): 141–47.

Chou, Hui-Tzu Grace, and Nicholas Edge. "'They Are Happier and Having Better Lives than I Am': The Impact of Using Facebook on Perceptions of Others' Lives." *CyberPsychology, Behavior and Social Networking* 15, no. 2 (2012): 117–21.

Cialdini, Robert B. "If You Want to Influence People Don't Try to Persuade Them. Use 'Pre-Suasion' Instead." *Los Angeles Times*, October 23, 2016. http://www.latimes.com/opinion/op-ed/la-oe-cialdini-presuasion -20161023-snap-story.html.

Cialdini, Robert B. *Pre-Suasion: A Revolutionary Way to Influence and Persuade.* New York: Simon & Schuster, 2016.

Cited (Podcast), accessed on August 8, 2018. http://citedpodcast.com.

Coates, Ta-Nehisi. "The Lost Cause Rides Again." *Atlantic*, August 4, 2017. https://www.theatlantic.com/entertainment/archive/2017/08/no -confederate/535512/?utm_source=atlfb.

Connolly, N.D.B. "Charlottesville Showed That Liberalism Can't Defeat White Supremacy. Only Direct Action Can." *Washington Post*, August 15, 2017. https://www.washingtonpost.com/news/made-by-history/ wp/2017/08/15/charlottesville-showed-that-liberalism-cant-defeat -white-supremacy-only-direct-action-can/?utm_term=.e6f479ff0db7.

Coontz, Stephanie. "Do Millennial Men Want Stay-at-Home Wives?" *New York Times*, March 31, 2017. https://www.nytimes.com/2017/03/31/opinion/ sunday/do-millennial-men-want-stay-at-home-wives.html?mcubz=0.

Crellin, Olivia. "Only Men at Your Event? This Blog Will Shame You." *BBC Trending*, May 27, 2015. https://www.bbc.com/news/blogs-trending-32789580.

Crenshaw, Kimberlé. "Mapping the Margins: Intersectionality, Identity Politics, and Violence against Women of Color." *Stanford Law Review* 43, no. 6 (1991): 1241–99.

Dahlstrom, Michael F. "Using Narratives and Storytelling to Communicate Science with Nonexpert Audiences." *Proceedings of the National Academy of Sciences of the United States of America* 111, no. 4 (2014): 13614–13620.

Daniels, Jessie. "Roundup of Responses to Kristof's Call for Professors in the Public Sphere." *Just Publics @365* (Blog), accessed on August 6, 2018. https://justpublics365.commons.gc.cuny.edu/02/2014/roundup-kristof -professors-public-sphere.

Dann, Naomi. "Richard Spencer Might Be the Worst Person in America. But He Might Also Be Right about Israel." *Forward*, August 17, 2017. https:// forward.com/opinion/380384/richard-spencer-israel.

Desch, Michael C., ed. *Public Intellectuals in the Global Arena: Professors or Pundits?*. Notre Dame: University of Notre Dame Press, 2016.

Dewey, Caitlin. "98 Personal Data Points that Facebook Uses to Target Ads to You." *Washington Post*, August 19, 2016. http://www.washingtonpost .com/news/the-intersect/wp/2016/08/19/98-personal-data-points-that -facebook-uses-to-target-ads-to-you/?tid=ss_tw&utm_term=.39353cd30f9f.

Dewey, Caitlin. "The Real Problem with David Brooks's Sandwich Column." *Washington Post*, July 11, 2017. http://www.washingtonpost.com/blogs/ wonkblog/wp/2017/07/11/the-real-problem-with-david-brooks -sandwich-column/?tid=ss_tw&utm_term=.745f62e28300.

DiAngelo, Robin. "White Fragility," *International Journal of Critical Pedagogy* 3, no. 3 (2011): 54–70. https://libjournal.uncg.edu/ijcp/article/viewFile/ 249/116.

DiAngelo, Robin. *White Fragility: Why It's So Hard for White People to Talk about Racism*. Boston: Beacon Press, 2018.

DiMeo, Nate. *The Memory Palace* (Podcast), accessed on August 8, 2018. http://thememorypalace.us.

Doucet, Andrea. "Scholarly Reflections on Blogging: Once a Tortoise, Never a Hare." *Chronicle of Higher Education*, January 3, 2012. https://www .chronicle.com/article/Scholarly-Reflections-on/130191.

Drezner, Daniel W. "A Professor and His Wife on Absorbing the Shock of Tenure Denial." *Chronicle of Higher Education*, July 3, 2011. https://www .chronicle.com/article/A-ProfessorHis-Wife-on/128077.

Drezner, Daniel W. "So Friday Was a Pretty Bad Day." October 8, 2005. http://www.danieldrezner.com/archives/002353.html.

Duca, Lauren. "How 'Nice White People' Benefit from Charlottesville and White Supremacy." *Teen Vogue*, August 14, 2017. https://www.teenvogue

.com/story/complacency-racism-white-supremacy-charlottesville-thigh
-high-politics-lauren-duca.

Duggan, Maeve, and Aaron Smith. "The Political Environment on Social
Media." Pew Research Center, October 25, 2016. http://www.pewinternet
.org/2016/10/25/the-political-environment-on-social-media.

Eisner, Jane. "Zionism Cannot Be Compared to Nazism—Even if Spencer
and JVP Say So." *Forward*, August 19, 2017. http://forward.com/
opinion/380526/zionism-nazism-richard-spencer-jvp.

Ellison, Nicole B., Jessica Vitak, Rebecca Gray, and Cliff Lampe. "Cultivating
Social Resources on Social Network Sites: Facebook Relationship
Maintenance Behaviors and Their Role in Social Capital Processes."
Journal of Computer-Mediated Communication 19 (2014): 855–70.

Eltagouri, Marwa. "Professor Who Tweeted, 'All I Want for Christmas Is
White Genocide,' Resigns after Year of Threats." *Washington Post*, December
29, 2017. https://www.insidehighered.com/news/2016/12/26/drexel
-condemns-professors-tweet-about-white-genocide.

Erickson, Amanda. "Iran's Protests Are Fading, but Iranians Are Still
Angry." *Washington Post*, January 4, 2018. http://www.washingtonpost.
com/blogs/worldviews/wp/2018/01/04/irans-protests-are-fading-but
-iranians-are-still-angry/?tid=ss_tw&utm_term=.5236ea2f4d30.

Eveleth, Rose. "How to Deter Doxxing: Newsroom Strategies to Prevent the
Harassment That Follows the Public Posting of Home Addresses, Phone
Number and Journalists' Other Personal Information." *Nieman Reports*,
June 1, 2015. http://niemanreports.org/articles/how-to-deter-doxxing.

Farber, Bernie M., and Mira Sucharov. "Ottawa Must Seek Justice for Hassan
Diab." *Toronto Star*, July 10, 2017. https://www.thestar.com/opinion/
commentary/2017/07/10/ottawa-must-seek-justice-for-hassan-diab.html.

Farber, Bernie M., and Mira Sucharov. "We Must Overcome Islamophobia in
2018." *Toronto Star*, January 2, 2018. https://www.thestar.com/opinion/
contributors/2018/01/02/we-must-overcome-islamophobia-in-2018.html.

Farber, Bernie M., and Mira Sucharov. "Why We Need a Parliamentary
Motion to Fight Islamophobia." *Toronto Star*, October 5, 2017. https://
www.thestar.com/opinion/commentary/2017/10/05/why-we-need-a
-parliamentary-motion-to-fight-islamophobia.html.

Farley, Robert. "Complicating the Political Scientist as Blogger." *PS: Political
Science and Politics* 46, no. 2 (April 2013): 383–86.

Farley, Robert. *Lawyers, Guns and Money* (Blog), accessed on August 6, 2018.
http://www.lawyersgunsmoneyblog.com/author/robert-farley.

Filipovic, Jill. "David Brooks' Fancy Sandwich Story Misses Point on
America's Divide." *CNN.com*, July 13, 2017. http://www.cnn

.com/2017/07/13/opinions/david-brooks-sandwich-misses-the-point
-filipovic/index.html.

Flaherty, Colleen. "Oberlin Ousts Professor." *Inside Higher Ed*, November 16,
2016. https://www.insidehighered.com/news/2016/11/16/oberlin-fires
-joy-karega-following-investigation-her-anti-semitic-statements-social#
.Wke6sbe-Ck4.link.

Forcese, Craig. *National Security Law: Canadian Practice in Comparative
Perspective* (Blog), accessed on August 6, 2018. http://craigforcese
.squarespace.com/national-security-law-blog.

Fortgang, Tal. "Checking My Privilege: Character as the Basis of Privilege."
Princeton Tory, April 2, 2014. http://theprincetontory.com/checking-my
-privilege-character-as-the-basis-of-privilege.

Frankely Judaic (Podcast). University of Michigan, accessed on August 8,
2018. https://lsa.umich.edu/judaic/resources/frankely-judaic-podcasts
.html.

Frenkel, Sheera, and Daisuke Wakabayashi. "After Florida School Shooting,
Russian 'Bot' Army Pounced." *New York Times*, February 19, 2018.
https://www.nytimes.com/2018/02/19/technology/russian-bots
-school-shooting.html.

Friedman, Thomas L. "Folks, We're Home Alone." *New York Times*, September 27,
2017. https://www.nytimes.com/2017/09/27/opinion/globalization
-trump-american-progress.html?smid=tw-share.

Gay, Roxane. "Dear Men: It's You, Too." *New York Times*, October 19, 2017. https://
www.nytimes.com/2017/10/19/opinion/metoo-sexual-harassment
-men.html.

Gladwell, Malcolm. *Revisionist History* (Podcast), accessed on August 8, 2018.
http://revisionisthistory.com.

Goffman, Erving. *The Presentation of Self in Everyday Life*. New York: Doubleday,
1959.

Goldman, Lisa. "Social Media Is Dangerously Undermining Our Democratic
Values." *Forward*, December 27, 2017. https://forward.com/opinion/391029/
social-media-is-dangerously-undermining-our-democratic-values.

Goldstein, Eric L. *The Price of Whiteness: Jews, Race, and American Identity*.
Princeton, NJ: Princeton University Press, 2008.

Goodman, Ryan, and Steve Vladeck, editors in chief. *Just Security* (Blog),
accessed on August 8, 2018. https://www.justsecurity.org.

Graber, Cynthia, and Nicola Twilley. *Gastropod* (Podcast), accessed on August
8, 2018. https://gastropod.com.

Graham Hunter, Anna. "Dustin Hoffman Sexually Harassed Me When I was
Seventeen." *Hollywood Reporter*, November 1, 2017. https://www

.hollywoodreporter.com/features/dustin-hoffman-sexually-harassed-me
-i-was-17-guest-column-1053466.

Green, Emma. "Are Jews White?" *Atlantic*, December 5, 2016. https://www
.theatlantic.com/politics/archive/2016/12/are-jews-white/509453/?utm
_source=twb.

Greenfield, Rebecca. "Judge Upholds *Huffington Post*'s Right Not to Pay
Bloggers." *Atlantic*, March 30, 2012. https://www.theatlantic.com/
business/archive/2012/03/judge-upholds-huffington-posts-right-not
-pay-bloggers/329891/?utm_source=twb.

Grigoriadis, Vanessa. "What the Weinstein Effect Can Teach Us about
Campus Sexual Assault." *New York Times*, November 15, 2017. https://
www.nytimes.com/2017/11/15/opinion/campus-sexual-assault
-weinstein.html.

Guillory, Sean. *Sean's Russia Blog Podcast*, accessed on August 8, 2018.
https://seansrussiablog.org.

Hall, Trish. "Op-Ed and You." *New York Times*, October 13, 2013. https://
www.nytimes.com/2013/10/14/opinion/op-ed-and-you.html?mcubz=0.

Hanif, Mohammed. "Not All Attacks Are Created Equal." *New York Times*,
June 9, 2017. https://www.nytimes.com/2017/06/09/opinion/london
-kabul-terrorist-attack.html.

Harris, Shane, Susan Hennessey, Benjamin Wittes, and Tamara Cofman
Wittes. *Rational Security* (Podcast), accessed on August 8, 2018. https://
www.lawfareblog.com/topic/rational-security.

"HBO's Controversial 'Confederate' Series Is 'Not Actively' Being Worked
On." *Shadow and Act*, November 30, 2017. https://shadowandact.com/
hbos-controversial-confederate-series-is-not-actively-being-worked
-on#shadowAndAct.

Healy, Kieran. "Public Sociology in the Age of Social Media." *Perspectives on
Politics* 15, no. 3 (2017): 771–80.

Hempel, Jessi. "The Problem with #MeToo and Viral Outrage." *Wired*,
October 18, 2017. https://www.wired.com/story/the-problem-with-me
-too-and-viral-outrage/?mbid=nl_101817_daily_list3_p.

Horwitz, Paul. "Of Mirrors and Media: The Blogger as Public Intellectual." In
Public Intellectuals in the Global Arena: Professors or Pundits?, edited by Michael
C. Desch, 214–246. Notre Dame: University of Notre Dame Press, 2016.

Hot and Bothered (Podcast), accessed on August 8, 2018. https://www
.hotandbotheredrompod.com/the-podcast.

"How Are Pledge-Takers Held Accountable?" *ProTruthPledge*, accessed on
August 6, 2018. https://www.protruthpledge.org/how-are-pledge-takers
-held-accountable.

H-Podcast. "Academic Podcast Roundup," accessed on August 6, 2018.
https://networks.h-net.org/node/84048/pages/111820/academic
-podcast-roundup.

Hudson, Laura. "Why You Should Think Twice before Shaming Anyone on
Social Media." *Wired*, July 24, 2013. https://www.wired.com/2013/07/
ap_argshaming/?mbid=email_onsiteshare.

Jacquet, Jennifer. *Is Shame Necessary? New Uses for an Old Tool*. New York:
Vintage, 2015.

Jaffe, Sarah, and Michelle Chen. *Belabored* (Podcast), accessed on August 8,
2018. https://www.dissentmagazine.org/tag/belabored.

Jarrar, Raed. "Why Won't Israel Let Me Mourn My Father?" *New York Times*,
November 23, 2017. https://www.nytimes.com/2017/11/23/opinion/
why-wont-israel-let-me-mourn-my-father.html?_r=0.

Jaschik, Scott. "Drexel Condemns Professor's Tweet." *Inside Higher Ed*,
December 26, 2016. https://www.insidehighered.com/news/2016/12/26/
drexel-condemns-professors-tweet-about-white-genocide#.Wke3W4V0sc0
.link.

Johnson, Maisha Z. "160+ Examples of Male Privilege in All Areas of Life."
Everyday Feminism, February 25, 2016. https://everydayfeminism
.com/2016/02/160-examples-of-male-privilege.

Karlsen, Rune, Kari Steen-Johnsen, Dag Wollebaek, and Bernard Enjolras.
"Echo Chamber and Trench Warfare Dynamics in Online Debates."
European Journal of Communication 32, no. 3 (2017): 257–73.

Karsten, Jack, and Darrell M. West. "Inside the Social Media Echo Chamber."
Brookings, December 9, 2016. https://www.brookings.edu/blog/
techtank/2016/12/09/inside-the-social-media-echo-chamber.

Keating, Joshua. "The Less You Know." *Slate*, May 20, 2014. http://www
.slate.com/blogs/the_world_/2014/05/20/the_depressing_reason_why
_hashtag_campaigns_like_stopkony_and_bringbackourgirls.html.

Kelly, Jason M. *Practicing History* (Podcast), accessed on August 8, 2018.
https://www.jasonmkelly.com/jason-m-kelly/2016/08/03/practicing
-history-podcast-episode-5-primary-sources.

Kennedy, Paul. *Ideas* (Podcast), accessed on August 8, 2018. http://www.cbc
.ca/radio/ideas.

Kestenbaum, Sam. "Richard Spencer Touts Himself as 'White Zionist' in
Israeli Interview." *Forward*, August 17, 2017. https://forward.com/fast
-forward/380235/richard-spencer-touts-himself-as-white-zionist-in
-israeli-interview.

Khera, Farhana, and Jonathan J. Smith. "How Trump Is Stealthily Carrying
Out His Muslim Ban." *New York Times*, July 18, 2017. https://www

.nytimes.com/2017/07/18/opinion/trump-muslim-ban-supreme-court
.html.

Koffler Fogel, Shimon. "How Anti-Zionism and Anti-Semitism Are
Converging." *Haaretz*, March 24, 2016. https://www.haaretz.com/
opinion/.premium-how-anti-zionism-and-anti-semitism-are-converging
-1.5422096.

Koffman, David S. "Suffering and Sovereignty: Recent Canadian Jewish
Interest in Indigenous Peoples and Issues." *Canadian Jewish Studies* 25
(2017): 28–59.

"Kony 2012." Invisible Children. YouTube, March 5, 2012. https://www.
youtube.com/watch?v=Y4MnpzG5Sqc&feature=youtu.be&noredirect=1.

Kristof, Nicholas. "Professors, We Need You!" *New York Times*, February 15,
2014. https://www.nytimes.com/2014/02/16/opinion/sunday/kristof
-professors-we-need-you.html?smid=tw-share.

Krupkin, Taly. "Linda Sarsour at Racial Justice March: 'It Is Not My Job
to Educate Jewish People That Palestinians Deserve Dignity.'" *Haaretz*,
October 2, 2017. https://www.haaretz.com/us-news/.premium-sarsour
-not-my-job-to-teach-jews-that-palestinians-deserve-dignity-1.5454882.

Kurtzer, Daniel C. "Donald Trump's Israel Ambassador Pick Is Hazardous
to Peace." *New York Times*, December 16, 2016. https://www.nytimes.
com/2016/12/16/opinion/donald-trumps-israel-ambassador-pick-is
-hazardous-to-peace.html.

Labott, Elise, Kevin Liptak, and Nicole Gaouette. "Ambassador Candidate
Dropped over Stark Warning on North Korea." *CNN*, January 30, 2018.
https://www.cnn.com/2018/01/30/politics/victor-cha-ambassador-to
-south-korea/index.html.

Larty, Jamiles. "Ta-Nehisi Coates Quits Twitter after Public Row with Cornel
West." *Guardian*, December 20, 2017. https://www.theguardian.com/
books/2017/dec/20/ta-nehisi-coates-quits-twitter-after-public-row-with
-cornel-west.

Lawler, Audra J., and Sara Ann Hook. "Developing a Social Media
Strategy for a Small Non-Profit Organization: More Conversation, Less
Marketing." (Poster), 23rd Indiana University Undergraduate Research
Conference, Indianapolis, Indiana, November 17, 2017.

Lee, Bruce Y. "Use Emojis in Work Emails? You May Be Tainting Your
Colleagues' Opinion of You." *Forbes*, August 15, 2017. https://www
.forbes.com/sites/brucelee/2017/08/15/using-emojis-at-work-beware-of
-this-risk/#1cbaa5113eca.

Lee, Frances. "Why I've Started to Fear My Fellow Social Justice Activists."
YES! Magazine, October 13, 2017. http://www.yesmagazine.org/people

-power/why-ive-started-to-fear-my-fellow-social-justice-activists
-20171013.

Lee, Sung-Yoon. "The Way to Make North Korea Back Down." *New York Times*, September, 6, 2017. https://www.nytimes.com/2017/09/06/opinion/the-way-to-make-north-korea-back-down.html.

Legam, Judd, editor in chief. *ThinkProgress* (Blog), accessed on August 8, 2018. https://thinkprogress.org.

Lenchner, Charles. "People for Bernie: An Answer to Some of Our Persistent Critics" (Facebook note). December 3, 2017. https://www.facebook.com/notes/charles-lenchner/people-for-bernie-an-answer-to-some-of-our-persistent-critics/10155982863849758.

Levitt, Stephen D., and Stephen J. Dubner. *Freakonomics Radio* (Podcast), accessed on August 8, 2018. http://freakonomics.com.

Lewis, Jeffrey, and Aaron Stein. *Arms Control Wonk* (Podcast), accessed on August 8, 2018. https://www.armscontrolwonk.com/archive/author/podcast.

Libenson, Daniel, and Lex Rofeberg. *Judaism Unbound* (Podcast), accessed on August 8, 2018. http://www.judaismunbound.com.

Loeffler, James. "The Zionist Founders of the Human Rights Movement." *New York Times*, May 14, 2018. https://www.nytimes.com/2018/05/14/opinion/zionism-israel-human-rights.html.

Lopez, German. "The Battle over Identity Politics, Explained." *Vox*, August 17, 2017. https://www.vox.com/identities/2016/12/2/13718770/identity-politics.

Mahmoud, Nervana. *From the Middle East to the British Isles* (Blog), accessed on August 8, 2018. https://nervana1.org.

Makarechi, Kia. "What the Data Really Says about Police and Racial Bias." *Vanity Fair*, July 14, 2016. https://www.vanityfair.com/news/2016/07/data-police-racial-bias.

Mallick, Heather. "Agree or disagree, I deserve an A+ for this column." *Toronto Star*, September 8, 2017. https://www.thestar.com/opinion/2017/09/08/agree-or-disagree-i-deserve-an-a-for-this-column-mallick.html.

Malloy, Jonathan. "How Ontario's NDP Is Setting Itself up to Repeat History." *Globe and Mail*, May 31, 2018. https://www.theglobeandmail.com/opinion/article-how-ontarios-ndp-is-setting-itself-up-to-repeat-history.

Marche, Stephen. "Canada Doesn't Know How to Party." *New York Times*, June 23, 2017. https://www.nytimes.com/2017/06/23/opinion/sunday/canada-doesnt-know-how-to-party.html.

Markel, Dan, et al. *PrawfsBlawg* (Blog), accessed on August 8, 2018. http://prawfsblawg.blogs.com.

Marshall, John. *Talking Points Memo* (Blog), accessed on August 8, 2018. https://talkingpointsmemo.com.

Marvin, Taylor, and Barbara F. Walter. "Where Are All the Female Bloggers?" *Political Violence @ a Glance: Expert Analysis on Violence and Its Alternatives* (Blog), June 28, 2013. http://politicalviolenceataglance.org/2013/06/28/where-are-all-the-female-bloggers.

Mathis-Lilley, Ben. "Times Columnist Says Confusing Sandwich Menus, Not Structural Inequality, Killed the American Dream." *Slate*, July 11, 2017. http://www.slate.com/blogs/the_slatest/2017/07/11/david_brooks_cites_foreign_ingredients_as_barrier_to_social_mobility.html.

Mayer, Brian. "Thomas Friedman Op/Ed Generator." Accessed on August 6, 2018. http://thomasfriedmanopedgenerator.com/about.php.

McCulloch, Gretchen, and Lauren Gawne. *Lingthusiasm* (Podcast), accessed on August 8, 2018. https://lingthusiasm.com.

McGlinchey, Stephen, editor in chief. *E-International Relations* (Blog), accessed on August 8, 2018. https://www.e-ir.info.

McIntosh, Peggy. "White Privilege and Male Privilege: A Personal Account of Coming to See Correspondences through Work in Women's Studies." Working Paper 189. Wellesley, MA: Wellesley College, Center for Research on Women, 1988.

McWhorter, John H. *Lexicon Valley* (Podcast), accessed on August 8, 2018. http://www.slate.com/articles/podcasts/lexicon_valley.html.

Mehl, Matthias R., Simine Vazire, Shannon E. Holleran, and C. Shelby Clark. "Eavesdropping on Happiness: Well-Being Is Related to Having Less Small Talk and More Substantive Conversations." *Psychological Science* 21, no. 4 (2010): 539–41.

"#MeToo: How a Hashtag Became a Rally Cry against Sexual Harassment." *Guardian*, accessed on August 8, 2018. https://www.theguardian.com/world/2017/oct/20/women-worldwide-use-hashtag-metoo-against-sexual-harassment.

Meyerson, Collier. "Can You Be a Zionist Feminist? Linda Sarsour Says No." *Nation*, March 13, 2017. https://www.thenation.com/article/can-you-be-a-zionist-feminist-linda-sarsour-says-no.

Monbiot, George. "Why Are the Crucial Questions about Hurricane Harvey Not Being Asked?" *Guardian*, August 29, 2017. https://www.theguardian.com/commentisfree/2017/aug/29/hurricane-harvey-manmade-climate-disaster-world-catastrophe.

Moon, Richard. "Pope's Refusal to Apologize for Residential Schools Evokes a Past Tragedy." *Ottawa Citizen*, April 4, 2018. https://ottawacitizen.com/opinion/columnists/moon-popes-refusal-to-apologize-for-residential-schools-evokes-a-past-tragedy.

Moore, Lela. "'It's Not the Fault of the Sandwich Shop': Readers Debate David Brooks's Column." *New York Times*, July 13, 2017. https://www.nytimes.com/2017/07/13/opinion/its-not-the-fault-of-the-sandwich-shop-readers-debate-david-brookss-column.html?smid=tw-share.

Morris, Tee, and Chuck Tomasi. *Podcasting for Dummies*. Hoboken, NJ: John Wiley & Sons, 2017.

Moser, Bob. "How Twitter's Alt-Right Purge Fell Short." *Rolling Stone*, December 19, 2017. http://www.rollingstone.com/politics/news/how-twitters-alt-right-purge-fell-short-w514444.

Muldowney, Decca. "Info Wars: Inside the Left's Online Efforts to Out White Supremacists." *ProPublica*, October 30, 2017. https://www.propublica.org/article/inside-the-lefts-online-efforts-to-out-white-supremacists.

Murphy, Rex. "Thinking of Dishing Out for Hillary's Book? I'll Save You the Expense." *National Post*, September 8, 2017. https://nationalpost.com/opinion/rex-murphy-thinking-of-dishing-out-for-hillarys-book-ill-save-you-the-expense.

Nexon, Daniel H. "ISQ Annual Report, 2016." December 12, 2016. https://www.isanet.org/Portals/0/Documents/ISQ/ISQ%20Annual%20Report%202016.pdf.

Nexon, Daniel H., et al. *Duck of Minerva* (Blog), accessed on August 8, 2018. http://duckofminerva.com.

Nguyen, Phan. "Reading Salaita in Illinois." *Mondoweiss*, August 13, 2014. http://mondoweiss.net/2014/08/reading-salaita-illinois-1.

Niezen, Ronald. "Inquiry into Violence against Indigenous Women Needs Teeth." *Toronto Star*, December 23, 2015. https://www.thestar.com/opinion/commentary/2015/12/23/inquiry-into-violence-against-indigenous-women-needs-teeth.html.

Nolan, Hamilton. "Thomas Friedman Writes His Only Column Again." *Gawker*, June 25, 2012. http://gawker.com/5921030/thomas-friedman-writes-his-only-column-again.

"No, We Won't 'Calm Down': Tone Policing Is Just Another Way to Protect Privilege." Robot Hugs (Webcomic), accessed on August 6, 2018. http://www.robot-hugs.com/tone-policing.

NYO Staff. "Write Your Own Thomas Friedman Column!" *New York Observer*, May 5, 2014. http://observer.com/2004/05/write-your-own-thomas-friedman-column.

Obeidallah, Dean. "'Black Panther' Inspires More than African Americans." *CNN*, February 18, 2018. https://www.cnn.com/2018/02/18/opinions/black-panther-minorities-opinion-obeidallah/index.html.

O'Carroll, Eoin. "How Digital Media Fuels Moral Outrage—And What To Do about It." *Christian Science Monitor*, September 22, 2017. https://www.csmonitor.com/Technology/2017/0922/How-digital-media-fuels-moral-outrage-and-what-to-do-about-it.

O'Connell, Joanne. "How to Stop Arguing and Actually Change Someone's Mind on Social Media." *Guardian*, January 28, 2017. https://www.theguardian.com/media/2017/jan/28/how-to-stop-arguing-and-actually-change-someones-mind-on-social-media.

Office of the Associate Vice-President (Teaching and Learning). Blog, accessed on August 6, 2018. https://carleton.ca/teachinglearning/blog.

Oliver, Kelly. "Education in the Age of Outrage." *New York Times*, October 16, 2017. https://www.nytimes.com/2017/10/16/opinion/education-outrage-morality-shaming.html?smid=fb-share.

O'Neill, Brendan. "I Hate to Break it to Feminists, but 'White Male Privilege' is a Myth." *Spectator*, January 5, 2016. https://blogs.spectator.co.uk/2016/01/i-hate-to-break-it-to-feminists-but-white-male-privilege-is-a-myth.

Oppenheim, Maya. "Alt-Right Leader Richard Spencer Worries Getting Punched Will Become 'Meme to End All Memes.'" *Independent*, January 23, 2017. https://www.independent.co.uk/news/world/americas/alt-right-richard-spencer-punched-anti-donald-trump-protest-meme-pepe-the-frog-inauguration-day-a7541461.html.

Ottoman History (Podcast), accessed on August 8, 2018. http://www.ottomanhistorypodcast.com.

Ouchlets. "First There Was Racism and Sexism, Now There's Ableism." *Ouch* (Blog), June 16, 2014. https://www.bbc.com/news/blogs-ouch-27840472.

Owen, Tayor, founder. *OpenCanada* (Blog), accessed on August 8, 2018. https://www.opencanada.org.

Page, Tiffany. "Vulnerable Writing as a Feminist Methodological Practice." *Feminist Review* 115, no. 1 (2017): 13–29.

Paris, Roland, and Thomas Juneau. "Read and Vote: Has Canada Drifted into a Combat Mission in Iraq?" *Globe and Mail*, January 29, 2015; updated June 19, 2017. https://www.theglobeandmail.com/opinion/read-and-vote-has-canada-drifted-into-all-out-combat-in-iraq/article22696704.

Patil, Anjuli. "Dalhousie Withdraws Disciplinary Action against Masuma Kham over 'White Fragility' Facebook Post." *CBC News*, October 25, 2017.

https://www.cbc.ca/news/canada/nova-scotia/dalhousie-withdraws
-complaint-against-masuma-khan-1.4371332.

Pepinsky, Tom. Blog, accessed on August 6, 2018. https://tompepinsky
.com/blog.

People of Color Also Know Stuff (Website), accessed on August 10, 2018.
https://sites.google.com/view/pocexperts/home?authuser=2.

Perez, Sarah. "Twitter Officially Launches 'Threads,' a New Feature for
Easily Posting Tweetstorms." *Tech Crunch*, December 12, 2017. https://
techcrunch.com/2017/12/12/twitter-officially-launches-threads-a-new
-feature-for-easily-writing-tweetstorms.

Pessah, Tom. "Men Who Are Silent after #MeToo: It's Time to Speak Up."
Guardian, October 20, 2017. https://www.theguardian.com/commentisfree/
2017/oct/20/men-silent-me-too-sexism?CMP=share_btn_link.

Pfeffer, Anshel. "What Kerry's Speech Says about the Obama
Administration's Israel Strategy." *Los Angeles Times*, December 29, 2016.
http://www.latimes.com/opinion/op-ed/la-oe-pfeffer-kerry-speech
-20161228-story.html.

Pfeffer, Fabian. "Multigenerational Approaches to Social Mobility: A
Multifaceted Research Agenda." *Research in Social Stratification and
Mobility* 35 (2014): 1–12.

Pittman, Matthew, and Brandon Reich. "Social Media and Loneliness: Why
an Instagram Picture May Be Worth More Than a Thousand Twitter
Words." *Computers in Human Behavior* 62 (September 2016): 155–167.

POCAlsoKnowStuff (Twitter Account), accessed on August 6, 2018. https://
twitter.com/pocalsoknow?lang=en.

Pryor, Lisa. "Heterosexual Couples Deserve Our Support." *New York Times*,
September 28, 2017. https://www.nytimes.com/2017/09/28/opinion/
heterosexuals-deserve-our-support.html?_r=0.

Reese, Hope. "Meet the Activist Who Wants to Stop HBO's Confederate
from Getting Made." *Vox*, August 4, 2017. https://www.vox.com/
conversations/2017/8/4/16098256/no-confederate-hbo-game-of
-thrones?.

Regan, Ruti. "The Rules for Responding to Call Outs Aren't Working." *Real
Social Skills* (Blog), October 24, 2017. https://www.realsocialskills.org/
blog/the-rules-about-responding-to-call-outs-arent.

Rennison, Callie Marie. "I'm the Professor Who Made Brock Turner the
'Textbook Definition' of a Rapist." *Vox*, November 17, 2017. https://www
.vox.com/first-person/2017/11/17/16666290/brock-turner-rape.

Respers France, Lisa. "Anthony Rapp 'Gratified' by Response to His
Allegations against Kevin Spacey." *CNN.com*, December 5, 2017. https://

www.cnn.com/2017/12/05/entertainment/anthony-rapp-kevin-spacey
-response/index.html.

Respers France, Lisa. "Dustin Hoffman Accused of Sexual Assault." *CNN*,
December 16, 2017. https://www.cnn.com/2017/12/15/entertainment/
dustin-hoffman-sexual-allegations/index.html.

Respers France, Lisa. "Mayim Bialik Responds to 'Victim Blaming'
Backlash." *CNN*, October 16, 2017. https://www.cnn.com/2017/10/16/
entertainment/mayim-bialik-weinstein-backlash/index.html.

Robb, Amanda. "Anatomy of a Fake News Scandal." *Rolling Stone*,
November 16, 2017. http://www.rollingstone.com/politics/news/
pizzagate-anatomy-of-a-fake-news-scandal-w511904.

Rofer, Cheryl. *Nuclear Diner* (Blog), accessed on August 8, 2018. https://
nucleardiner.wordpress.com.

Ronson, Jon. "How One Stupid Tweet Blew Up Justine Sacco's Life." *New
York Times*, February 12, 2015. https://www.nytimes.com/2015/02/15/
magazine/how-one-stupid-tweet-ruined-justine-saccos-life.html.

Ronson, Jon. *So You've Been Publicly Shamed.* New York: Riverhead Books,
Penguin, 2015, 78–79.

Rosenberg, Yair. "Confessions of a Digital Nazi Hunter." *New York Times*,
December 27, 2017. https://nyti.ms/2pLYdEQ.

Rothman, Joshua. "The Origins of 'Privilege.'" *New Yorker*, May 12, 2014.
https://www.newyorker.com/books/page-turner/the-origins-of
-privilege.

Rum, Jeff. "A Civil Rights Organization That Does Social Media Right."
Social Media Today, August 24, 2017. https://www.socialmediatoday.com/
news/a-civil-rights-organization-that-does-social-media-right/504245.

Sacks, Oliver. "Sabbath." *New York Times*, August 14, 2015. https://www
.nytimes.com/2015/08/16/opinion/sunday/oliver-sacks-sabbath
.html?smid=tw-share.

Saideman, Stephen M. *Saideman's Semi-Spew: International Relations, Ethnic
Conflict, Civil-Military Relations, Academia, Politics in General, Selected
Silliness* (Blog), accessed on August 6, 2018. http://saideman.blogspot.ca.

Sasley, Brent E., and Mira Sucharov. "Scholarly versus Activist Identities:
What Standards Should Govern Academic Engagement in the Public
Sphere?" *LSE Impact Blog*, accessed on August 6, 2018. http://blogs.lse
.ac.uk/impactofsocialsciences/2014/08/18/scholarly-versus-activist
-identities-standards.

Schneider, Jordan. "Why I Curse in Class." *Chronicle of Higher Education*,
October 26, 2016. https://www.chronicle.com/article/Why-I-Curse-in
-Class/238164.

Schreier, Joshua, and Mira Sucharov. "If Israel Lets in Palestinian Refugees, Will It Lose Its Jewish Character?" *Forward*, October 17, 2016. https://forward.com/opinion/352075/if-israel-lets-in-palestinian-refugees-will-it-lose-its-jewish-character/?attribution=author-article-listing-2-headline.

Schuessler, Jennifer. "Ta-Nehisi Coates Deletes Twitter Account Amid Feud with Cornel West." *New York Times*, December 19, 2017. https://www.nytimes.com/2017/12/19/arts/ta-nehisi-coates-deletes-twitter-account-cornel-west.html?_r=0.

"Seeing White." *Scene on Radio*, (Podcast), accessed on August 6, 2018. http://www.sceneonradio.org/seeing-white.

Seidman, Gwendolyn. "Self-Presentation and Belonging on Facebook: How Personality Influences Social Media Use and Motivations." *Personality and Individual Differences* 54, no. 3 (2013): 402–407.

Shafer, Jack. "The Op-Ed Page's Back Pages." *Slate*, September 27, 2010. http://www.slate.com/articles/news_and_politics/press_box/2010/09/the_oped_pages_back_pages.html.

Shane, Scott, and Vindu Goel. "Fake Russian Facebook Accounts Bought $100,000 in Political Ads." *New York Times*, September 6, 2017. https://www.nytimes.com/2017/09/06/technology/facebook-russian-political-ads.html.

Shariatmadari, David. "'Virtue-Signalling'—The Putdown That Has Passed Its Sell-By Date." *Guardian*, January 20, 2016. https://www.theguardian.com/commentisfree/2016/jan/20/virtue-signalling-putdown-passed-sell-by-date?CMP=share_btn_link.

Shechet, Ellie. "Members of 'UES Mommas' Facebook Group Threaten Legal Action after Being Called Racist." *Jezebel*, August 23, 2017. https://jezebel.com/members-of-ues-mommas-facebook-group-threaten-legal-act-1798309160.

Shire, Emily. "Does Feminism Have Room for Zionists?" *New York Times*, March 7, 2017. https://www.nytimes.com/2017/03/07/opinion/does-feminism-have-room-for-zionists.html?_r=0.

Shire, Emily. "We Were Kicked Off Chicago's Dyke March For Not Being 'the Right Kind of Jew.'" *Daily Beast*, July 2, 2017. https://www.thedailybeast.com/we-were-kicked-off-chicagos-dyke-march-for-not-being-the-right-kind-of-jew.

Sibley, Robert. "Do We Really Think Our Universities Are Full of Sexual Attackers?" *Ottawa Citizen*, August 29, 2016. https://ottawacitizen.com/opinion/columnists/sibley-do-we-really-think-our-universities-are-full-of-sexual-attacker.

Sides, John. "About the Monkey Cage." *Washington Post*, January 1, 2014. http://www.washingtonpost.com/news/monkey-cage/wp/2014/01/01/about-the-monkey-cage/?utm_term=.e7e7beb3d15a.

Sides, John. "Why this Blog?" Monkey Cage, November 20, 2007. http://themonkeycage.org/2007/11/why_this_blog.

Socolow, Michael J. "A Profitable Public Sphere: The Creation of the *New York Times* Op-Ed Page." *Journalism and Mass Communication Quarterly* 87, no. 2 (2010): 281–96.

Spangler, Todd. "HuffPost Shuts Down Unpaid Contributor Blogger Program." *Variety*, January 18, 2018. https://variety.com/2018/digital/news/huffington-post-ends-unpaid-contributor-blogger-program-1202668053.

Steele, Brent J. "Making Words Matter: The Asian Tsunami, Darfur, and 'Reflexive Discourse' in International Politics." *International Studies Quarterly* 51, no. 4 (2007): 901–25.

Stephens, Bret. "Tips for Aspiring Op-Ed Writers." *New York Times*, August 25, 2017. https://www.nytimes.com/2017/08/25/opinion/tips-for-aspiring-op-ed-writers.html?_r=0.

Sucharov, Mira. "Anti-Occupation Jews: Time to Do Some Bible Thumping of Your Own." *Haaretz*, November 27, 2016. https://www.haaretz.com/opinion/.premium-anti-occupation-jews-time-to-do-some-bible-thumping-of-your-own-1.5466232.

Sucharov, Mira. "Are Israel's Jewish-Arab Coexistence Schools Setting Kids Up for a Cruel Fall?" *Haaretz*, September 8, 2016. https://www.haaretz.com/opinion/.premium-are-jewish-arab-schools-setting-kids-up-for-a-cruel-fall-1.5438547.

Sucharov, Mira. "A Shoah Survivor Who Found Kindness in Unexpected Place." *Canadian Jewish News*, February 11, 2015. http://www.cjnews.com/perspectives/opinions/guest-voice-shoah-survivor-found-kindness-unexpected-places.

Sucharov, Mira. "As They Celebrate Independence, Israelis Should Remember the Nakba." *Haaretz*, May 11, 2016. https://www.haaretz.com/opinion/.premium-israelis-remember-the-nakba-on-independence-day-1.5382192.

Sucharov, Mira. "Canada 150 and 50 Years of Israel's Occupation Need Sober Reflection." *Canadian Jewish News*, May 3, 2017. http://www.cjnews.com/perspectives/opinions/this-year-deserves-sober-reflection-in-canada-and-israel.

Sucharov, Mira. "Can Jewish Institutions Survive without Mega-Donors?" *Haaretz*, October 11, 2015. https://www.haaretz.com/blogs/the-fifth -question/.premium-1.679802.

Sucharov, Mira. "Hashtag Protests against IDF Sexual Assault Case Inspire Backlash." *Forward*, December 7, 2016. https://forward.com/ sisterhood/356383/hashtag-protests-against-idf-sexual-assault-case -inspire-backlash.

Sucharov, Mira. "How Can Israel End 'Jewish Privilege' When Most Citizens Believe They Deserve It?" *Forward*, March 28, 2016. https://forward. com/opinion/337152/how-can-israel-end-jewish-privilege-when-most -citizens-believe-they-deserve.

Sucharov, Mira. "In Diaspora Jewish Communities, Just Don't Call It the 'Occupation.'" *Haaretz*, May 10, 2017. https://www.haaretz.com/ opinion/.premium-in-diaspora-jewish-communities-just-don-t-call-it-the -occupation-1.5470414.

Sucharov, Mira. "Israel's Travel Ban: How Banning Settlement Boycotters Is Driving Me into the Arms of BDS." *Haaretz*, March 7, 2017. http://www .haaretz.com/opinion/.premium-1.775717.

Sucharov, Mira. "Let's Keep Israel Lobbying Out of Jewish Youth Groups." *Canadian Jewish News*, April 3, 2017. http://www.cjnews.com/ perspectives/opinions/keep-lobbying-israel-out-jewish-youth-groups.

Sucharov, Mira. "Parental Involvement." *Ottawa Citizen*, October 27, 2008: A12.

Sucharov, Mira. "Peres's Vision for Peace Reached Too Far, and Not Far Enough." *Globe and Mail*, September 28, 2016. https://www .theglobeandmail.com/opinion/peress-vision-for-peace-reached-too-far -and-not-far-enough/article32102765.

Sucharov, Mira. "Poison by PowerPoint: Reading between the Lines of Islamophobic Emails." *Haaretz*, July 31, 2013. https://www.haaretz .com/.premium-poison-by-powerpoint-reading-between-the-lines-of -islamophobic-emails-1.5315039.

Sucharov, Mira. "The Shavit Story, Sadly, Hits Too Very Close to Home." *Canadian Jewish News*, November 10, 2016. http://www.cjnews.com/ perspectives/opinions/shavit-story-sadly-familiar.

Sucharov, Mira. "The Trouble with the King Who Was Cosby." *Haaretz*, December 4, 2014. https://www.haaretz.com/.premium-the-trouble-with -cosby-1.5340462.

Sucharov, Mira. "Thoughts (for 'Both Sides') on the Academic Boycott." *Duck of Minerva* (Blog), January 12, 2017. http://duckofminerva.com/2017/01/ thoughts-for-both-sides-on-the-academic-boycott.html.

Sucharov, Mira. "Uncovering the Lost Palestinian Villages underneath Glitzy
    Tel Aviv." *Forward*, July 19, 2017. https://forward.com/opinion/345430/
    uncovering-the-lost-palestinian-villages-underneath-glitzy-tel-aviv.
Sucharov, Mira. "Upper East Side Moms Facebook Group in Turmoil—Over
    Israel and the Palestinians." *Forward*, November 20, 2017. https://forward
    .com/life/tech/387997/upper-east-side-mothers-facebook-group-in-turmoil
    -over-israeli-palestinian/?utm_content=sisterhood_Newsletter_MainList
    _Title_Position-1&utm_source=Sailthru&utm_medium=email&utm_campa
    ign=Sisterhood+Redesign+2017-11-21&utm_term=Sisterhood.
Sucharov, Mira. "Values, Identity and Israel Advocacy." *Foreign Policy
    Analysis* 7, no. 4 (2011): 361–79. doi:https://doi.org/10.1111/j.1743
    -8594.2011.00145.x.
Sucharov, Mira. "Why I'm Resigning my CJN Column." *Canadian Jewish
    News*, June 2, 2017. http://www.cjnews.com/perspectives/mira
    -sucharov-cjn-column.
Sucharov, Mira. "Why Jews Must Defend Muslim Women's Right to Wear
    the Burqa." *Haaretz*, October 19, 2017. https://www.haaretz.com/
    opinion/.premium-why-jews-must-defend-muslim-women-s-right-to
    -wear-the-burqa-1.5458940.
Sucharov, Mira. "Why Would Jews Have a Problem with the Term
    'Islamophobia'?" *Haaretz*, February 20, 2017. https://www.haaretz.com/
    opinion/.premium-why-would-jews-have-a-problem-with-the-term
    -islamophobia-1.5439026.
Sucharov, Mira, and Brent E. Sasley. "Blogging Identities on Israel/Palestine:
    Public Intellectuals and Their Audiences." *PS: Political Science and Politics*
    47, no. 1 (2014): 177–81.
Sullivan, Jake, and Victor Cha. "The Right Way to Play the China
    Card on North Korea." *Washington Post*, July 5, 2017. https://www
    .washingtonpost.com/opinions/the-right-way-to-play-the-china-card-on
    -north-korea/2017/07/05/6d223aa0-6187-11e7-a4f7-af34fc1d9d39_story
    .html?utm_term=.625cd6ef8cf9.
Sunstein, Cass R. *#Republic: Divided Democracy in the Age of Social Media.*
    Princeton: Princeton University Press, 2017.
Tajfel, Henri, M.G. Billig, R.P. Bundy, and Claude Flament. "Social
    Categorization and Intergroup Behaviour." *European Journal of Social
    Psychology* 1, no. 2 (1971): 149–78.
Taylor, Laurie. *Thinking Allowed* (Podcast), accessed on August 8, 2018.
    https://www.bbc.co.uk/programmes/b006qy05.
Tel Aviv Review (Podcast), accessed on August 8, 2018. https://tlv1.fm/
    podcasts/tel-aviv-review-show.

The Nostalgia Trap (Podcast), accessed on August 8, 2018. https://nostalgiatrap
.libsyn.com.

The Scholarly Kitchen Podcast, accessed on August 8, 2018. https://scholarly
kitchen.sspnet.org/category/podcast.

Thompson, Nicholas. "Exclusive: Facebook Opens Up about False News."
Wired, May 23, 2018. https://www.wired.com/story/exclusive-facebook
-opens-up-about-false-news.

Tierney, Allison. "I Took a Social Media Break and You Should Too." *Vice*,
October 5, 2017. https://www.vice.com/en_us/article/43a55j/i-took-a
-social-media-break-and-you-should-too.

Tiezzi, Shannon, editor in chief. *The Diplomat* (Blog), accessed on August 8,
2018. https://thediplomat.com/category/blogs.

Todahl, Jeffrey L., Elaine Walters, Deepa Bharwdi, and Shanta R. Dube.
"Trauma Healing: A Mixed Methods Study of Personal and Community-
Based Healing." *Journal of Aggression, Maltreatment and Trauma* 23, no. 6
(2014): 611–32.

Trần, Ngọc Loan. "Calling In: A Less Disposable Way of Holding Each
Other Accountable." *BGD*, December 18, 2013. http://www.bgdblog
.org/2013/12/calling-less-disposable-way-holding-accountable.

TREYF Podcast. "Short: Mira Sucharov." June 7, 2017. https://soundcloud
.com/treyfpodcast/short-mira-sucharov.

Tsipursky, Gleb. "The Pro-Truth Pledge: An Effective Strategy for Skeptics to
Fight Fake News and Post-Truth Politics." *Skeptic*, accessed on August 6,
2018. https://www.skeptic.com/reading_room/take-pro-truth-pledge-fight
-fake-news/?utm_source=eSkeptic&utm_campaign=7bf26f20da-EMAIL
_CAMPAIGN_2017_11_28&utm_medium=email&utm_term=0_8c0a740eb4
-7bf26f20da-73259197&mc_cid=7bf26f20da&mc_eid=cc296fe2ae.

Tufekci, Zeynep. "Does a Protest's Size Matter?" *New York Times*, January 27,
2017. https://www.nytimes.com/2017/01/27/opinion/does-a-protests
-size-matter.html.

Twitter. "How to Mute Accounts on Twitter," accessed on August 6, 2018.
https://help.twitter.com/en/using-twitter/twitter-mute.

Uberti, David. "The Real History of Fake News." *Columbia Journalism Review*,
(December 15, 2016). https://www.cjr.org/special_report/fake_news
_history.php.

Uncivil (Podcast), accessed on August 8, 2018. http://www.gimletmedia.
com/uncivil.

Utt, Jamie. "Income versus Wealth: How Privilege Is Passed Down from
Generation to Generation." *Everyday Feminism*, May 26, 2014. https://
everydayfeminism.com/2014/05/income-vs-wealth.

Verman, Alex. *"Canadian Jewish News* Loses Last Regular Left-Leaning Columnist over Word 'Occupation.'" *Canadaland*, June 30, 2017. http:// www.canadalandshow.com/cjn-loses-mira-sucharov.

Voeten, Erik. "Dear Nicholas Kristof: We Are Right Here!" *Washington Post*, February 15, 2014. https://www.washingtonpost.com/news/monkey -cage/wp/2014/02/15/dear-nicholas-kristof-we-are-right-here/?utm_ter m=.754dc7ffa3c7&noredirect=on.

Volokh, Eugene. "Who Are We?" *Washington Post*, January 16, 2014. https:// www.washingtonpost.com/news/volokh-conspiracy/who-are-we/?utm _term=.cb76145e8c26.

Walker, Benjamin. *Theory of Everything* (Podcast), accessed on August 8, 2018. https://theoryofeverythingpodcast.com.

Wang, Vivian. "Erica Garner, Activist and Daughter of Eric Garner, Dies at 27." *New York Times*, December 30, 2017. https://www.nytimes .com/2017/12/30/nyregion/erica-garner-dead.html?smid=tw-share.

War on the Rocks (Podcast), accessed on August 8, 2018. https:// warontherocks.com/podcasts.

Ward, Michael. "Create Your Own Theme Friedman Op-ed Column." April 28, 2004. https://www.mcsweeneys.net/articles/create-your-own -thomas-friedman-op-ed-column.

Wardle, Claire, and Hossein Derakhshan. "Information Disorder: Toward an Interdisciplinary Framework for Research and Policy Making." Council of Europe report DGI(2017)09, September 27, 2017. https://firstdraftnews .org/wp-content/uploads/2017/11/PREMS-162317-GBR-2018-Report -désinformation-1.pdf.

Wente, Margaret. "Why Treat University Students Like Fragile Flowers?" *Globe and Mail*, September 19, 2017; updated September 20, 2017. https:// www.theglobeandmail.com/opinion/why-treat-university-students-like -fragile-flowers/article36292886.

West, Cornel. "Ta-Nehisi Coates Is the Neoliberal Face of the Black Freedom Struggle." *Guardian*, December 17, 2017. https://www.theguardian.com/ commentisfree/2017/dec/17/ta-nehisi-coates-neoliberal-black-struggle -cornel-west.

West, June. "Strategic Communication to Inform or Persuade." *Darden Ideas to Action*, February 12, 2015. https://ideas.darden.virginia.edu/2015/02/ strategic-communication-to-inform-or-persuade.

Wiener, Jon. "A Forgotten Hero Stopped the My Lai Massacre 50 Years Ago Today." *Los Angeles Times*, March 16, 2018. http://www.latimes.com/ opinion/op-ed/la-oe-wiener-my-lai-hugh-thompson-20180316-story .html.

Winseck, Dwayne. *Mediamorphis: Network Media Industries and the Forces of Change and Conservation* (Blog), accessed on August 6, 2018. https://dwmw.wordpress.com/about.

Wittes, Benjamin, editor in chief. *Lawfare* (Blog), accessed on August 6, 2018. https://www.lawfareblog.com/masthead.

Wong, Julia Carrie. "Facebook Overhauls News Feed in Favor of 'Meaningful Social Interactions.'" *Guardian* (international edition), January 12, 2018. https://www.theguardian.com/p/7qeaf/stw.

Woolley, Frances. *Worthwhile Canadian Initiative: A Mainly Canadian Economics Blog*, accessed on August 6, 2018. http://worthwhile.typepad.com/worthwhile_canadian_initi/about-frances-woolley.html.

Wright, Tolly. "Mayim Bialik Apologizes for her Controversial Harvey Weinstein Op-ed." *Vulture*, October 18, 2017. http://www.vulture.com/2017/10/mayim-bialik-apologizes-for-controversial-weinstein-op-ed.html.

Young, Helen. "Game of Thrones: Race, Racism, and the Middle Ages." *Public Medievalist*, July 21, 2017. https://www.publicmedievalist.com/game-thrones-racism-problem.

Zak, Paul J. "Why Inspiring Stories Make Us React: The Neuroscience of Narrative." *Cerebrum* (January–February 2015). https://www.ncbi.nlm.nih.gov/pmc/articles/PMC4445577.

Zaki, Jamil, and Paul Bloom. "Does Empathy Guide or Hinder Moral Action?" *New York Times*, December 29, 2016. https://www.nytimes.com/roomfordebate/2016/12/29/does-empathy-guide-or-hinder-moral-action.

Zook, Jason. "Do a Social Media Detox." *Jason Does Stuff* (Blog), accessed on August 6, 2018. https://jasondoesstuff.com/social-media-detox-recap.

Index

Printed and bound by CPI Group (UK) Ltd, Croydon, CR0 4YY

13/04/2025

14656517-0001